SALLY PHIPPS

Silent Film Star

By Her Son

Robert L. Harned

ISBN-13:
978-1511915922

ISBN-10:
1511915927

Published by: Robert L. Harned, Brooklyn, New York, June 2015.

Printed by: CreateSpace.

Available from: Amazon.

For Arthur Schwartz, my hero

With special thanks to my dear friend Billee Stallings,
patient editor and enthusiastic cheerleader

TABLE OF CONTENTS

PREFACE

John Roberts, a writer for the cinema history and nostalgia publication, *Classic Images*, wrote a career article about Sally Phipps, the silent film star, in the November 1984 issue. He commented:

> **Remember Sally Phipps? Not really. Phipps starred in a handful of silents as a teenager under contract to Fox and belongs to silent obscuredom, one of many who enjoyed a small piece of the spotlight ... went from leading lady to the background ... [and] drifted out of films. ...**
>
> **Phipps' life after Hollywood is relatively unknown, and she was all but forgotten until her obituary appeared in the trade papers.**
>
> **Sally Phipps died March 17, 1978 in New York, leaving a son, Robert Harned.**
>
> **The case of Sally Phipps brings to mind a number of obscure silent actors, and we wonder whatever became of them.**

This book was written to answer John Roberts' question -- Whatever became of Sally Phipps? And the answer is that, after Hollywood, Sally Phipps led a fascinating life, much of it chronicled in newspapers and magazines. Her Hollywood portraits and pin-up images continue to be highly collectible today. She was on Broadway twice and on national radio. She worked for the Federal Theatre Project during the WPA era. She spent a year travelling in India.

She married twice and, with her second husband, became a mother – to my sister, Maryanna, and to me. I am Sally's son, Robert L. Harned, and I can testify that she was never completely forgotten. In fact, less than a year and a half before her death, she was honored with an award for her silent film work and a few months later with a screening of one her films. As recently as 2008, the *New York Times Style Magazine "T"* did a feature article about her.

As a professional librarian and archivist, I made a point of collecting and organizing the many artifacts of my mother's life, including photographic, painted and drawn portraits, scene stills, lobby cards, letters, newspaper and magazine articles, and family history. My parents separated before I was two years old, and my father raised my sister and me. During most of my life, my mother lived far away, but as an adult I found ways to visit her to get to know her better, during which time she filled me with many stories and reminiscences about her early life. I also learned much about her early life from contemporary newspaper and magazine articles.

What follows is my mother's unique life story – both personal and professional – derived from sources both private and public.

Robert L. Harned

PORTRAIT GALLERY

AUTREY

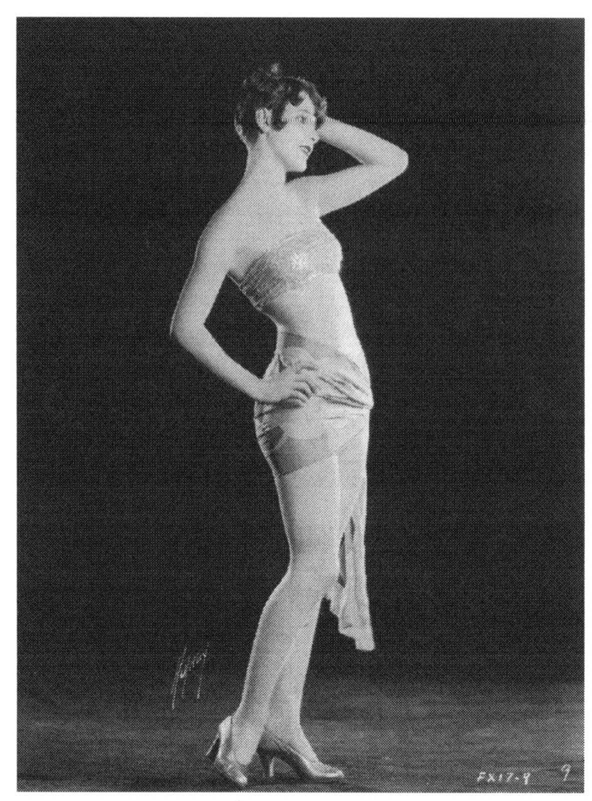
FX17-9 9

Chapter 1
Early Years – San Francisco Bay

Sally Phipps was less than two years old when she won a beautiful baby contest in 1913 and, according to the newspaper report, performed in the contest's evening program. Later articles called her "a child of beauty" and continued to follow her activities.

By the age of three and a half, she was already on the road to stardom. Her career began in late 1914 when she performed in three Broncho Billy films. She remembered watching Charlie Chaplin work and had the specific delight of sitting on his lap. This early work was followed by a Fox Film studio contract at age 14. While still only 15, she became one of the 13 WAMPAS Baby Stars of 1927, an honor given to starlets who showed the most promise. The adorable child had grown into an enchanting young woman, delighting newspaper reporters who loved to follow her antics, travels, and romances. Following stardom in many films, she moved on to Broadway where she played the movie-struck ingénue Susan Walker in the Kaufman and Hart Hollywood stage spoof *Once In A Lifetime.* The comedy ran a full year, closing after 406 performances.

Through these early years, she was shuttled back and forth between biological, foster and adoptive families, and it is amazing that she achieved such success in spite of an incredibly unstable upbringing. Somehow, as far as her career was concerned, with a lot of good luck, she was always in the right place at the right time. In fact, in the January 1931 issue of the famous movie magazine, *Picture Play*, in the "Over the Teacups" column by "The Bystander," it was said, "She is undoubtedly the luckiest girl I've ever known."

SALLY'S PARENTS

Sally had show business in her blood. Her father, Albert Edward Bogdon, was, in his early life, a professional magician in amusement parks and on the vaudeville, lyceum, and Chautauqua circuits. Her mother, Edithe Alois Lane, appeared in community performances, had a beautiful singing voice, and played several musical instruments, especially the piano and guitar.

It is a mystery how this young couple, from such diverse backgrounds, came together. Albert was from a poor Russian/Lithuanian family from Pittsburgh, Pennsylvania, started performing magic on stage at age 13, and by age 14 was advertising himself as "The World's Greatest Boy Manipulator." Edithe was the cherished adopted daughter of a prominent Oakland, California couple.

When they met, Albert saw Edithe, this attractive, talented young woman not yet out of her teens, as a brilliant addition to his magic act. She was undoubtedly transfixed by this stunningly handsome young man, who traveled the country and had the ability to woo her with his silver tongue.

After a brief courtship, they were married on Wednesday, July 27, 1910 in Oakland. Albert was only nineteen. Edithe was eighteen. Neither imagined that their new life together would be interrupted, in a little less than a year, with the birth of a cranky, sick baby.

Sally was born on May 25, 1911, 10 months after their marriage, at Acropolis Hospital in Oakland. She was named Nellie Bernice Bogdon, the Nellie in honor of Edithe's adoptive mother, Nellie Cleary Lane. But, Sally's name was to change several times during her life.

Sally's father, Albert E. Bogdon

Sally's mother, Edithe Alois Lane Bogdon

SALLY'S FATHER

Sally's father, Albert Bogdon, was born in Mahanoy City, Pennsylvania, on February 19, 1891 to a Russian-born father named William and a Russian-born mother of Lithuanian ancestry, whose maiden name, according to sources, was either Anna or Franciska Kirklis. He had one sister, Helen.

He was a beautiful boy with blond hair and blue eyes and grew up to be a handsome young man, about five feet seven inches tall. There are many photographs of him taken over the years, most of them obviously publicity portraits related to his show business career.

In his theatrical flyer dated to mid-1914, Bogdon included two photos that showed him "as he appeared at the age of thirteen [around 1904] during an extended tour of four years in the Orient." In another part of the flyer, he states that he had toured "China, Japan, Philippine Islands, Russia and Guam." No official documentation has ever been found for any of these trips.

When he was 14, he began advertising his theatrical activities in several professional publications. Some of his earliest ads were in the July, August, and September 1905 issues of *The Sphinx; a Monthly Illustrated Magazine Devoted to Magic and the Kindred Arts. The Sphinx* was the official publication of the Society of

Bogdon performing magic, age 13

Bogdon performing magic, age 22

American Magicians, founded in 1902. On pages displaying the business cards of various contemporary magicians, there appears the following:

Albert E. Bogdon
World's Greatest Boy Manipulator
Permanent Address: N.Y. Clipper.

He billed himself as a "manipulator," a word used to describe a magician who does magic tricks with his hands. The "N.Y. Clipper" address refers to the weekly theatrical publication, the *New York Clipper*, which was the predecessor to *Variety*. This magazine was frequently used as a kind of post office, where performers could get mail sent from producers desiring their services, if the performer advertised in the publication, as Bogdon certainly did.

An advertisement in the *New York Clipper's* October 14, 1905 issue gives a performance reference at a Luna Park in Pittsburgh:

ALBERT E. BOGDON
World's Greatest Boy Manipulator
Headliner at Luna Park, last week, Pittsburgh; With Hill's Concert Co. until Nov. 1, 1905; after that, ALL OPEN. Per. Address, Care CLIPPER.

This ad shows that he was connected with Hill's Concert Company, obviously some kind of booking organization, and it also indicates exactly when his current contract expires, November 1, 1905. Another similar advertisement gives the name of his manager with this company, Jack Sampselle. It is obvious that he was a true professional when he was only 14, with a manager and even a business address.

Early on, his family moved to Pittsburgh, Pennsylvania, where they were enumerated in the 1900 federal census, showing them situated in a southeast section of the city called Homestead. Albert kept Pittsburgh as his hub throughout his magic career, even while travelling in various theatrical circuits. Even after marrying Edithe, he still considered Pittsburgh his home base, although Edithe was living in Oakland.

The May 26 *New York Clipper* revealed some of Albert's 1906 bookings in its "Vaudeville Route List":

Bogden [sic], Albert E. Novelty. Denver, Col., [May] 21-26; Chicago, [May] 28-June 2.

The "en" ending of Bogdon's name was a frequent accidental misspelling. The "Novelty" designation after Bogdon's name refers to the particular vaudeville circuit that had booked him to perform his act in Denver and Chicago in late May and early June 1906. The Novelty Circuit was affiliated with a larger circuit, called the Western States Vaudeville Association, which comprised a network of theaters scattered throughout cities in the western part of the United States, including Missouri, Colorado, Utah, Nevada, Washington State, Oregon, and California. There was even a Novelty Theatre in Oakland, where Bogdon might possibly have met Edithe at a later booking.

These 1906 dates are the last printed theatrical references found about Bogdon before he married Edithe in 1910. He may have devoted the years after 1906, from age 15 on, to finishing high school.

SALLY'S MOTHER

Sally's mother, Edithe Alois Lane, was born in Sacramento, California on January 28, 1892. Later in life, she changed the spelling of her first name from "Edith" to "Edithe," adding an "e" at the end, the form used throughout this book. Edithe had brown eyes and dark auburn hair, and she was not much taller than five feet. Her family, and later her husband, Albert Bogdon, preferred to address her by her middle name, "Alois."

In 1892, Edithe was the third of three children born to Louis Bassett Green and Emily Alberta Weaver. Her older brother, Harold Louis Green, was born October 18, 1888, and her sister, Ida Alberta Green, was born April 25, 1890.

Edithe's father, Louis Green, was born in Quincy, Illinois on April 8, 1855. Her mother, Emily, was born in Omaha, Nebraska in August 1864. All that Edithe knew about her mother's parents was that Emily's father was "tall, dark, and handsome and from Tennessee." Louis and Emily were married some time in 1887.

Edithe's mother, Emily Green, died of typhoid fever on August 10, 1892, when Edithe was about 7½ months old. She was buried in Sacramento in Helvetia Park Cemetery.

Louis was not able to care for his three young children after Emily died and found foster homes for them. Edithe was taken in by Jacob and Nellie Lane, a childless couple who lived in Oakland, California.

Still living in Sacramento, Louis married Mamie Virginia Rausch within two years. He then tried to reclaim his three children from their foster homes. He got back Harold and Ida, but the Lanes had fallen in love with their baby Edithe and did not want to give her up. So Louis let the Lanes keep her as their own daughter. The Lanes adopted her, and she became Edithe Alois Lane.

Louis, with his new wife, fathered two more daughters, Lulah Marie, born May 14, 1895, and Nell, born August 11, 1898. Edithe continued to keep in touch with her father, over the years, also with her sister, Ida, her brother. Harold, and her half-sisters, Lulah and Nell.

SALLY'S MATERNAL GRANDPARENTS

Edithe's adoptive parents, Sally's maternal grandparents -- Jacob Cooper Lane (1851-1901), and Nellie Cleary Lane (1853-1932) -- lived in the East section of Oakland, California. They met in Salt Lake City and got married on July 31, 1871, when he was nineteen and Nellie was eighteen. In the 1900 census, the entire Lane family is included in the record: Jacob, Nellie, and, for the first time, "Edith A. Lane," recorded as "daughter."

Edithe's adoptive father, Jacob Cooper Lane

Edithe's adoptive mother, Nellie Cleary Lane

Jacob Lane was born on November 21, 1851 in Greens Fork, Clay Township, Wayne County, Indiana. His parents were Ira D. Lane and the Hannah Cooper, both from Illinois. He was the youngest of their nine children.

His family became well known in San Francisco. His mother's brother, Elias Samuel Cooper (1819-1893), and Jacob's own brother, Levi Cooper Lane (1828-1902), were both practicing physician/surgeons in San Francisco. In 1859, they collaborated on opening the first medical school in the western United States. The school was originally called the Medical Department of the University of the Pacific. It soon expanded to become Toland Medical College, then Cooper Medical College, adding on Lane Hospital. In 1908, the medical complex was acquired by Stanford University as the nucleus of its Department of Medicine. Today it is called the Stanford University School of Medicine. The University's medical library is named Lane Medical Library in Levi's honor.

Sally never knew her grandfather Jacob, who died before she was born. However, her grandmother Nellie became an extremely important figure in her life. In addition to being named after her grandmother, Sally was brought home from the hospital to the bungalow in the rear of her grandmother's house, where her parents lived after their marriage. Later, when she was ill and could not digest her food, her grandmother purchased a goat that provided the milk that sustained her. Although in time her family broke apart, circumstances brought Sally back to live with her grandmother when she was four, and she stayed until she was 11 years old.

Jacob and Nellie Lane were pioneers in California. They had moved to San Francisco some time in the mid-1870s, when they were in their early twenties, and lived there at several addresses. In the mid-1880s, they made their first move to Alameda County, across the Bay from San Francisco. Like so many of the newcomers to California, the Lanes were attracted to fruit farming and bought land for that purpose.

Apparently they were successful, because they were able to purchase a very nice home when they decided to move to Oakland. The following paragraph appeared in the newspaper *Daily Alta California*, September 7, 1887, in a column called "The Eastern Shore; News from Berkeley, Alameda, Oakland, and Environs" under the "Oakland" section:

> **For $14,000 Nellie Lane, a resident of Mendocino, has bought the handsome residence and grounds of William Parker on East Seventeenth Street, near Nineteenth Avenue. The lot is 75 x 140.**

This "handsome residence and grounds," mentioned in the above article, was 962 East 17th Street and comprised a two-story house with enough land for a couple of subordinate buildings. This was the house where baby "Edithe Green" was first received when she arrived to live with the Lanes in 1892.

In 1890, Jacob C. Lane was calling himself a "Book Publisher," as recorded in the *California Voter Register*, dated August 29, 1890. He published the *Sacramento City And County Directory* for 1888-1889, 1889-1890, and 1891-1892.

Jacob's most well-known directories, however, are the Hawaiian ones. The first one appeared in November 1888 with his name prominently displayed on the title page, "Edited by J. C. Lane" and signed in the preface, "J. C. Lane, Editor." His second Hawaiian directory appeared in October 1890. Hawaii, at that time, was not yet part of the United States but was a separate country, the Kingdom of Hawaii, with its own sovereign, King Kalakaua (1836-1891). Jacob spent quite of bit of time in the islands working on the directories. He even met King Kalakaua and dedicated his Hawaiian directories to the monarch.

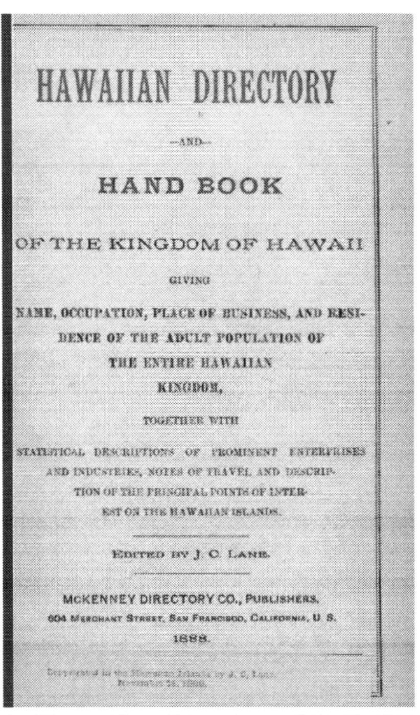

HAWAIIAN DIRECTORY

—AND—

HAND BOOK

OF THE KINGDOM OF HAWAII

GIVING

NAME, OCCUPATION, PLACE OF BUSINESS, AND RESIDENCE OF THE ADULT POPULATION OF THE ENTIRE HAWAIIAN KINGDOM,

TOGETHER WITH

STATISTICAL DESCRIPTIONS OF PROMINENT ENTERPRISES AND INDUSTRIES, NOTES OF TRAVEL AND DESCRIPTION OF THE PRINCIPAL POINTS OF INTEREST ON THE HAWAIIAN ISLANDS.

EDITED BY J. C. LANE.

McKENNEY DIRECTORY CO., PUBLISHERS,
604 MERCHANT STREET, SAN FRANCISCO, CALIFORNIA, U. S.
1888.

J. C. Lane's *Hawaiian Directory* (1888 title page)

By the time Edithe came into their lives, Jacob was settled back in Oakland, where his occupation, as listed in the *California Voter Register,* was no longer "Book Publisher" but "Travelling Salesman."

It is interesting to note that many years later Edithe, Sally, and Sally's second husband and children all ended up living for a time in Hawaii.

Jacob died in April 1901 at age 49. Family correspondence reports that Jacob was diabetic and that he was in chronic ill health in his last few years, very possibly aggravated by an incident in 1895 when he was thrown from a street car and sustained a broken leg.

NELLIE CLEARY LANE

Nellie was now alone at age 48 with a nine-year-old daughter to bring up.

She herself had a fascinating background. She was born Ellen Cleary Phelps on March 26, 1853 in Salt Lake City, but always preferred to use the name "Nellie." She was named after her maternal grandmother, Ellen Cleary. After her marriage, she continued to use the middle initial "C." as part of her official name, "Nellie C. Lane."

Nellie was the daughter of William Wines Phelps (1792-1872), a famous Mormon personage of Salt Lake City, and Sarah Betsina "Betsy" Gleason (1827-

1916). Sarah was born in Newly, Tipperary County, Ireland and became Phelps' fifth wife. Polygamy was customary in the Mormon Church at that time.

Nellie C. Lane's father, William Wines Phelps

William Phelps, born in Hanover Township, New Jersey, was in his early life the colleague and scribe of the founder of Mormonism, Joseph Smith. Phelps is alluded to four times quite prominently in the *Book of Mormon's* important *Doctrines And Covenants* section. He became a publisher for the Mormon Church and was also a composer of many of the Mormon hymns still in use today. Sally inherited a book of these hymns, given to her by her grandmother Nellie:

> ***Sacred Hymns and Spiritual Songs for the Church of Jesus Christ of Latter-Day Saints.*** **14th ed. Salt Lake City: Published by George Q. Cannon, 1871.**

It is a small 3½ x 5-inch volume including 36 hymns, which Nellie's father, William Phelps, wrote. This hymnal was personally inscribed by her mother, Sarah, on Nellie's 18th birthday and was given to her as a birthday present. Although the inscription is in black ink, the entire page is also decorated in charming red, blue, and green pencil markings.

SACRED HYMNS

AND

SPIRITUAL SONGS.

FOR THE

CHURCH OF JESUS CHRIST

OF

LATTER-DAY SAINTS.

FOURTEENTH EDITION.

SALT LAKE CITY:

FOR SALE AT DESERET NEWS OFFICE, THE CHURCH BOOK DEPOT.

PUBLISHED BY GEORGE Q. CANNON.

1871.

Mormon hymnal, 1871 edition

Phelps' married his first wife as early as 1815. He married Nellie's mother, his fifth wife, Sarah, on December 22, 1847 at Winter Quarters, Douglas County, Nebraska. William and Sarah had three children -- two boys, Gleason and Enon, and a girl, Nellie. He even took a sixth wife before he died in 1872 at the age of 80.

Nellie became totally disillusioned with Mormonism and ended up turning against all organized religions – not against God and spirituality, but against what she saw as the evils of organized religions. She imparted this attitude to Edithe as well as to Sally.

Even though she was now a lapsed Mormon living in Oakland, she kept up her contacts with relatives and friends in Salt Lake City. Her mother and brother Enon continued to live there until both of them died within days of each other in 1916. Her brother Gleason died in infancy.

Nellie became a civic force in Oakland. There are numerous newspaper articles reporting her activities, which today would be considered quite progressive and liberal for a woman of her day. Being a real crusader, she frequently challenged the "powers that be" and won.

EDITHE

Probably because of her mother's civic prominence, Edithe was also actively involved in community affairs at an early age. Her name appeared in the local Bay Area newspapers several times. The first time was in the *Oakland Tribune*, July 7,

1897, in a list of little girls and boys who appeared in a patriotic dance at a performance held during the Third Oakland Exposition, a trade show organized by the local Board of Trade. In the dance, according to the article, "Edith Lane" represented the state of Connecticut.

The *San Francisco Call*, February 21, 1903, reported a legal case involving Edithe in an article entitled "May Contest Dr. Lane's Will; Sister Of Late Physician Dissatisfied With Document." Levi Cooper Lane, Jacob Lane's brother, had died, leaving everything to his widow, Pauline. Pauline died a few months after Levi, leaving the entire estate of $500,000 to the Lane Hospital, which was partly founded by her husband Levi. The immediate family decided to contest the will and Edithe was included in the newspaper list as, "a niece, Edith A. Lane, in Oakland." She was only eleven years old, and it is not known if there was ever any kind of settlement, or if she received any amount of money.

Much of Edithe's early life is preserved in reminiscences that she shared with her grandson Robert. Because of Robert's parents' separation before he was two, Edithe served as a surrogate mother to Robert, and he spent a lot of time in her company. He was always eager to hear her stories of the "old days": Remembering the time she fell out of the apricot tree in the family backyard and breaking her arm. Feeding her favorite livery horse sugar lumps. Playing the guitar and singing with a lovely voice until her voice got ruined through overuse during a childhood disease. Remembering seeing photographs of her father posed with King Kalakaua, the King of Hawaii. Having the specific household chore of cleaning the soot out of all the glass kerosene lamp chimneys. In 1898, when she was six years old, watching the U.S. Navy ships leave San Francisco Bay from the Oakland side, as they sailed out to fight in the Spanish American War. Living through the 1906 earthquake. Having an enormous crush on a handsome Portuguese boy in the neighborhood, and Nellie not allowing her to date him.

EDITHE IN THE NEWS

Several newspaper articles reveal Edithe's developing musical talent. In 1907, all of Oakland was on a fund raising mission to find a suitable home for young girls who had to live and work outside of their parents' homes, and Nellie was actively involved with the effort. One solution was to purchase a former mansion, the Playter home, and put it under the aegis of the newly formed local Y.W.C.A. The *Oakland Tribune*, April 4, 1907, covered this effort in an article entitled: "Benefit For Girls' Home; Program to be Given at Entertainment to Raise Charity Funds." It stated that the entertainment was given in order "to assist Mrs. Nellie C. Lane in procuring funds to buy the Playter Home for the Y. W. C. A., for the benefit of the working girls." Fifteen-year-old Edithe is listed twice in the program, once for playing the guitar, and again for portraying Mrs. Brown, the leading character in a "Dialogue" called *The Unappreciated Genius*. "Dialogues" were short, one act plays, no more than a few pages long, with very few characters.

Three years later, 18-year-old Edithe appeared in a concert that was publicized in the *San Francisco Call*, April 3, 1910: "Series of Concerts by Harmonie Club; Initial

Musicale to Be Given at Loring Hall." This series was comprised of weekly concerts held throughout the month of April 1910 in Loring Hall, an auditorium in downtown Oakland. In the program, there were several instrumental and vocal solos accompanied by a small orchestra made up of violins, violoncello, clarinet, trombone, trumpet, and piano. "Edith A. Lane" is listed as the pianist. Concerning her piano activities, Edithe's grandson Robert remembers her telling him how difficult it was for her to curl her fingers high enough during piano practice to satisfy her strict piano teacher.

The Harmonie Club concerts were held only three months before she married Albert Bogdon. Nothing is known about how or when they met, but Albert might have seen her play at one of the concerts. They may also have met when Albert was in the San Francisco Bay Area performing as a magician in a vaudeville, lyceum, or Chautauqua gig.

EDITHE AND ALBERT

Edithe was always reluctant to talk to her family about her life with Albert. Their life together, therefore, has to be reconstructed from other sources, such as Sally's memoirs, Sally's baby book, letters, photographs, legal documents, newspaper articles, and even educated assumptions.

They were married on July 27, 1910 in Oakland. Edithe had just graduated from high school. Albert was obviously attracted by the fact that Edithe was a pianist and was accomplished enough to play in an orchestra. It is clear from correspondence that he expected her to join him in his magic act as a pianist, and he continued to count on it for several years. As late as July 16, 1914, he wrote to her from Pittsburgh, where he was preparing himself for another tour on the performance circuit:

> **If things turn out as I anticipate, you will be here in Sept. and start out with me with my show.**
> **Keep yourself in shape on the piano, practice, practice, practice.**

SALLY'S PARENTS' MARRIAGE

After Edithe and Albert married, the newlyweds moved into the bungalow in back of Nellie's house in Oakland. It had its own address, 975 East 19th Street. It did not take long for Albert to resume his magic career. This meant Albert would have to be away for long periods of time on the road performing in various theaters. He would now have two major home bases, one in Oakland with his wife Edithe, and another in Pittsburgh with his mother and sister Helen. Nellie was not happy about the situation. In fact, Nellie was never in favor of the marriage. She only tolerated Albert because of her daughter, but she may have kept her true feelings to herself in the early stages of the marriage.

On his part, Albert tried to ingratiate himself to his mother-in-law as indicated by a letter he sent to Nellie from Pittsburgh, only six months after his marriage to Edithe. In the letter dated January 28, 1911, Albert addressed Nellie as "My beloved Mother" and signed off as "Your beloved son, Albert." Nellie must have asked him to pay a social visit on her behalf to a particular Pittsburgh family and to report back in a letter about their current situation. He complied dutifully in detail:

Pittsburgh, Pa.
January 28, 1911

My beloved Mother:

At Mrs. Hamilton's special instance and request, I gave her a call at her beautiful home on Fifth Avenue yesterday afternoon. I got there at three and stayed till six, before I was able to break away. Unfortunately her son was not at home, so am unable to pen any observations of him. Mrs. Hamilton says he is not studious, nor methodical, and his crowning glory is his love for play and to be looked after.

She had a great deal to say about her daughter, who was at the skating rink with her brother while I was interviewing her. She spoke of her daughter graduating at Vassar and her experiences while there.

Mr. Hamilton got home about five and [I] had a chat with him. He seemed to be full of prejudices about California and seemed to be dissatisfied with everything in general. From what I could gather from his speech, it seemed to appear that competition in the glass business is quite keen, and he has [a] lot of difficulty to stand the strain. With such a cause, it naturally follows that the effect is financial difficulties, and when they weigh on one's shoulders, <u>we</u> know what that means. So much for Mr. Hamilton.

Now, to concentrate on Mrs. Hamilton. She has had rheumatism for a number of years, that means she is in bad health, <u>we</u> know what [that] means. Her daughter is about eighteen and very much fond of the boys. <u>You know</u> of course know what that means. Her son causes her a great deal of anxiety. Mr. Hamilton is seventy-three years of age, and they commence to notice it. On leaving, she told me to tell you that they didn't expect to go to California this winter, and send their hearty regards to you. So much for the Hamiltonian visit.

Personally, I am about to embark on the circuit. Shall give you the details in my next letter.

Your loving son,
Albert

#806 Home Trust Bldg.,
Pittsburgh, Pa.

The letter indicates that Albert is still doing the performance "circuit," whichever circuit that may be at the time, and is politely keeping Nellie informed of his performance dates.

However, by this time, Edithe was five months pregnant with Sally, very likely interfering with Albert's plans for Edithe to join the act.

SALLY'S BIRTH

Sally's baby book, which Edithe meticulously maintained, gives an abundance of details about her birth and early years. She was born at 8 a.m. and weighed 8¼ pounds. Albert was in town for the birth. Edithe and Sally stayed in the hospital until June 8 and then finally came home by automobile to the bungalow in back of grandmother Nellie's house. Edithe and Albert very quickly came up with pet names for Sally: Bunny, Violet, and Bumbums.

Sally summarized the first seven months of her life succinctly in her diary-like memoirs, which cover her life from birth through 1933:

> **Birth - 5/25/1911 - Acropolis Hospital, Oakland, Calif. – near Lick Observatory. Mother/Father & I returned to Grandma's bungalow – in back of main house. – I was deathly ill first 6 months – nutrition problem. – I was dying – nothing nourished me. A German Dr. suggested goats' milk. They bought a goat, which gave them a bad time – butting Grandma off steps etc. I survived.**

Another quote from the baby book reveals other interesting facts about the goat:

> **"Annie" Goat was bought September 7th, 1911, a present from Grandma. The goat's milk was the first thing that would stay in our Bunny's stomach after trying every kind of food and milk. "Annie" went dry December following – cow's milk and graham crackers taking her place.**

The bungalow on Nellie C. Lane's property

“Annie” the goat

Edithe and baby Sally

Regardless of Sally's delicate health condition, indomitable grandmother Nellie found a way to introduce Sally publicly to the world. According to Sally's baby book, a little over a month after her birth, Nellie showed her off in a 1911 July 4th celebration parade: "July 4: Bunny rode with Grandma in an auto at head of procession."

The baby book also reveals that Bogdon left their home in Oakland as early as 2½ months after Sally was born: "Papa went to Pittsburgh, Pa., August 9, 1911." The baby book does not give any explanation. Was he returning right away to the performing stage? Was he finding his home life difficult, with Sally not being able to ingest food well, and with Edithe and Nellie at odds with each other over Albert's plans?

PITTSBURGH TRIP

It was becoming obvious that Nellie was upset over Albert's apparent desertion of Edithe, and she was not concealing her dislike of him. The relationship between Edithe and her mother was deteriorating rapidly. On April 1, 1912, Edithe and Sally left for Pitttsburgh, perhaps hoping to stay there or else to convince Albert to come back to Oakland. Edithe, in her meticulous notes in Sally's baby book, recorded that visit. The following are some miscellaneous verbatim notes from various pages in the baby book, with "mama" referring to Edithe and "Nellie" referring to Sally, because, at that time, it was Sally's given name:

> **April 1, 1912. Mama & Nellie left California for Pittsburgh.**
> **Mama & Nellie arrived in Pittsburgh, April 6, 1912.**
> **Places Nellie had lived [in Pittburgh]:**
> > **Fifth Avenue, Pittsburgh, Pennsylvania**
> > **At #25 Ulysses St., Pittsburgh, Pa.**
> > **At Chalfants, #18 Bigham St., Pittsburgh, Pa.**
>
> **This is the day when our baby learned to creep. Date: May 15, 1912, Pittsburgh, Pa.**
>
> **Our baby took her [first] steps without any assistance on November 27, 1912. The day before Thanksgiving [November 27, 1912] - at Chalfants', Pittsburgh, mama started her to walk two or three steps to papa [Albert] – then across the room, and then anywhere.**
>
> **Dec. 4, 1912. Mama & Nellie left Pittsburgh for Oakland, California. Mama and Nellie went West to California on December 4, 1912, stopping off at Chicago, Omaha, Denver, and Salt Lake City enroute. We arrived in Oakland, Monday December 23rd, 1912.**

After Edithe and Sally had been away in Pittsburgh for almost five months, grandma Nellie sent her the following, rather emotional letter. As was the family custom, Nellie always referred to Edithe as Alois:

Oakland, Aug. 22nd, 1912

Dear Alois,

Just 20 years ago today, you came into my life, & brought the sweetest joy I have ever known, & down the long vista of years, we traveled hand in hand, with our hearts trussed in perfect harmony – there was no note of discord & life was a joy to me. I lived to make you happy. Your happiness meant mine, & the future was woven with yours. – There was no suspicion of [a] storm that was to come and sweep away everything that life held for me, love, confidence, my future happiness. I was so unprepared – for there was no note of warning. I was engulfed before I could get my bearings. I have been & am yet dazed. Many times I have taken the pen to write, but my hand seemed paralyzed, & I could not write.

August 29th. I could not finish this letter as you see – but in course of time, I may.

I wonder if your mind turns to the pictures that hang on "memories walls." They at least will give you comfort & perhaps help you to awaken to the fact that you have missed something in your life that can never be replaced, -- that you are under the influence of a "Svengali." I do not doubt, for you never could have acted as you have done, otherwise.

Cloth[e]s & amusements – do not bring happiness. They only tend to stifle ones feelings for the time being. – True happiness comes from right living, & right doing, in making others happy. You have experienced the feeling – when you made the little pin-cushion, & many other things that I have stored away in memories' treasure box.

I cannot believe that tender memories of the happy past do not rise up & long to make these things manifest. It is only a miserable bluff, a defiant attitude that are against the laws of nature, & when you come back to your normal senses, you will see how blind you have been, how you have cheated yourself & baby out of your birth-right.

The school of experience is free, but the incidentals are very expensive.

The awful premonitions I had when you were married have come true. Indeed I have walked alone, in a great abyss & in my loneliness, I have prayed for death – for the joy of living has gone, to return no more. Oh, the pity of it all.

All the honors that have come to me (& they are many) are as empty as air, for you do not share them with me.

[. . .]

I went to the ranch for 10 days. We drove over the mountains. They look lovelier than ever. The day was a perfect one, the lake with its blue winding waters, the mountains, the trees & the shrubs. I feasted my soul. At the ranch, the threshers were there a month earlier, the hay balers, & the

peas were being threshed out for the great Jersey seed corn. Horace has so many lovely colts & calves. There is fine fishing. Dr. Murray came & he caught 31 fine trout. The finest vegetable garden they ever had, lots of cream and fruit. I took down 24 empty jars, brought them back full [with] wild black berries, huckleberries, string beans, honey, spiced cherries. I brought home one hundred & fifty lbs. Crullers, crumpets, suet pudding, chicken. I was loaded down. All around her house are flowers, a perfect bower. It is lovely there. ...

[. . .]

I have no future. There is only the past for me.
But, it is better to have loved & lost than never to have loved at all.

With love,
I am the same yesterday to-day & forever,

Mama

Edithe certainly does not appear to have been in a rush to come home after receiving that letter. According to her notes in the baby book, she did not arrive back in Oakland until near the end of December 1912, almost four months later. She had been with Albert a little over eight months, and Albert stubbornly persisted in staying in Pittsburgh. When she returned to Oakland, she was already in her fifth month of pregnancy with another Bogdon child.

Sally's baby book has another list entitled: "Places Nellie [Sally] has lived," covering roughly the first four years of her life. The Pittsburgh addresses are repeated:

First home -- The Bungalow -- #975 E. 19th St., Oakland.
Second home -- At Grandma's -- #1369 20th Ave., Oakland [later renumbered to 1749 20th Ave.]
Third home -- Fifth Ave., Pittsburgh, Pennsylvania
Fourth home -- At #25 Ulysses St., Pittsburgh, Pa.
Fifth home -- At Chalfants, #18 Bigham St., Pittsburgh, Pa.
Sixth home -- At #2335 E. 17th St., Oakland, California
Seventh home -- At Sawyers. 22d Ave. & 16th St., Oakland
Eight home -- Niles, California

There is no mention of either the bungalow address or of grandma Nellie's address after they returned from Pittsburgh. Edithe and baby Sally immediately moved in with friends in the same neighborhood, at 2335 East 17th Street. Sally, in her memoirs, says that Nellie "had locked the door on her [Edithe]." When her friends, whom Edithe was living with, found it difficult to deal with baby Sally, pregnant Edithe continued to stay with them but temporarily put Sally in a foster home.

Albert E. Bogdon, Jr., Edithe's and Albert's second child, was born on May 27, 1913, almost exactly two years after Sally's birth. Edithe would later change his name from "Albert" to "Lane" in honor of her adoptive parents. Edithe put her son Lane into a foster home not long after he was born. She chose the home of a local German couple, and always remembered how uncomfortable she felt hearing Lane speak German when she visited him.

Sally reports this in her memoirs:

> **My first memories occur at about 2 yrs. Lane was born 5/27/1913. Mother showed him to me where she was staying with some friends in Oakland. Grandma had locked the door on her. I was placed with neighbors . . . Later Lane was put to board with an Oakland German couple, as she [Sally's mother Edithe] went with photography work in San Francisco.**

EDITHE AT WORK

There was not a lot of work available for young women in 1913 in the Bay Area, and Edithe, who needed to support herself and her two children, found work difficult to find. Because of her talent in art, however, she got a job as a commercial artist, coloring black and white photographs using transparent oil paints designed specifically for photographic paper. She worked in an art studio across the Bay in San Francisco and lived in an apartment-hotel nearby. She quickly became quite proficient in this work. She visited her children frequently.

JACK LONDON – A FAMILY FRIEND

In Nellie's letter of August 22, 1912 to Edithe in Pittsburgh, she says:

> **I went to the ranch for 10 days. We drove over the mountains. They look lovelier than ever.**

This was undoubtedly a reference to the ranch in the Sonoma Mountains that her family friend, Jack London, acquired in 1905. He eventually owned 1,400 acres and built a mansion there, "Wolf House," that was destroyed by fire in 1913. He spent a lot of time there, even after the fire, until his death in 1916, once saying it was an escape from Oakland, which he called "the man trap." The ranch is now a National State Historic Park.

Jack London (1876-1916), the famous American novelist, journalist, and social activist, knew the Lanes well, possibly ever since he was a little boy. His mother, Flora, and his step-father, John London, lived in Oakland in the late 1880s. James L. Haley, in his 2010 book, *Wolf; The Lives Of Jack London*, mentions that "The house the Londons took on East 17th Street in March 1886" was in East Oakland, and that "Johnny was now ten and attended the Garfield School across the street from their house." The Garfield School was located on the corner of 17th Street and 22nd Avenue, on the same street, and only three blocks from, the Lane residence at 962 East 17th

Street. East Oakland was sparsely populated in the 1880s, and it is highly likely that the Lanes and Londons got to know each other quite well.

Nellie received the following letter from Jack London the same year he bought the Sonoma property:

Jack London
Glen Ellen
Sonoma Co., Cal.
Sep. 12, 1905

Dear Mrs. Lane – Glad you liked my bed and Noel's "Sea Wolf."
It wasn't my "Sea Wolf" – O, Gawd!
Story was all right – a dandy.
Thanks for your kind words.
Awfully rushed.
Jack London

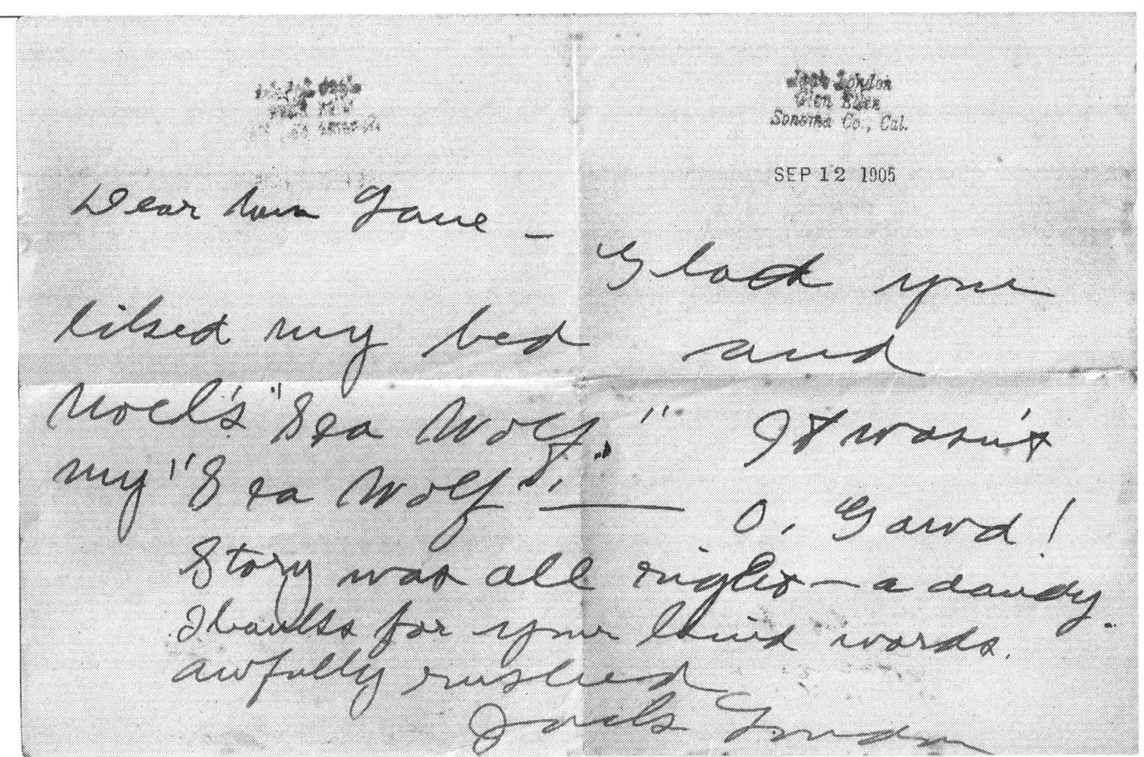

Jack London
Glen Ellen
Sonoma Co., Cal.
SEP 12 1905

Dear Mrs Lane – Glad you liked my bed and Noel's "Sea Wolf." It wasn't my "Sea Wolf." — O, Gawd! Story was all right – a dandy. Thanks for your kind words. Awfully rushed.
Jack London

Jack London letter to Nellie C. Lane

This original handwritten letter is in Edithe's grandson Robert's possession. It is written in ink, although the upper-right-hand corner address and dates were rubber-stamped. Robert also has its original handwritten envelope, displaying a 2-cent-stamp and a postmark of September 13, 1905.

The content of the letter requires some explanation. London addresses Nellie as "Mrs. Lane" rather than "Nellie" -- totally understandable considering the 23-year age difference. There are two "Glad you like" references in the letter. The first is to "my bed," probably referring to some recent visit for overnight or longer. The second is to "Noel's 'Sea Wolf,'" which he says is not his "Sea Wolf." "Noel" refers to Joseph Noel, the dramatist, novelist, and newspaperman, who was also a friend and associate of Jack London. Joseph Noel had recently written his first play, a dramatization of London's famous 1904 novel *The Sea Wolf.* This play had its premiere in Oakland on Monday, September 4, 1905 at the Ye Liberty Theatre and then opened the following Monday, September 11, in San Francisco at the Majestic Theater -- to disastrous reviews. *The San Francisco Call*, September 12, said: "Joseph Noel, the dramatist, has neither done justice to himself nor the author." However, when the play closed, although a critical failure, it turned out to be a tremendous financial success. Nevertheless, since the London letter was written the same day that the negative reviews came out for the play, it is interesting to know that Jack London was glad that Nellie liked the play. But did he like the play? His letter seems to indicate he did not. "Not my Sea Wolf" and "O Gawd! – Story was all right – a dandy. – Thanks for your kind words." Regardless of the content of this letter, it definitely reveals a close, warm, informal relationship between Jack London and Nellie.

In November of the same year, 1905, after divorcing his first wife Elizabeth "Bessie" Maddern (1876-1947), Jack married Charmian Kittredge (1871-1955). Edithe, who was 13 years old at the time, had a crush on Jack. She told her grandson Robert how she jokingly threatened Jack London with a "breach of promise suit" because of his marriage to Charmian. Nellie kept up her friendship with both Jack and Charmian. In 1912 she was still visiting the ranch. Charmian gave Nellie a number of her own copies of Jack London's books with her name written in them. Robert remembers seeing them in Edithe's book collection.

SALLY IN FOSTER HOME

In 1913, when she was not quite two years old, Sally was placed in the home of Warren Sawyer (1877-1952) and Eva Sawyer (1882-1955). In her brief memoirs, Sally refers to them as "neighbors," for they lived only a few blocks away at 1551 22nd Avenue, at the corner of 16th Street. It was just a short walk from Nellie's house at 1749 20th Avenue. Warren worked on the stage crew at the Orpheum and Ye Liberty Theatres in downtown Oakland. He was also a set designer, prop man, and sometime actor at a small movie studio in Niles, California -- Essanay Film Company. Warren's wife Eva was an actress with Essanay. Charlie Chaplin worked in the Niles Essanay studio for a short time in late 1914 and early 1915.

NELLIE BERNICE BOGDON

Sally had developed into an extraordinarily beautiful and good-natured little girl, and the Sawyers must have been thrilled to be foster parents to such a child. By this time, Sally's hair had grown out into a beautiful shade of red. Being theatrically minded, the Sawyers began entering her into local baby contests.

On April 1, 1913, when Sally was 22 months old, there appeared in the *Oakland Tribune*, the following newspaper article, "'Mother Goose' Baby Show To Be Attractive Church Entertainment." It was an announcement of a children's entertainment day to be held on Friday, April 4, which was to have a beautiful baby contest in the afternoon and a theatrical program in the evening. In addition to picturing eight of the adult female participants involved in the day-long entertainment, Sally was pictured right in the center, below the participants, in a charming oval frame showing her head and shoulders resting on her little hands. In the article, she is referred to as "Bernice Bogdon."

'MOTHER GOOSE' BABY SHOW TO BE ATTRACTIVE CHURCH ENTERTAINMENT

ALAMEDA BELLE TO WED IN JUNE

Miss Adele Winks, Assistant Librarian, Announces Engagement.

ALAMEDA YOUNG FOLKS WED AT SAN RAFAEL

FINE PROGRAM IS ARRANGED

Many Children Will Take Part in Affair Next Friday Evening.

ANNIVERSARY OF CENTER OBSERVED

Melrose Civic League Workers Celebrate One Year of Activity.

CONVALESCENT AFTER THIRD OPERATION

***Oakland Tribune* article featuring Sally, April 1913**

The Sawyers had dropped Sally's first name, "Nellie," and were using "Bernice Bogdon" as her billing. She was also listed in the article as a young miss "who will take part in the program for the evening." On the night of the contest, Sally won the first prize ribbon in the beautiful baby contest.

Four months later, Sally appeared again in the *Oakland Tribune*, August 17, page 39, in connection with another baby contest. This time she is referred to as Nellie Bogden, with an incorrect spelling of her last name:

Pretty Infant Is Prize-Winner

*****

Baby Show Carnival Feature

*****

Fair at Elmhurst Will End Tonight After Successful Run

*****

Elmhurst, Aug. 16.—Nellie Bogden, a winsome two-year-old girl of East Oakland, was first-prize winner in the baby show held in Redman's Hall yesterday in connection with the Elmhurst fair and carnival. Nellie carried off the honors in the face of stiff opposition from other pretty children, for Elmhurst boasts many babies eligible for prizes for beauty, chubbiness, prettiness and other commendable qualities in babydom. A sweet expression and pretty face probably won over the hearts and the judgment of the baby show arbiters in Nellie's favor. Elmhurst babies figured high in the prize list at the show, for which there was a large entry.

The article is accompanied by a photograph of baby Sally's head and shoulders, with her hands folded neatly in front of her as she gazes gently downward. The photo is attributed to "Graves Photograph."

OAKL

RA COSTA

PRETTY INFANT IS PRIZE-WINNER

BABY SHOW CARNIVAL FEATURE

Fair at Elmhurst Will End Tonight After Successful Run

ELMHURST, Aug. 16.—Nellie Bogden, a winsome two-year-old girl of East Oakland, was first-prize winner in the baby show held in Redmen's hall yesterday in connection with the Elmhurst fair and carnival. Nellie carried off the honors in the face of stiff opposition from other pretty children, as Elmhurst boasts many babies eligible for prizes for beauty, chubbiness, prettiness and other commendable qualities in babydom.

A sweet expression and pretty face probably won over the hearts and the judgment of the baby show arbiters in Nellie's favor. Elmhurst babies figured high in the prize list at the show, for which there was a large entry.

Today was one of the biggest days of the carnival week in Elmhurst, parades and other events causing a stir of excitement in the fair ground and streets throughout the day. Crowds from Oakland and other centers visited the East Oakland carnival city to witness the big parade and enjoy the fair attractions.

The parade, which started from the carnival center on Ninety-sixth avenue at 3 o'clock, was headed by Captain Thorwald Brown and Lieutenant [illegible], who led a platoon of police. In the procession were Queen Edna, Miss Edna Knight, and her maids of honor, Miss Mamie Smith and Miss Genevieve Knight, members of Moose lodges from Fruitvale and other districts, wearing their insignia, Elmhurst school children dressed in white, a band and a number of expert

NELLIE BOGDEN. —Graves Photograph.

Oakland Tribune **article featuring Sally, August 1913**

On December 27, 1913, again in the *Oakland Tribune*, under the heading "Oakland Boys And Girls", there is a feature article about Sally, with the same photograph as in the August 17th article, and with the same incorrect spelling of her name:

> **Is Much Admired**
> **Child Of Beauty**
> **NELLIE BOGDEN**
> **Nellie Bogden of East Oakland, a child about three years, has perhaps attracted more attention on this side of the Bay than any other tot of her size and age. She had been admired in baby shows, where she carried off prizes because of her beauty. Nellie is a brunette [sic] and is a delightful child.**

From the start of her professional career Sally was introduced with different names. She was born Nellie Bernice Bogdon, but as previously mentioned, she was first billed as "Bernice" Bogdon. A few months later, the billing went back to Nellie Bogden; Bogden with an "en" ending rather than "on", a frequently used incorrect variation. (Her father and mother encountered the same problem.) For the rest of Sally's life, she would deal with many different variations of her name, both professionally and personally. In fact, she was not given the name Sally until October 1926, when she was 15.

ESSANAY FILM COMPANY

The Essanay Film Company in Niles, California, where both Sawyers worked, was a branch of the main Essanay production studio in Chicago. This small movie studio was located in southeast San Francisco Bay and had been producing films in Niles since April 1912. Today, Niles is a suburb of the city of Fremont. In mid-1914, the Niles studio needed a little girl to act in several of its two-reel westerns. The Sawyers suggested using Sally, who was still living with them as their foster child. She was hired. Rather than using her real name, Nellie Bernice Bogdon, in the film credits, the Sawyers and the studio used "Bernice Sawyer," combining her middle name with her foster parents' last name. By age three, she had already been given four names.

BRONCHO BILLY

Sally made three Broncho Billy films at Essanay. The first was *Broncho Billy and the Baby,* starring an early western character played by Gilbert M. Anderson (1880-1971), whose real name was Max H. Aronson. Sally, of course, was the baby. Lee Willard (1873-1940) and Evelyn Selbie (1880-1950) played her parents. It was released on January 23, 1915. Two other films followed a few months later, also starring Broncho Billy. They were *The Western Way* and *The Outlaw's Awakening. The Western Way* co-starred Lee Willard and Hazel Applegate (1886-1959) and was released on March 20, 1915. *The Outlaw's Awakening,* with Broncho Billy as the outlaw and Neva West (1883-1965) as his wife, was released on March 27, 1915.

Sally's work at Essanay, under the name Bernice Sawyer, resulted in her appearance in national film magazines. For *Broncho Billy and the Baby*, the reviewer, in the January 23, 1915 issue of *Motography*, said:

> **The acting of a little child, Bernice Sawyer, and the building of an exciting climax, together with a realistic portrayal of an outlaw by G. M. Anderson, makes this an acceptable film.**

Sally portrait (ca. 1915)

***Broncho Billy And The Baby* scene still with Sally burying her doll**

The review also included a scene still from the film that showed Sally as the focus of attention. Sally can also be seen in a scene still from *The Western Way* in the March 20, 1915 issue of *Motography. Moving Picture World* mentions Bernice Sawyer in the February 6, 1915 and April 10, 1915 issues in reviews for *Broncho Billy and the Baby* and *The Outlaw's Awakening*.

Sally also appeared in *Technical World Magazine*, June 1915, in an article titled "Bad Men of the Movies," by Harold Cary. The article is a well-illustrated career article about Gilbert M. Anderson, who co-formed the Essanay Film Company, created the idea of Broncho Billy as the "good bad man," and portrayed him in the films. Sally is pictured in two scene stills from her second Broncho Billy film, *The Western Way*. However, in the picture captions, she is not identified by name but only referred to as "the little girl."

Then came a notorious stagecoach accident that ended Sally's stint at Essanay. David Kiehn, in his book *Broncho Billy and the Essanay Film Company* (Berkeley, California: Farwell Books, c2003), relates the pertinent facts:

> **The worst accident in the Western Essanay's history occurred on November 3, 1914, during a rehearsal for *Broncho Billy's Christmas Spirit*. The coach was top-heavy with seven people on the roof; it hit a rut in the Niles Canyon road, lost its front wheels and turned over. Lila McClemmon hit the ground face first. Florence Cato and Eva Sawyer piled on top of her. Everyone involved suffered scrapes and bruises, but Eva Sawyer also dislocated her**

> **shoulder and sprained her back. A full month passed before she was able to move around on crutches.**

Eva Sawyer was, of course, Sally's foster mother, and Kiehn also mentions that it took her two months to recover from the accident.

Sally was on the stagecoach too, but only hurt her little finger. However, back in Oakland, the accident scared Sally's grandmother, Nellie Lane, out of her wits, and she insisted Sally be taken out of any more filming. She also decided that Sally should now come and live with her. This was certainly a solution to the family's dilemma – Sally's own mother, Edithe, was now working, and her foster mother, Eva Sawyer, was currently recuperating from a very bad accident.

SALLY MOVES IN WITH HER GRANDMOTHER

Thus, when she was four years old, Sally began a new life with her grandmother. Sally remembers Nellie as being quite erudite and impressive. Nellie was active in the chamber of commerce and on the school board, very rare for a woman those days. In her memoirs, Sally says she was "happy at Grandma's." But, also in her memoirs, she recalls the family unrest in those early years:

> **I remember a <u>horrible</u> fight between Father and Mother in her Art Studio. I ran to Mother and confronted Father! He left angry. By this time, I had persuaded Grandma to let me live with her, & Mother visited Oakland often – especially for Xmas. She whistled as she approached the house.**

Sally's name continued to appear in the *Oakland Tribune*. On October 3, 1915, there was an article: "Oakland Girl Winner Of Exposition Prize." The Exposition referred to was the San Francisco World's Fair of 1915, more officially named the Panama-Pacific International Exposition of 1915, which ran from February to December of that year. Robert remembers hearing his grandmother Edithe bragging about how her daughter, his mother Sally, won the beautiful baby contest at the San Francisco World Fair. According to one newspaper article, she definitely won, but it was only fifth place. In Sally's memoirs, she mentions visiting the World's Fair often with her grandmother. In addition, several pictures of Albert Bogdon in Robert's possession also show him visiting the San Francisco World's Fair. Apparently, their paths never crossed.

Sally was again in the news on July 2, 1916, in an article entitled: "Civic Committees Plan for Big July 4 Celebration; Announce Novel Events for Day of Patriotism." The celebration included many events: an elaborate parade, harness races, water sports, military bands, a literary program, all ending with a fancy dress ball. Both Sally and her grandmother had major roles in the parade:

> **Little Nellie Bernice Bogden, the moving [picture] star and grandchild of Mrs. S. D. [i.e. N. C.] Lane, "the mother of the parade," will play an important part. She is an extremely beautiful child and will serve as one of the attendants of the goddess of liberty, whose name will be announced Monday.**

Both the functions of "mother of the parade" and "attendant of the goddess of liberty" were certainly positions of high honor and reveal the Oakland community's reverence for Nellie, one of their "pioneers," and her beautiful movie star granddaughter.

Sally and grandmother Lane, ready for an automobile outing

Another article, which ran on the front page of the September 24, 1917 issue, announced a "Garden Benefit Fete Tomorrow":

> **Music, dancing and many other diversions have been added to an already well-filled program for the benefit of the Woman's Section of the Navy League ...**
> **A feature of the program will be the dancing of little Nellie Lane, 5-year-old [sic] movie star.**

Sally was actually six years old.

Sally told her son Robert that, as a little girl, she studied Isadora Duncan style dance for a short while in a school in San Francisco. There is a photograph of Sally, very likely from the same time period, in which she is dressed up in a very Isadora Duncan-like Grecian one-shouldered draped costume. This may have been a way for her to show off some of her dance training.

At that time, Isadora Duncan (1877-1927) was wildly popular all over America and the world, and dance schools sprung up everywhere to teach the new revolutionary free modern style. Duncan was born in San Francisco and lived much of her early life in both San Francisco and Oakland. She left the San Francisco area completely in 1895 and did not return until November 1917 when she was scheduled to perform several dance concerts at the Columbia Theater in San Francisco. Unfortunately, her expected concert in Oakland was cancelled. When Sally performed her Isadora Duncan-like dance, the Bay area must already have been abuzz with excitement over Duncan's eagerly anticipated return engagement to take place in just a couple of months.

Sally *a la* Isadora Duncan

Sally also remembered appearing in local pageants and operettas. One theatrical company that she recalled in her memoirs is the Ferris Hartman Company of Oakland, with such productions as "The Toymaker" and "The Snow Queen," among others. These large children's productions were usually staged in the enormous Oakland Civic Auditorium Theater, which opened in 1915.

Grandmother Lane decided that Sally should be home schooled. Sally says she did not go to real school until she was about seven years old. The year was 1918, and she entered the third grade at the neighborhood Garfield School where Nellie had volunteered for years and served as president of the Mother's Club. Sally did not get into the *Oakland Tribune* again until 1922, when she won an essay contest about the early Spanish life of Alameda County, of which Oakland is the county seat. The contest was sponsored by Oakland's East Side Board of Trade, and the winner was announced at an enormous outdoor Spanish barbecue on Friday evening, June 9, 1922, a few weeks after Sally's 11th birthday. The barbecue party and essay contest results were announced in the *Oakland Tribune*, June 13, 1922, "Eastbay Barbecue Proves Success." Sally was referred to as "First prize, Nellie Bogdon, 1749 Twentieth Avenue." On June 14, 1922, there was a follow-up article, "East Oakland Revives Old Spanish Days: Here Is Prize Essay On Early Days In County: Nellie Bogdon, 1749 Twentieth Avenue, Wins Board of Trade Contest":

> **At the East Side Board of Trade barbecue, Friday evening, June 9, first prize was awarded Nellie Bogdon, 1749 Twentieth Avenue, for the best essay on early Spanish life in Alameda Country. This interesting and informative essay is printed below in full.**
>
> **In 1822 a vessel sailed into the Oakland estuary between 15th and 19th Avenues, this being the only port on the Pacific. This vessel came direct from the Sandwich Islands (their name then) [i.e. Hawaii]. On it were Spanish people of the best class. They had a mixed cargo of tools, trees, shrubs, plants and seeds. They had heard about this promised land and had come prepared to stay.**
>
> **William Heath Davis, who is our only authority on the early history of California, was one of the passengers. He helped to locate the village of San Antonio at about E. 12th and 15th Avenue. E. 14th Street was a slough. The Embarcadero was at or near E. 12th Street and 14th Avenue. There were about five hundred inhabitants in the village.**
>
> **BIRTH OF ALAMEDA**
>
> **For many miles it was all Contra Costa County. Not until 1852 was there a division of counties. Alameda was the name chosen for the new county. The county seat was Alvarado (or Union City, as it was called). In 1854, the county seat was moved to San Leandro, where it remained until 1871.**
>
> **There was a fine large spring on 21st Avenue between 17th and 19th Street, from which more than a hundred people got their water supply. When the street was macadamized, the spring was filled in.**
>
> **A large bull ring was located near 20th Avenue and E. 16th Street. Wild bulls were driven into this large enclosure, and the Dons, gaily dressed and their horses attractively decorated, chased the bulls around the ring, and when they caught them, twisted their tails, which caused the bulls to fall upon their noses. They were then conquered. Other bulls were reserved for the genuine bull fights.**
>
> **The slaughter house was at the foot of 23rd Avenue. The bears used to wander all around here and get their meat. They caught the bears by digging deep trenches, covering them with brush, and suspending a good-sized chunk of meat**

over the pit from the limb of an oak tree. Then the bear would jump for the meat, and in this way it was caught. There was a great demand for bear skins and oil, which was rendered after the meat was cooked. Bear meat is very much like pork.

TRADING PORT BORN

A great trading port was soon established. Hides for shoes and tallow for candles were shipped in great quantities to Boston. Their mode of conveyance was by huge sleds, and all had to pass under the great Chileno Gateway at 18th Avenue and E. 14th Street.

The Esplanade, which is now called San Antonio Park, was where people sat and watched the bull fights. In the spring, it was one splash of gold. The California poppy was everywhere, also baby blue eyes, yellow and purple lupins, Indian paint brush, and trembling grass. The song of the meadow lark made one feel that it was good to be alive in such an enchanted land.

The senoritas had the most luxuriant heads of hair with a permanent wave. This was accomplished by using bear's grease. The hair was four and five feet in length. Everyone had beautiful teeth. Men, too, had heavy heads of hair, there being no baldness among them. Outdoor exercise, wholesome food, tamales, enchiladas, together with highly perfumed garlic, onions with the barbecued meat, and a peaceful life kept the system in fine condition. All the ropes, halters, and bridles were made from the hair taken from the horses' tails, and they were beautiful as well as useful.

The Indians taught the white people many useful things -- how to make beads out of stones and nuts; the medicinal use of many shrubs, plants, and flowers, as well as the bark of trees.

This was, and is, indeed, the promised land.

I love you, California.

And now in memory of the pioneers of San Antonio, a school is to be built, named the Roosevelt High School, overlooking the Estuary and taking in the panorama that spreads before our gaze. Six counties can be seen from the heights just above the famous old bull ring. It is justly due these pioneers that we should show our appreciation after a lapse of a hundred years from 1822 to 1922 – that we should recognize their efforts on our behalf – and erect this temple of learning, so that those who follow us will know that we followed the trail which was blazed for us by the Spanish pioneers of San Antonio.

NELLIE BOGDON
1749 20th Avenue,
Oakland, California

Sally was well prepared for writing this essay. Sally had always loved hearing Nellie's stories about the early days, especially because they lived right in the middle of the historic district. She could repeat the stories that had enchanted her over the years, even though the story she was told about the founding of Oakland in 1822 by William Heath Davis is not historically accurate. However, the new school referred to at the end of the essay, the Theodore Roosevelt High school, was soon to have ceremonies in which her very own grandmother would have the honor of raising the flag and breaking the ground for the first time.

NELLIE IN THE NEWS

Nellie C. Lane appeared dozens of times in newspapers in the early decades of the twentieth century, in the *Oakland Tribune* and in other Bay area newspapers, such as the *Daily Alta California*, the *San Francisco Call*, and the *San Francisco Chronicle*. Most of the articles describe her activities in connection with her civic and club work, which was of the crusading type – good education, good libraries, strong mothers, healthy families, good food, homes for working girls – and her participation in bond issuances to accomplish this work.

Her main concentration, however, was on the education and welfare of children, to whom she seemed to be intensely devoted. In mid-May 1911, when she was elected president of the Garfield School Mother's Club, her adopted daughter Edithe was already married and pregnant with Sally.

She also fought hard and worked for years to have a school built in her section of East Oakland – the Theodore Roosevelt High School. After groundbreaking ceremonies were held on November 11, 1922, she appeared the next day pictured in an *Oakland Tribune* article. Later she was featured in a *San Francisco Chronicle* story, also in a large photograph, showing her holding a shovel of dirt at the ceremony (after she had first raised the flag), surrounded by all the major dignitaries of the city, including the mayor, the president of the board of education, and a congressman-elect:

> **I have dreamed of this school for years, worked for it, planned it, and I feel that I helped to put it there. It's to be the greatest school in Oakland and will be named after what I consider America's greatest President – Theodore Roosevelt. I'm proud of having had something to do with the work of conceiving it, and it certainly will be a memorial to the pioneers who settled this portion of the city.**

After the school's opening in 1924, Nellie's name continued to appear regularly in the newspapers, in 1925 and 1926 as judge or inspector in her polling place precinct. After Sally came to visit her in September 1927, however, she entered the Crocker Old

Peoples Home, located at 2507 Pine Street in San Francisco. She lived there from October 1927 until she died on Saturday, January 30, 1932.

Ground Breaking Ceremonies at East Oakland School

FRED M. HUNTER, superintendent of schools, at the extreme left of the main picture, is watching MRS. NELLIE LANE, [illegible] *president of the Board of Education. In the circle is seen ERNEST J. ENGLER, president of the Civic League, addressing the crowd. Congressman-elect JAMES MacLAFFERTY occupies the upper left insert, and MRS. F. V. VOLLMER is seen at the lower right.*

"Ground Breaking Ceremonies At East Oakland School." (*Oakland Tribune - 1922*)

SALLY'S PARENTS' SEPARATION

Sally's mother Edithe worked hard to set up a new life for herself after her separation from Albert. She could no longer depend on her mother, Nellie. She found a place to live, and, more importantly, she found a profession – commercial art. She was eventually to become one of the most expert colorists of black and white photographs in the country, as continuing sales of her oil-painted photographs on eBay can attest.

During their period of separation, Albert wrote letters to Edithe, as usual addressing her by her middle name "Alois." Four of these letters from 1914 have survived. From January 26, 1914:

HOTEL STEIM
KITTANNING, PA.

Jan. 26, 1914

My darling Alois:

On my arrival from my two weeks trip, your three letters and a telegram were waiting for me at Pgh. [Pittsburgh].

Of course, you readily can appreciate the anxiety your letters and first telegram caused, hence the method I pursued in getting information via Mother Lane; much to my displeasure, I assure you.

Since this has passed, I am only too glad to bury it together with other foolishness.

As none of your letters have asked for anything specific that have not been answered, therefore comment unnecessary.

Now:

The date was Thursday Jan. 22nd, weather rather cool and crisp, with ice here and there. I woke up early and said to myself: -- This is the day I am to be made a Mason. . .

[*He continues with a description of his induction to the Masons.*]

It means hard study you can readily perceive. No tomfoolery of foolishness in Masonry. No bluff works.

I have the brains to absorb all the knowledge – enough money to pull me through completely with your co-operation. I shall win out. My personality is invincible. It is now where all my hard study is going to be rewarded fructuously.

So much for Masonry.

When I finish up, I am positively going to launch out in the Show Business. Magic it will be. Whether it is going to be vaudeville – Chautauqua – or my own show has not been fully decided as yet. From the way things look now, it is going to be the latter.

Since you have broken all your promises to me and have been excused by me from all you pledged to do, you can perceive I am not justified to include you in my show as one of the fellow workers.

But before making arrangements with someone else at Vassar or Wellesley College, I give you your last chance. I do this because you are my lawful wife and because you still have enough time to prepare yourself.

Also bear in mind, when you are prepared and start out with the show, you will have no cinch – but there will be hard work for everybody, particularly for me.

Your prompt reply touching this subject thoroughly and carefully will be greatly appreciated.

Please:

Do not make any promises that you are unable or will not fulfill.

As you well know, I shall never ask the impossible of you.

For if you will not carry out your promise solemnly and sincerely – [I] shall lose faith in you forever.

Better not make any promise at all than to make one and disappoint me. Better keep my love warm for you than to cool it with a disappointment.

Be serious in your answer. Just as I am now.

With love to you all.

Your true lover,
Albert

From June 13, 1914:

FORT PITT HOTEL
FORT PITT HOTEL CO.
PENN AVENUE & 10TH STREET
PITTSBURGH, PA

June 13, 1914

My darling Alois:

As to portion of your last letter wherein you mentioned to drop operations of going along further in Masonry for reasons that I cannot financially afford it and not befitting my finances or station.

Believe me, once I land it, I will soon make it fit my finances and station. It will be the means of working a certain system towards a certain goal by a unique method – "higher masonry."

I sure do know how to play the game of life.

My only bad quality is – that I want to push things. And for this you do not blame me.

Things look quite propitious for my receiving 32o. All I have to do is to hold tight and let the powers of B keep working, which have been started by me about six months ago.

As to what kind of letter to write Helen [Albert's sister], would suggest nothing for the present – concerning topic of you coming here.

Just let things – circumstances – adjust themselves. I will make the proper move at the right time. Trust me. Nothing so far is definite. But I know what I would like to do. That is all.

However I am busy.

Your true lover,
Albert

1000 X X X X AS.
" " for Nellie
" " " Junior

From July 16, 1914:

FORT PITT HOTEL
FORT PITT HOTEL CO.
PENN AVENUE & 10TH STREET
PITTSBURGH, PA

July 16, 1914

My darling Alois:

Have mailed my Masonic apron to you yesterday A.M. Under the flap, you will find name, number and location of my lodge. This will give you a faint idea of just what I had to go through to become a Master Mason.

I first made application in Pennsylvania and was turned down.

Then attempted it in Ohio, with same result.

Then West Virginia and made it.

Should I [have] failed in W. Va., I would next have tackled Indiana state. I would have kept trying in every state in the union until I arrived.

There are [a] lot of clandestine lodges, but they should be sidestepped.

You might ask your secretary of Eastern Star Lodge to find out for you if Nelson #30 A.F. & A.M. Lodge is a legal lodge and recognized by California state. I would do this for your information; in this way, you will know just where Sonny [Albert, Jr./Lane] will stand for [the] future.

Enclosed you will find a picture of Dick's [family friend] baby boy. Hamlin is his last name, I believe. They roomed with us at Chalfants.

Everything is coming along fairly well and the big move will be made shortly.

Hoping to hear from you soon. I am as ever,

Your true lover,
Albert

P.S. It is coming to a point soon with me where my love for you is becoming stronger than my ambition for big things; and life without your presence is impossible. How I ever endured your absence, I do not know. If things turn out as I anticipate, you will be here in Sept. and start out with me with my show.

Keep yourself in shape on the piano, practice, practice, practice. Be prepared for any emergency. I see success. Expect to get money for apparatus middle of next month; -- sure – sure – sure – sure – sure – sure— sure. So be happy with me and share my joy.

From September 16, 1914:

AEB [monogram]

Valparaiso, Ind.
Sept. 16, 1914

My darling Alois:

Sorry to not have received response to my letter before this.

Just as soon as I get straightened out a little here, shall write you a long letter.

However, would be pleased to hear from you first, so as to know whether or not you are interested in me any more.

Have entered University here yesterday. Passed one of the best entrance examinations here for some time. Of course I knew I could make it or never would have come. Really, if I had cared to, I could pass one good enough to enter Harvard, Yale, or Princeton.

Of course, you are wondering, I know, what possessed me to start school, etc. But, if I had you here for a few minutes, I could explain in a jiffy.

I am taking medicine. First year's work will be: Anatomy, Histology, Physiology, Medical chemistry, Material medica & Pharmacy.

Took my first lessons today and greatly enjoyed same to be sure. I find these studies comparatively easy on account of my dandy previous preparation and good brain.

In addition to above subject, am studying advanced Philosophy and Spanish and French. I know you like Spanish, so you will realize your wish for me.

Propose to study here two years, then last two years to finish up at Johns Hopkins University.

Of course, this is problematical, as it all depends on you my dear whether I shall be called Dr. Bogdon or not in the future.

As suggested some time ago, that I may finish as a Physician and Surgeon in the United States Navy. And while there, you know what it will mean to Nellie [Sally] – Sonny [Albert, Jr./Lane] and yourself.

Again, I repeat, it is up to you, whether the Bogdon name is to be blessed or not.

You have it in your power to have me dismissed etc. from this university for non-support etc. etc.

But, should you do anything of this nature, I shall gladly leave and will head for New York -- thence to Russia where I shall enter medical school there and be safe.

Am determined to become one of the brilliant intellects of the century.

As ever,
XX 1000 AS. **Your true lover,**
address: **Albert**

Valparaiso University
Valparaiso, Indiana

P.S. Am solely self-supporting. Including work & study, shall take 14 hours per day.

It was obvious that Bogdon was still not returning home, so Edithe decided to divorce him and ask for child support. She was not able to do so until early 1917, and was not able to reunite her family until she remarried in the early 1920s.

Although Sally did not see her father after the separation, except for short visits when she was still a little girl, she remembered enough to cry out for her "real father" when she was seriously ill as a child. She was also aware of what was happening in his later life, including his second marriage and the birth of his daughter Violet, Sally and Lane's half sister.

ALBERT BOGDON AFTER SEPARATION

Bogdon's magic career was starting to thrive at the same time that his young daughter's theatrical career was just beginning. He started by joining, through correspondence, a prestigious magic society in England called The Magic Circle, on October 1, 1913.

Bogdon's magician brochure (cover page)

From the time that Bogdon was accepted into The Magic Circle in 1913 until he joined the U.S. Navy on April 4, 1917, his name and/or photo appeared in 49 issues of magazines devoted to magic and/or the performing arts: *The Conjuring Record*, *The Lyceum World*, *The Magic Circular*, *The Magic Wand*, *The New York Clipper*, *The New York Dramatic Mirror*, and *The Sphinx*. In the year 1915 alone, he had as many as 22 mentions. Of all these magazines, only *The Magic Circular*, founded in 1906, continues to publish. It is the longest-running magic-related periodical in the world.

The Magic Circular reported in the March 1914 issue that Bogdon was given full membership in the Inner Magic Circle on February 10, 1914, allowing him to use the designation "M.I.M.C." The July 1914 issue stated:

> **Our best thanks to Mr. Bogdon, of Pittsburgh, U.S.A., for contributions to hand [sic], which we hope to use shortly.**

Two articles by him (his "contributions") appeared in 1914 – a short story entitled "The Legerdemaniacs" in August and "The Magician's Creed" in October.

209

As a finale, Linga-Singh introduces a light carriage (four-wheeled), which is examined by committee from audience, one of whom sits in the carriage. With the aid of a piece of string fastened to front of carriage the performer then drags the vehicle across the stage with his eyes, the ends of the string being fastened in either eye. The illusion act is silent, but this last item was given with some witty patter in excellent English. It was, however, unduly prolonged, and being scarcely in the best of taste, might well be omitted.

H.L.L.

THE LEGERDEMANIACS.

By Albert E. Bogdon, M.I.M.C.

In the outer office, her nimble fingers running the gamut of a typewriter keyboard, Miss Marian Polk strained her ears in vain. She could distinguish no word that was being spoken on the other side of the ground-glass door. What went on the other side of that door is of more importance at present than Miss Polk's curiosity. So, consider the scene shifted to a commonplace, ten-by-twelve, oak-finished and furnished, private office.

"Well, let him in. I'll see what he wants. Are there many waiting ? "

"No, only three or four, Sir. I'll show him in at once."

Elwood Hughes swung his capacious office-chair around as a young man was ushered in.

"Well ? " queried Hughes. "Who are you, that you can't announce your name and business ? And what do you want ? "

"If I'd sent in my name," the young man replied, complacently, "you might not have cared to see me ; so I chose a more novel way of announcing myself. My card, Mr. Hughes, you will find in the lower left-hand drawer of your desk, if you care to look."

Hughes leaned over with a grunt and inserted a key in the lock of the lower drawer, all the while regarding the youth curiously from the corners of his eyes.

"This drawer is locked," he said. "What sort of a game are you trying to work on me ? "

"Open it."

Hughes turned the key and pulled the drawer out with an effort —it was rather tightly encased. On top of a thick bundle of letters lay a small business card :

Bogdon's short story "The Legerdemaniacs" (first page)

For Private Circulation only.

THE MAGIC CIRCULAR.

A Monthly Review of the Magic Art.

Vol. 8 OCTOBER, 1914 *Nos. 95 & 96.*

THE MAGICIANS' CREED.

I believe in Magic Magic the Art the Original—the Progressive. I believe in the Past of Magic—and in the Future, founded on the heritage of that Past ; of clean living ; frugal, industrious—the magician of poise, power, purity, genius and courage. I believe that Magic's dominant spirit is, has been, and always will be, instructive and entertaining enlightment.

I believe that my brother stands for the same faith in Magic, although his expression may vary from mine. I believe in Magic of the present, and her professors possessing the wisdom of past generations, purified through the melting pot into a greater potency for good.

I believe in taking pride in our Art, her Students, her Professionals, her Entertainments. I believe in the great plans, born of initiative, foresight and invention, created by the great Magicians of to-day—here—now.

I believe that the Magicians who truly represent her Art are those of God-fearing lives, who scorn ostentation and the seats of the ungodly ; building surely, quietly and permanently. I believe that those who really know her—love her her Art—her Science, discovered and expressed through her instrument of speech—Brother John Nevil Maskelyne.

This philosopher has done the greatest work for us in the history of Magic, and my supreme desire is that my brother artistes will absorb, reflect upon and welcome the true spirit of his message, and will realize in it peace, power and plenty. So mote it be.

Albert Edward Bogdon, M.I.M.C.,
Pittsburgh, Pa.

Text of Bogdon's "The Magician's Creed"

For the *Lyceum World*, Bogdon wrote a series of three articles on the history of magic that were published in the January, March and June 1915 issues. This magazine was the official organ of the Independent Lyceum Bureau, a talent booking organization, with which Bogdon was registered. Bogdon also advertised his magician work regularly in this magazine between 1913 and 1917.

Helps and Hints for our Lyceum Entertainers

Ancient, Mediaeval and Modern Magic.

By Albert Bogdon, M.I.M.C.

ARTICLE I.

EDITORIAL NOTE—With this number we begin a series of articles on "Magic," by the talented magician, Mr. Albert Bogdon. These articles are among the most interesting we have published in THE LYCEUM WORLD, and will prove to many to be the most interesting ever read in any magazine. The articles have been carefully prepared by the author, and will cover the entire field of magic in a way not attempted before this. Many people will understand better the real nature, purpose, and character of the performance of a modern magician, and will realize that such a number of a lecture course or chautauqua program is not merely "amusement and entertainment," but of educational value.

We have given Mr. Bogdon permission to express himself freely in these articles, and while we may differ from him in some views expressed, shall not change materially the articles as submitted, but present them to our readers for careful study and consideration. We always hear from our readers as to what they like and dislike, and expect to hear from them about these articles, and hope to hear many favorable things. These articles will continue in THE LYCEUM WORLD during the new year, and those who wish all the articles may date back their subscriptions and we shall supply back numbers as long as we have any copies left.

Magic! There is no word in the language which has a more alluring and fascinating sound. The very word itself is suggestive of mystery. Magic is one of the oldest forms of amusement. Its practice as an art has survived through the ages and will never lose its attraction for the people's mind. It is to be borne in mind, however, that the magic of the ancient and mediæval days is separated by a deep chasm from the modern magic; and while it is true that the modern magic has been evolved from the former, yet there is the well-defined and easily ascertainable line of damarcation between the two. Modern magic is diametrically opposed, both in principle and practice, to the ancient magic, and the foundational conceptions in no manner compare with those upon which rested the magic of the past.

The word magic was given us by the Romans and the Greeks. To them it meant priestcraft. The word came to them from the Persians. The Babylonians gave it to the Persians, and they in their turn got it from Assyria. Further back than that its history is hazy and uncertain, save that it was the language of the Sumero-Akkadians.

"Maga" to the Akkadians meant priest; in the language of the Assyrians the meaning was practically the same, they calling their high priest "Rab-Mag"; and considering the fact that the main business of the priests in ancient times consisted in fortune-telling, miracle-working, and giving out oracles, it seems justifiable to believe that the Persian term, which in the Latin version is "Magus," is derived from the Chaldeans, and is practically the same; for the connotation of a wise man endowed with supernatural powers has always been connected with the word "Magus," and even today means wizard, sorcerer, or miracle-worker.

While the belief in and practice of magic are not entirely absent in the civilization of Israel, we find that the leaders of orthodox thought have set their faces against it—at least as it appeared in its crudest form, and went so far as to persecute sorcerers with fire and sword.

Goethe introduces the belief in magic into the very plot of Faust. In his despair at never finding the key to the world-problem in science, which as he thinks does not offer what we need, but useless truisms only, Faust hopes to find the royal road to knowledge by supernatural methods. He says:

"Therefore, from magic I seek assistance,
That many a secret perchance I reach
Through spirit-power and spirit-speech,
And this the bitter task forego
Of saying the things I do not know,—
That I may detect the inmost force
Which binds the world, and guides its course;
Its gems, productive powers explore,
And rummage in empty words no more!"

Faust follows the will-o'-the-wisp of pseudo-science, and so finds his efforts to gain useful knowledge balked. He turns agnostic and declares that we cannot know anything worth knowing. He exclaims:

Bogdon's January 1915 article on the history of magic (first page)

THE LYCEUM WORLD. 621

THE INDEPENDENT LYCEUM BUREAU

—PRESENTS—

ALBERT BOGDON

MASTER MAGICIAN

MEMBER OF THE INNER MAGIC CIRCLE OF LONDON, ENGLAND

This is an attraction committees and audiences are looking for, want and will enjoy. Will please the most fastidious. Is a standard and recognized.

Has toured China, Japan, Corea, Manchuria, Philippine Islands, Guam, Territory of Hawaii and Russia successfully last four years. Now is in the field to fill dates in the United States.

PROGRAM IN THREE PARTS:

Spectacular array of high-class

SLEIGHT-OF-HAND,

CONJURING

and ILLUSIONS

SEND FOR CIRCULAR, SPECIMEN PROGRAM AND PARTICULARS AT ONCE.

INDEPENDENT LYCEUM BUREAU

CINCINNATI. : CHICAGO. : INDIANAPOLIS.

Bogdon's full-page ad in *Lyceum World*

Around the same time, he produced two versions of his official stationery. Both versions have the same heading:

ALBERT BOGDON, Europe's MASTER MAGICIAN

All headings include a sepia-colored framed oval photo of Bogdon in "white tie," in three quarter bust profile facing right. In the photo, he also wears the Magic Circle membership pin. On the right of the name is a ribbon sporting a crowned double-headed eagle. At the bottom of the stationery is the Independent Lyceum Bureau logo, as is also found in the flyer. The date is printed on the stationery as an open date of "191-," to cover any date in the 1910s. In one version, the center of the page is blank. In the other version, flush left, is a list of previous gig locations and theaters in which Bogdon presumably performed in the past:

HONOLULU, T-H.
"Orpheum"
SAMOAN ISLANDS
"Tutuila"
AGANA, GUAM
"Adrian"
MANILA, P. I.
"Manzanilla"
SANDAKAN, BRITISH N. B.
"Naval Hall"
HONG KONG, CHINA
"Empire"
TOKIO, JAPAN
"Alladin"
DALNY, MANCHURIA
"Dairen"
VLADIVOSTOK, RUSSIA
"Rusticana"
SEOUL, KOREA
"Sienpi"

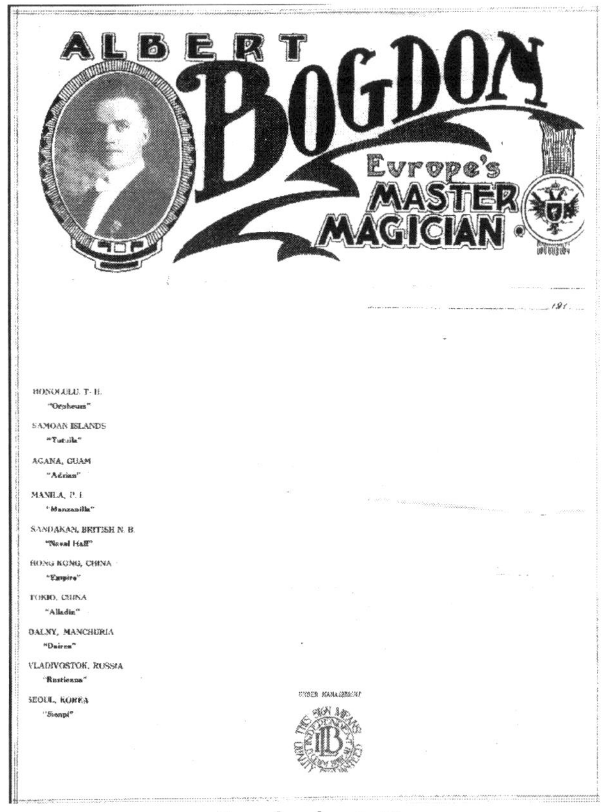

ALBERT BOGDON
Europe's MASTER MAGICIAN

HONOLULU, T-H.
"Orpheum"
SAMOAN ISLANDS
"Tutuila"
AGANA, GUAM
"Adrian"
MANILA, P. I.
"Manzanilla"
SANDAKAN, BRITISH N. B.
"Naval Hall"
HONG KONG, CHINA
"Empire"
TOKIO, CHINA
"Alladin"
DALNY, MANCHURIA
"Dairen"
VLADIVOSTOK, RUSSIA
"Rusticana"
SEOUL, KOREA
"Sienpi"

Bogdon's stationary

The September 6, 1913 issue of the *New York Clipper* ("Out Of Town News" column) included his photo and a news item saying he had been awarded a $500 prize and was selected to compete with Howard Thurston at the I. M. A. Convention in Cleveland, Ohio in 1914. Thurston was the most famous magician of his day, even more famous that Harry Houdini.

Sally remembers hearing somewhere that Bogdon toured with Howard Thurston, but she was never sure whether that was true or not. However, a small collection of objects relating to Thurston was found in the Bogdon family memorabilia. It included a photo of Bogdon and Thurston arm-and-arm taken on the back porch of a house during a weekend, which was reported in the September 15, 1915 issue of *The Sphinx* magazine, the official organ of the Society of American Magicians. In a column entitled "Notes from Baltimore, Md.," Charles Fulton Oursler describes the weekend when this and other photographs were taken:

> **Magic would not come to Baltimore in July, so in emulation of Mahomet, two residents of Baltimore, in the persons of Thomas C. Worthington, Jr., arch demon of the Demon Club of Baltimore Magicians, and yours truly, went to magic. That is to say, at the invitation of Mr. Howard Thurston, we spent the week-end at his villa in Beechhurst, L. I., and we had a delightful time. Mrs. Thurston is as charming and interesting a hostess as there is in the land. And then there was their baby Jane, a most interesting little lady, at whose birthday party we were privileged to be present; whose birthday cake we helped destroy, and whose favor we enjoyed throughout her visit. And Dr. Bogdon of Moscow, a scholarly magical adept, whom Mr. Thurston laughingly introduced as a "Russian spy" who is a houseguest of Mr. and Mrs. Thurston, also helped make our stay pleasant.**

The "week-end" referred to in the above column, during the period when Bogdon was a house guest, was Saturday and Sunday, July 24 and 25, 1915. Thurston's villa was in Beechhurst, a section of Whitestone, Queens, in New York City.

Besides the arm-in-arm photo of Bogdon and Thurston found in the Bogdon family memorabilia, another photo taken during the same weekend and showing a group of six people was found in a Brooklyn-based Thurston collector's private collection. In this photo, in addition to Bogdon and Thurston, there is Thurston's wife, Leotha; their six-year-old daughter, Jane; Charles Fulton Oursler (1893-1952), a promising young Baltimore journalist; and Thomas C. Worthington (1882-1953), also a magician and head of the famous club of magicians, the Demon Club.

Bogdon and Howard Thurston together at Thurston's Beechhurst cottage

Other articles in the 1915 and 1916 issues of *The Sphinx* help to better describe the Bogdon-Thurston relationship. In the June 15, 1915 issue's editorial column, written by its editor and publisher, A. M. Wilson, he refers to Bogdon as Thurston's advisor and literary assistant:

> **Among the celebrities I met at Martinka's Powers and other places, were: Karl Germain, Harry Houdini . . . and Howard Thurston whom I had the pleasure of meeting in his commodious workshop, where he is rebuilding his show and getting ready for the coming season. In addition to his regular corps of mechanics, etc., Thurston has secured the services of Frank Heines (The White Yogi), a skillful worker in all branches of magic craft. Thurston is also fortunate in having with him as advisor and literary assistant Dr. Albert**

> **Bogdon, late attaché of the Russian Embassy to Italy. There is no truth in the report that Mr. Thurston will return to vaudeville.**

In an earlier article, Charles Fulton Oursler referred to Bogdon as "Dr. Bogdon of Moscow," and Howard Thurston laughingly referring to Bogdon as "a Russian spy." A. M Wilson, stated, in the previous article, that he was the "late attaché of the Russian embassy to Italy." What was all this about? There is no clue. However, Bogdon was always conscious of his Russian roots. His marriage document for his second wife claims that both his parents were born in Russia, although his mother was ethnically Lithuanian. His letterhead displayed the Tsarist crowned double-headed eagle. In his advertisements, he includes Russia as one of his "four-year" tour stops. In one letter to his wife Edithe, he talks about escaping from her "to Russia where I will enter medical school and be safe."

In the July 15, 1915 *The Sphinx* issue, A. M. Wilson extols Bogdon's talents:

> **Magic needs an exponent, a demonstrator of theory and principle, one who can teach or explain to the public just what magic is, what relationship it sustains to other forms of art as produced on the public stage. ... there is hope, for Thurston has associated with him Dr. Albert Bogdon who I believe is thoroughly qualified to take up such a work as I hint at and I believe he will do it and that right soon.**

The entire impetus for the 1915 Bogdon-Thurston relationship could well have originated with the publication of an article by Robert Grau (1858-1916) entitled "The Passing of the Magician," in the May 19, 1915 issue of *The New York Dramatic Mirror*. Although Robert Grau was a prominent writer in the field of show business activity, people in the magic profession considered his article unfairly pessimistic and irresponsibly full of falsehoods and misrepresentations.

Albert Bogdon and the famous magician, Harry Houdini (1874-1926), were awarded the writing assignments to defend the entire magic profession. Their articles appeared on the first page of the June 16, 1915 issue of *The New York Dramatic Mirror*. Bogdon's article, entitled "The Rise of the Magician," comes first and takes up about two-thirds of the page. Houdini's article, entitled "The Magicians In Review," is positioned below Bogdon's, takes up the final third of the page, and then continues on another page.

The two writers have different approaches in their articles. Bogdon wrote about magic, the magician, and the profession in more general terms, similar to the way he wrote about the history of magic in *The Lyceum World* in his Article I of January 1915. In only the last paragraph did he refer to Grau's article:

> **The writer of an article which appeared in this periodical recently was evidently misinformed as to the true status of the present day magician. Realizing that THE MIRROR is an authority on things theatrical, and has a broad circulation, even reaching the universities and Lyceum's public, with**

> **whom the writer is connected as professor and exponent of this worthy art for many years, he feels it his duty to correct the erroneous impressions received from the article called "the Passing of the Magician," by Robert Grau.**

Houdini, in his article, chose to be extremely specific in his attacks. He carefully corrected and explained all the mistakes and falsehoods that Grau had made in his original article. Taken together, the two articles work well as a complementary defense of the magic profession.

THE NEW YORK DRAMATIC MIRROR

ESTABLISHED JANUARY [illegible] 1879

VOLUME LXXIII — NEW YORK, WEDNESDAY, JUNE 16, 1915 — No. 1904

THE RISE OF THE MAGICIAN

By ALBERT BOGDON, LL.B., M.D.

MUSIC, Painting, Sculpture, Acting—each and every art has its own persuasive eloquence—a method of appeal peculiar to itself. The more perfect the art, the more clearly does it convey its message to the human mind.

Magic that interests is no less an art, dependent for its human appeal on the ideal which the magician has wrought into his work. However, it does not exist for art's sake; it exists to entertain, inspire and enlighten.

Magic as it is practiced by its artists to-day originated from the old magic, when the belief in sorcery began to break down in the eighteenth century, which is the dawn of rationalism, and marks the epoch since which scientists have been working out a scientific world conception.

While magic as a superstition and a fraud is doomed, magic as an art will not die. Science has taken hold of it and permeated its own spirit, changing it into scientific magic, which is destitute of all mysticism, occultism, and superstition, and comes to us now as a witty play for our recreation and diversion.

The spread of modern magic and its proper understanding are an important sign of progress, and in this sense the feats of our Herrmanns, Kellars, and Thurstons, are a work of great educational significance. They are instrumental in dispelling the fogs of superstition by exhibiting to the public the astonishing but natural miracles of the art of magic; and while they amuse and entertain they fortify the people in the conviction of the reliability of science.

The study of magic is wonderfully fascinating. It possesses, too, a decided pedagogic value, which eminent scholars have not been slow to recognize. Those who obtain an insight into its principles are preserved against infection from many psychical epidemics of the age. My friend, Dr. G. Stanley Hall, at one time professor of experimental psychology at the Johns Hopkins University, Baltimore, at present president of Clarke University, Worcester, Mass., used to exhibit conjuring experiments to his classes, to illustrate the illusion of the senses. Professor Joseph Jastrow, of the University of Wisconsin, has from time to time subjected a number of students to careful tests, to ascertain their "tactile sensibility, sense of textures, accuracy of vision perception," and other mental processes.

The literature of magic is not extensive and all the artists that have made a success of this profession have had to take a course at the school of experience to get the A B C of their work coupled with a most thorough training in the university of hard knocks.

The magician no less than the actor, has to bring his audience into a responsive mood. But it is more difficult for the magician to do this. Usually there is no initial antagonism to the actor, but the magician's audience is at first in a watchful and critical state of mind. By the very conditions of his performance, he challenges the spectators' sharpness of perception. Virtually it is understood that he is about to delude them, and that they will not see through his effects. So they summon all their keenness and resolve to find out if they can. For a while they scrutinize him coldly, but if he succeeds in mystifying them, they surrender completely and give him generous applause.

It is estimated that there are at least 500 professional magicians in the United States. Of this great number, it is said, not more than ten are able to earn a good living in their special line, and scarcely more than five are really making money. Considering the multitude of performers, many of them expert, it is evident that only exceptional skill could enable one to win a place among the foremost. This is shown by the fact that America has had but one successful magician at a time, excepting those, of course, engaged on the Lyceum platform. At the retirement of Kellar in 1907, he proclaimed Thurston to the world as his legitimate successor, and Mr. Thurston has held the field to himself for the last eight years with unquestionable success.

The writer of an article which appeared in this periodical recently was evidently misinformed as to the true status of the present day magician. Realizing that THE MIRROR is an authority on things theatrical, and has a broad circulation, even reaching the universities and Lyceum's public, with whom the writer is connected as professor and exponent of this worthy art for many years, he feels it his duty to correct the erroneous impressions received from the article called "The Passing of the Magician," by Robert Grau.

[illegible], New York.

KELLAR AND THURSTON,
The Picture of the Two Noted Magicians Was Taken on the Occasion When Kellar, Retiring, Conferred His Sceptre Upon Mr. Thurston.

THE MAGICIANS IN REVIEW

By HARRY HOUDINI

I READ with great astonishment the article in your issue of May 15, 1915, captioned "The Passing of the Magician," and cannot understand how Mr. Grau could have signed such a bunch of incongruities.

He is wrong in almost every statement.

In Paris there is no Musee Grevin for Illusionists. Very likely he means the Theater Robert Houdin on Boulevard Des'Italiens. This is still in existence and controlled by the Melis Brothers, the well-known moving picture exploiters and manufacturers. They started the mystery pictures, and the vogue for this style of picture has long passed away.

Very few manufacturers appeared on the stage, and very few performers of the magical craft have ever been successful as manufacturers.

Among the notable manufacturers I may mention Voisin, of Paris; the Anglo-Frenchman, C. Devere, who is still very much alive and in Paris; Ernest Basch, of Hannover, Germany; Conradi-Horster, of Berlin (still living); A. Herman, known as Berlin Herman; Lischke; Carl Willmann, Hamburg, Germany; in England, Hamleys, Frank Blum, Goldston and Munroe rarely appeared as performers; only on state occasions for charity. In America: Martinka, Otto Maurer, Jr., W. D. Leroy, Augustus Roterberg, Yost, Hartz and Judd, Hartz being the only really prominent manufacturer who ever became extra well known as a clever sleight-of-hand performer. Basch, however, traveled for years as mysterious entertainer. This will dispose of the [illegible] that some performers made money as manufacturers.

Harry Kellar retired, not because business was bad, but he explained to me he had money enough to enjoy himself for the rest of his life. The younger generation were getting a bit speedy, and by the sudden reversal of steel bonds he nearly lost his fortune, and by the self same, only in a different direction of reversing of steel, he made a fortune, and, with what he had, bought an annuity for his good wife and himself and moved to Los Angeles to enjoy same. Fate, however, decreed that Mrs. Kellar was to pass away about a year after the annuity had been bought, and Kellar takes life easy in sunny California.

Regarding Robert Heller, Mr. Grau is all wrong. Heller never presented spiritualism in any of his programmes, at least not among my programme collection, and I have without a doubt the only collection in the world of magician's programmes.

Anderson, the Wizard of the North, with a number of other performers, exploited the "spiritualism exposed," or "the Davenport Brothers shown up."

(Continued on page 6.)

Bogdon's and Houdini's articles defending the magic profession

Reading Bogdon's article, one could consider it quite a good public relations placement for Howard Thurston. Thurston is mentioned in it twice. The first quote is:

> **The spread of modern magic and its proper understanding are an important sign of progress, and in this sense the feats of our Herrmanns, Kellars, and Thurstons, are a work of great educational significance.**

The other is:

> **At the retirement of Kellar in 1897 [i.e. 1908], he proclaimed Thurston to the world as his legitimate successor, and Mr. Thurston has held the field to himself for the last eight years with unquestionable success.**

Not only is Thurston mentioned twice, but he and Kellar are pictured in the middle of the article in a three-by-three-inch photo. The photo shows Kellar (on the left) and Thurston (on the right), from the waist up shaking hands, with the following caption:

KELLAR AND THURSTON
The Picture of the Two Noted Magicians Was Taken on the Occasion When Kellar, Retiring, Conferred His Scepter Upon Mr. Thurston

However, during the six months after Bogdon visited Thurston, something puzzling happened to their relationship, as evidenced by the following declaration by Thurston, reported by A. M. Wilson in the January 15, 1916 issue of *The Sphinx*:

> **Mr. Thurston authorizes me to state that Dr. Albert Bogdon is not now, never has been, nor never will be connected with him in a business way. Dr. Bogdon was the guest of Mr. Thurston for a while last summer, but never connected with the show or any other business venture of Thurston.**

Regardless of what precipitated this statement, Bogdon's name continued to appear regularly in the talent list of *The Lyceum World* as "Prof. Albert Bogdon, Magician" throughout 1916 and lastly in the January 1917 issue.

At the same time, however, he began to explore other careers. Much earlier, *The Sphinx*, in a column concerning the Pittsburgh Association of Magicians, reported in its August 15, 1914 issue:

> **The matter of our association securing a charter is being agitated and same will be given prompt consideration as soon as all data pertaining thereto has been compiled, which work is being taken care of by Attorney Albert Bogdon, who is interested in our association to no small extent.**

In the Bogdon family memorabilia, there is a certificate which indicates that Bogdon was "admitted to the bar" for the "District Court of the United States of America in and for the Southern District of California." It is dated September 29, 1916, in Los Angeles, California. Furthermore, a few months earlier, he was able to find a position as a financial representative. The family memorabilia contains the following flyer:

> **Important Announcement**
> **Berkeley Bible Seminary**
> **Berkeley, California**
> **March 17, 1916**

> **Mr. Albert Bogdon, whose picture is shown herewith, has been elected Financial Representative of Berkeley Bible Seminary. In a short time he will call upon you in the interest of the Seminary, and we bespeak for him your cordial and fraternal assistance . . .**

Soon, the Navy beckoned, but, before moving on, Bogdon had a major family matter to settle. He had deserted a wife, a daughter, and a son back in Oakland. An official divorce was obtained between Bogdon and Edithe on January 16, 1917. Edithe was awarded custody of the two children. A court-ordered child-support-payment decree, signed on February 23, 1917, required Bogdon to pay $30 a month to Edithe. The payments, according to the decree, were to begin on March 1, 1917. Bogdon probably made only two payments, for March and April 1917, before enlisting in the U.S. Navy on April 4, 1917, just two days before America declared war on Germany, April 6, 1917. While in the service, support payments were automatically deducted from his military pay and then sent directly to Edithe.

Chapter 2
Hollywood Years – Los Angeles

EDITHE MARRIES BEUTLER

Edithe started a new life in the 1920s. She married again, in early 1922, to a man also named Albert – Albert Sprague Beutler (1896-1969). He, like Edithe, was a commercial artist but did other jobs, such as real estate agent, to make ends meet. When they moved to San Francisco later that year, Edithe took advantage of the opportunity to bring her family together. Sally and Lane left their foster homes and joined Edithe and Albert in their new home, but the children never warmed up to their stepfather. Sally said in her memoirs, "Lane and I began to hate Beutler."

THE BEUTLERS MOVE TO LOS ANGELES

Edithe, Albert, and the children moved again in mid-1924, this time to Los Angeles. Edithe got a job coloring black and white photographs at First National movie studio, and Albert continued as a commercial artist. Sally began school in the fall in the newly built Fairfax High School. She said in her memoirs that she initiated the first school newspaper there.

In the 1925-1926 school year, Sally was cast as the lead in the school's major dramatic production of the year. She played the title role in *The Queen's Enemies* by Lord Dunsany. This one-act play was written in 1913 and is based on a passage in Herodotus. In the story, a cleverly deceptive Egyptian queen of the Sixth dynasty B.C.E. invites a group of generals, who have just conquered her country, to a feast in an underground temple where she succeeds in drowning them all by opening the floodgates of the Nile.

Sally's theatrical talent was soon lost to Fairfax High because, at some point during that year, Fox Film studio called, and her high school classes were replaced by on-the-set private tutors. Sally was still underage and, by law, required continued schooling.

MELBA BROWN – DANNY BORZAGE – FRANK BORZAGE

Sally's connection with Fox began with a visit from Melba Brown. Melba was a close friend of Sally's grandmother, Nellie Lane, and, like Nellie, was from Salt Lake City. Sally remembers Melba visiting her grandmother years earlier in Oakland, and Melba continued to be a close friend of Edithe and the Beutler family. Melba was now living in Los Angeles and was married to Danny Borzage, a Fox studio musician who was hired to play mood music, mainly on the accordion, during filming. Danny often came along with Melba on her visits to the Beutler home, and he got to know Sally quite well. He was impressed with her considerable beauty, charm, and maturity, for a girl of only 14.

Sally and Danny Borzage playing his accordion

Danny, like Melba, was born in Salt Lake City. He and two of his brothers, Frank and Lew, all ended up working in Hollywood at Fox studio. Frank Borzage became a famous film director, in silent films as well as talkies, winning Oscars in both media. Danny Borzage, besides working as an "on set" musician, was a sometime actor. Lew Borzage became an assistant director and also sometimes acted.

SCREEN TEST & BIT PARTS

Danny Borzage sent word about Sally's potential to his brother Frank, who arranged for Fox to give her a screen test. The test was a great success, and this eventually led to a contract. In essence, Sally also owed her Hollywood career to Melba Brown of Salt Lake City.

Frank Borzage

This Salt Lake City connection caused confusion about Sally's true hometown origin and early place of residence. When, on November 28, 1926, the *Salt Lake Tribune* ran an article entitled, "Dainty Little Sally Phipps, Flapper Of Brand New Type, Former Salt Lake City Girl," the reporter wrote:

> **Sally was born in San Francisco, on May 25, 1909. With her parents, she moved to Salt Lake City when she was 2 years of age, returning after two years to San Francisco.**

The only correct information in the whole paragraph is her studio-given name and the day of her birth, May 25. Several biographies record her birth date as 1909 rather than 1911. Fox Film studio, obviously aware of her extreme youth, purposely added two years to her age.

Another article in the *Salt Lake Tribune*, from January 16, 1927, entitled "Three Salt Lake Girls Given High Recognition by 'Movie' Organization," created even more mythology about Sally:

> **Miss Phipps was born in San Francisco, but went to Salt Lake when very young, and was largely educated in the Utah metropolis.**

The same article also gave full credit to Frank Borzage as the first person to put Sally in a film:

> **... Frank Borzage, whom Salt Lakers know so well, couldn't resist seeing her in films. He is an old friend of the family, and Sally's beauty attracted the Fox producer-director at the outset. He insisted on a test and Sally showed to such advantage that she was put to work. Her first work was in "Early To Wed," ...**

Early To Wed was a feature film starring Matt Moore and Kathryn Perry. Sally had an uncredited bit part. It was released on April 25, 1926, a month shy of Sally's 15th birthday. Despite the family connection, this was the only film that Sally made with Frank Borzage. She was cast the same year in another uncredited part in *The Family Upstairs*, released August 29. By February 15, 1927, her name was in big type in an advertisement in the *Salt Lake Tribune*. It called her "Salt Lake's Own Sally Phipps," although she was only one of the billed featured players, not the star.

NEW NAME – SALLY PHIPPS

Fox studio had a problem with Sally's real name – Nellie Bernice Bogdon. In any case, by 1926, Sally had already dropped "Nellie." In its place, she revised the spelling of her middle name to "Byrnece" and adopted her stepfather's last name, to become "Byrnece Beutler."

The movie studios considered their stars' names to be vital to the marketing of their stars' personalities. Many, if not most, stars had their names changed to match their images. When she signed her Fox contract, Sally was immediately given the name "Byrnece Beautler," a slight variation of the name she was already using. Only once can that name be found in print -- in *Motion Picture News*, October 30, 1926. However, Fox studio soon began to see Sally as an attractive young flapper and quickly changed it to "Sally Phipps," thinking it more fitting for her peppy, perky image.

An article in the *Salt Lake Tribune*, October 15, 1927, discussed the important role of casting directors in naming new contract players. The column entitled, "Sidelights Of The Stage And Screen," was written by Motion Picture Feature Editor Wade Werner:

> **James Ryan, casting director at Fox, can recall many such studio christenings. There was the time, for instance, when it was decided that a new player named Byrnece Beutler should henceforth flicker across the screen as Sally Phipps. Byrnece didn't like the new name, and her mother agreed with her. They had to be persuaded [that] Sally Phipps was a film name that would help her to film fame. Numerology turned the trick: Ryan proved by the 'science' of numbers that Sally Phipps was a lucky label, so it stuck.**

It is not surprising that Sally accepted the name change after its numerological benefit was pointed out, for she was already interested in such things as astrology. The aforementioned article from the *Salt Lake Tribune*, November 28, 1926 said:

> **Sally is the original 'ology' girl, and that's why it is said she represents a new type of flapper. When other little girls were playing with their dolls, Sally at the age of 7 was having the time of her life playing with heavy volumes on astrology, psychology, neurology, physiology, biology, pathology, geology, and a lot of other 'ologies.' Her grandfather ... kept his books in the attic, and there, Sally used to hide for hours, while she was living with her grandmother, and play with the books. Of course, she didn't know a great deal about the contents of the volumes at the time, but when she grew older, she began to read them.**

SALLY TYPED AS A COMEDIENNE

Frank Borzage, in several sources, touted his protégé, Sally, as the new Clara Bow. However, in her memoirs, Sally says, "Fox typed me as a comedienne," and she was put to work right away in the comedy department making two-reel shorts. She was paired in these films with whichever male comedian was on hand at the time, using several different directors. Starting a starlet's career with comedy shorts was a common studio practice at the time.

STUDIO PHOTOGRAPHS

Between 1926 and 1929, Sally made 22 films at Fox - 10 comedy shorts and 12 features, all silent, except for the last, a talkie comedy short made in mid-1929. Although only a small percentage of these films has survived, hundreds of scene stills and publicity photos, including many of the pin-up variety, taken by Fox staff photographer Max Munn Autrey, have survived. Autrey is considered one of the foremost photographers of Hollywood stars, and Sally was obviously one of his favorite subjects. Concentrating on her greatest assets to the studio -- her youth, beauty, and sex appeal -- Fox had the studio's esteemed photographer take hundreds of photos of her. Because of Sally's lovely face and curvy figure, much of what he shot resulted in Sally becoming a favorite pin-up subject in the late 1920s into the early 1930s. Much of Autrey's work, in 8x10 portraits and studio-sold postcards, is still being collected and auctioned on eBay. In her black and white films and photographs, her striking red hair appears brunette.

Fox studio liked to show off this beautiful young girl. Headshots of Sally and five other Fox players, billed as the "stars of today and tomorrow," appeared in a full-page advertisement, "Youth in Fox Pictures," placed in the December 1926 issues of *Cinema Art* and *Theatre Magazine*. Sally was pictured with Madge Bellamy, Janet Gaynor, Charles Farrell, George O'Brien, and Olive Borden, good company for a 15 year old, while the others ranged in age from 23 to 26. Sally also appeared in January 1927 with Madge Bellamy in the feature, *Bertha, the Sewing Machine Girl,* and in the following September with Janet Gaynor and George O'Brien in another feature, *Sunrise,* a role that earned Gaynor an Academy Award.

LIGHT WINES AND BEARDED LADIES

The first film in which Sally got billing was the two-reel comedy short, *Light Wines And Bearded Ladies.* It was released November 14, 1926, was directed by Jules White, and was produced as part of Fox's prestigious Imperial Comedy series. *Moving Picture World,* November 29, 1926, referred to Sally as: "A new and attractive leading lady..."

The film co-starred Gene Cameron, who played a barber recently graduated from barber college. Sally played his girlfriend "Minnie Root," the daughter of a crackpot inventor of a hair-growing tonic. Sally's rival suitor, the local grocer, played by Harrison Martell, constantly thwarts the barber's advances toward Sally. The zany action that follows set the pattern for most of the Sally's films: she would play a beguiling girl who either has or gets a boyfriend, only to have him challenged by a rival suitor. She smiles winningly, laughs easily, and performs physical comedy, such as pratfalls, with great agility.

At this point in her career, she was never asked to emote much beyond some "damsel in distress" screams. Her beauty and charm were often mentioned by reviewers, with such comments as "cute," "nice appearance," "attractive heroine," and "pretty as can be."

***Light Wines And Bearded Ladies* scene still, with Gene Cameron and Sally**

After *Light Wines And Bearded Ladies* was completed, she autographed a publicity picture from the film for her best friend Dorothy Day (1909-2000) saying:

Well Dot –

I have a new name and this is the first time that I have signed it. This is from "Light Wines and Bearded Ladies."

Love,

Sally Phipps

Sally and Dorothy had been friends since their time together at Fairfax High School, and they remained friends for life. Dorothy's family was from Salt Lake City, and, like the Beutlers, she had recently moved to Los Angeles. Dorothy stayed on and graduated from Fairfax High School in June 1927, well after Sally dropped out to begin work at Fox Film studio.

Scene still inscribed to Dorothy from Sally

Dorothy Day, later Zohmah Charlot

BIG BUSINESS

Sally's next appearance was in a two-reel comedy, *Big Business*, another in Fox's Imperial Comedy series. It was released December 26, 1926 and starred Harold Austin, who played an umbrella salesman in a rainless town. Mark Sandrich directed.

Big Business **scene still, with Harold Austin and Sally**

BERTHA, THE SEWING MACHINE GIRL

Sally was then cast in a feature-length film, *Bertha, The Sewing Machine Girl.* It was an updated version of the play by Theodore Kremer, and premiered in New York in early January 1927. Sally received third billing in the film's opening credits. She played the part of "Jessie," the friend of the leading character Bertha, played by Madge Bellamy. She follows along when Bertha goes to work for a dress designer, and, when Bertha is promoted to chief model, Sally has an opportunity to do many glamorous fashion modeling scenes.

***Bertha, The Sewing Machine Girl* scene still, featuring Sally**

WAMPAS BABY STAR OF 1927

Each year, beginning in 1922, the Western Association of Motion Picture Advertisers (WAMPAS or Wampas) chose 13 starlets who showed the most promise. Roy Liebman in his book, *The Wampas Baby Stars: A Biographical Dictionary*, 1922-1934, writes:

> **The idea was conceived to select 13 young women with potential star power and to publicize them to a fare-thee-well. The future stars were to be known as the Wampas Baby Stars; the "Baby" not meaning infants but rather "junior" stars. At first, the organization's desire to publicize Wampas, rather than the actresses, was undoubtedly at the forefront. Its members may not have been prepared for what followed. The studios realized the inherent promotional value of this hoopla and gave the idea their enthusiastic blessing. The concept took off and became wildly popular.**

Sally was selected as one of the Wampas Baby Stars of 1927, a high honor in itself, but even more so for a girl of only 15 years old (the studio continued to claim she was 17). The Wampas Baby Star winners were announced in *Moving Picture World* magazine, January 15, 1927 and were presented at a ball held at the Ambassador Hotel on February 17, 1927. Sally had only two starring two-reel comedies, and one supporting role in a feature film to her credit, so the promotional boost to her career was tremendous. Fox then increased her publicity, placing glamour photos and stories about her in magazines, newspapers, and postcards.

WAMPAS Baby Stars of 1927, with Sally second from left

LOVE MAKES 'EM WILD

Love Makes 'Em Wild is another feature that came out early in 1927, following *Bertha the Sewing Machine Girl*. Sally played the role of Mary O'Shane, with Johnny Harron as her leading man. *Moving Picture World*, March 19, 1927, said: "…Sally Phipps is an exceptional, attractive, and likable heroine." In the *Appleton Post-Crescent*, a Wisconsin newspaper, May 4, 1927, the reviewer for the film said:

> **Sally Phipps plays the girl, and we want to go on record right now as saying that Miss Phipps is one of the most charming actresses we have had the privilege of seeing in many a day. She has a personality which is distinctly individual, to say the least, and flirts across the silver screen with a grace which would become an actress of many more years' experience.**

Love Makes 'Em Wild **scene still, with Johnny Harron, Ben Bard, and Sally**

GIRLS

Girls, a two-reel comedy based on an O. Henry story, was directed by Eugene Forde and released on March 27, 1927. Sally played Louise Anna, a college co-ed who pursues a male student, played by Richard Walling, who has taken a vow never to be kissed by any female. She runs after him and endures many pratfalls, until she finally gets her big kiss. Taking falls is the price a silent film comedienne had to pay for appearing in two-reel comedies.

Girls is commercially available on DVD, as unannounced special material accompanying the feature film, *O. Henry's Full House*, a 1952 film re-released in 2006.

***Girls* scene still, with Sally Eilers, Sally, and Richard Walling**

THE CRADLE SNATCHERS

Sally's next film assignment was an uncredited role, playing one of the flapper girlfriends of a philandering husband in the feature *The Cradle Snatchers*, starring Louise Fazenda and J. Farrell MacDonald. It was directed by Howard Hawks and released on May 28, 1927.

Alice L. Tildesley, in a 1930 *Times-Picayune* newspaper article, explains why Sally and other Fox contract players were given uncredited parts:

> **The Fox Studio has a policy with its young players that is very wise. All players under contract to them must have extra parts or bits in other people's pictures when there isn't a lead for them. ... Before Janet Gaynor was starred and while she was playing leads, she often played extra [parts] in other pictures. This gives the youngster the balance necessary to keep off an attack of swelled cranium.**

The Cradle Snatchers was followed by five more two-reel comedies and, by the end of the year, two more feature films.

***The Cradle Snatchers* scene still, with J. Farrell MacDonald, Sally, and Louise Fazenda**

THE KANGAROO DETECTIVE

The first of the five comedies was *The Kangaroo Detective* released on May 15, 1927. She was again paired with Gene Cameron, her co-star in *Light Wines And Bearded Ladies.* (Sadly, Cameron, one of Fox's most popular comedians, died in a car crash in mid-November 1927.)

***The Kangaroo Detective* scene still, with Gene Austin and Sally**

Around the time of the filming of *The Kangaroo Detective*, Fox was using kangaroos in several of its two-reel comedies. One day, as a publicity stunt, Fox staged a mock boxing match on the lot between Sally and one of the kangaroos and sent out the story to the newspapers. A number of months later, on January 14, 1928, the *Daily Star* (Brooklyn, New York) published the quirky story with the title, "Sally Phipps Robbed In Kangaroo Bout":

> **In the matter of Jack Dempsey and the "long count," Sally Phipps has grounds for sympathy with the ex-champ. This vivacious little actress, just announced as one of a newly-signed group of a dozen young screen players, was robbed of the kangaroo championship by a ring referee.**
>
> **Any referee who would act like that, Sally feels, when such an important matter as the kangaroo championship is at stake, is positively uncouth.**
>
> **It happened when she was matched to put on the gloves with the boxing kangaroo, which Harry Adby brought to the Fox lot from Australia. Sally was the only one of her sex willing to exchange smacks with the kangaroo.**
>
> **She's only five feet, two inches in altitude, whereas the kangaroo is tall for his age. Moreover, he had a large tail on which he could sit and rest while delivering haymakers. But Sally didn't mind – the kangaroo might score a hit, but she had "it."**
>
> **So Young Kid Kangaroo was sent in against Slippery Sally Phipps, the Fox flash, winner take all. It was nip and tuck, or give and take, from the start. Wallops were swapped, nasty looks were exchanged. Sally certainly beat the kangaroo on points when it came to making faces.**
>
> **And then, just as she was all set to hand the young smart aleck kangaroo a sleeping potion, the timekeeper rang the end of the round before it was really over. And the referee, upholding the timekeeper and maintaining the reputation of referees for being mean horned toads, declared "no decision" and short-changed Sally out of her rightful place in pugilistic history.**

A MIDSUMMER NIGHT'S STEAM

In the next two-reel comedy, *A Midsummer Night's Steam*, also an Imperial Comedy, Sally is one of six bathing beauties hired to jazz up a theater that is about to flop. It starred Eddie Clayton, was directed by Mark Sandrich, and was released on June 5, 1927.

CUPID AND THE CLOCK

The comedy short, *Cupid And The Clock*, was another based on an O. Henry story, co-starred Nick Stuart, was directed by Eugene Forde, and was released on June 19, 1927. Stuart is a reporter sent to a girls school to get a photo of a girl's legs, which have been insured for a large sum of money -- an opportunity for many leg shots.

A Midsummer Night's Steam **scene still, featuring Sally in the center**

Cupid And The Clock **scene still, with Nick Stuart and Sally**

GENTLEMEN PREFER SCOTCH

During a flashback in *Gentlemen Prefer Scotch,* Sally plays Sally McTavish, a blonde-wigged Scottish girl. This was the fourth of the two-reelers in the Fox Imperial Comedy series. It again co-starred Nick Stuart, was directed by Jules White, and was released on June 26, 1927.

***Gentlemen Prefer Scotch* scene still, with Nick Stuart and Sally in Highland costume**

This film had an important personal significance for Sally, because it was during its filming that she received the news that her father had died. As she told the story, the cast and crew were on location on June 10, 1927 when Edithe suddenly arrived in her automobile. Edithe interrupted the filming, saying she had to urgently discuss something with Sally. Her arms were full of Denver newspapers carrying front-page stories with many large pictures announcing that Sally's father and Edithe's ex-husband, Albert Bogdon, had been shot to death the previous evening in Denver, Colorado. Bogdon, now a prominent lawyer and state senator for the Denver area, was advising a female client about her divorce in a meeting in her apartment. The woman's husband, suspecting a love tryst, burst into the apartment and shot Bogdon to death in a jealous rage.

Besides being terribly upset by her father's death, Sally was also embarrassed by Edithe's bursting in and breaking the news in front of the cast and crew. Sally, however, was just past her 16th birthday and still too young and naive to understand how damaging her father's scandalous story could be to a star's personal life and career. She only later realized that Edithe wanted Sally and the studio personnel to get the news as soon as possible so they would be prepared before any press people arrived in pursuit of a sensational story.

Sally knew that her father had remarried and had another daughter, Sally's seven-year-old half-sister, Violet. She was also aware that he had been paying support payments for herself and Lane ever since Edithe's divorce from him ten years earlier. Even though Sally had not seen him for more than 12 years, she was proud of him, and she always referred to him as the lawyer and senator. For a while, she even wanted to become a lawyer herself.

The news of his death, and the manner in which it was delivered, was devastating. She realized that there would be a murder trial in a few months. With her filming work commitments, however, it was difficult for her to keep on top of the events that followed. Although she was curious about them and about Bogdon's life after his divorce from Edithe, she put these things aside for the sake of her career, hoping that someday she would have a chance to learn more. Eventually she did.

MUM'S THE WORD

Nick Stuart had co-starred with Sally in her last three films and did so again in *Mum's The Word.* It was another Imperial Comedy, released on July 31, 1927. It seems that Fox had finally decided on a suitable co-star for Sally and continued to team them almost exclusively in two-reel comedies and features until the middle of 1928. Nick and Sally made an attractive couple. He was the proverbial tall, dark, and handsome leading man, a perfect match for Sally.

Mum's the Word **scene still, with Nick Stuart and Sally**

The story involves efforts of "The Boy" to discover the identity of "The Girl," with the action moving from a department store to her apartment house. *Moving Picture World*, August 20, 1927, said in the review of this film: "... it may seem to those who admire Miss Phipps that she is glimpsed in altogether too few scenes."

In August 1927, Fox offered Sally a five-year contract, which would take her well into 1932. According to the contract, her salary range for the five-year period was to increase from $125 a week in 1927 to $600 a week in 1932. The contract also contained a clause that allowed her employers to cancel her contract if her weight passed 130 pounds. This so impressed Sally that she kept a newspaper article naming her as one of the young starlets with this clause in their contracts.

SUNRISE

Sunrise, which is considered one of the greatest silent films ever made, was another of Sally's 1927 features. She was not billed, and her appearance is brief, but her scene is poignant and pivotal.

Fox brought the famous German director F. W. Murnau (Friedrich Wilhelm Murnau, 1888-1931) from Germany especially to direct *Sunrise*. It took many months to film, because Murnau had several elaborate sets built on the Fox back lot, including one simulating a big city like Berlin. His most famous film was *Nosferatu* (1922), an adaptation of Bram Stoker's 1897 novel *Dracula*.

In *Sunrise*, a wicked city woman (Margaret Livingston) tries to lure a young farmer (George O'Brien) into killing his wife (Janet Gaynor) so he can take up with her. After an attempt to drown his wife, the farmer finds he cannot go through with the deed, and they reconcile. They then go to an amusement park to renew their vows and spend a happy day together. While there, the farmer becomes pre-occupied with an amusement park game while his wife patiently gazes over the joyful surroundings. At one point, she looks dreamily over her shoulder into a floor-to-ceiling window and watches couples dancing.

One couple, played by Sally Phipps and Barry Norton, appears inside the window, slowly dancing across the floor from the left to the right side of the screen. The camera zooms in, showing their faces clearly as they dance cheek to cheek and then slowly dance off the screen. The farmer's wife looks admiringly and longingly at the young couple and tries in vain to get her husband interested in taking her dancing. Later, after a comedy chase involving a fleeing pig, the dancing couple, Sally and Barry, is caught in an embarrassing kissing clinch by the farmer.

Sunrise had its New York premiere on September 23, 1927, and won several Academy Awards at the first Academy Award ceremony, which was held on May 16, 1929. It won "Most Unique Artistic Production," "Best Cinematography," as well as "Best Actress" for Janet Gaynor (shared with her roles in *Seventh Heaven* and *Street Angel*).

Sunrise scene still, with Barry Norton and Sally

Sunrise scene still, with Sally, Barry Norton and George O'Brien

HIGH SCHOOL HERO

Sally and Nick's first feature film as co-stars was *High School Hero*, directed by David Butler and released on October 16, 1927. The usual "competitive suitors" plot was enhanced by the casting of John Darrow, David Rollins, the famous Olympic track runner, Charles Paddock, as the coach, and character actor, Brandon Hurst, as the students' Latin teacher.

***High School Hero* scene still, featuring Sally and some adoring men**

The critics said Sally was "comely," "cute," and "looks her role of high school flapper." One reviewer noted that Sally, already a veteran of two-reel comedies, played her part "with much comic sense."

Sally attained the height of her movie career in 1928. She was the female star in one two-reel comedy and three feature films.

HOLD YOUR HAT

In early 1928, she appeared in *Hold Your Hat*, another in Fox's Imperial Comedy series. It was her last silent two-reel comedy, was directed by Billy West, again co-starred Nick Stuart, and was released on January 15, 1928.

***Hold Your Hat* scene still, with Nick Stuart and Sally**

WHY SAILORS GO WRONG

She again co-starred with Nick Stuart in the feature film *Why Sailors Go Wrong*. It was directed by Henry Lehrman and released on March 25, 1928. The true stars of the film, however, were the comedians Sammy Cohen and Ted McNamara, who got top billing and received most of the best footage in the film. (Tragically, Ted McNamara died of pneumonia in early February, almost two months before the film's opening.)

The story involves the usual competing suitors, a storm at sea, and an island full of angry natives and wild animals, punctuated by the antics of Cohen and McNamara. It was reviewed by *The New York Times*, April 9, 1928, in an article referring to Sally as "an attractive heroine." UCLA owns a copy of the film.

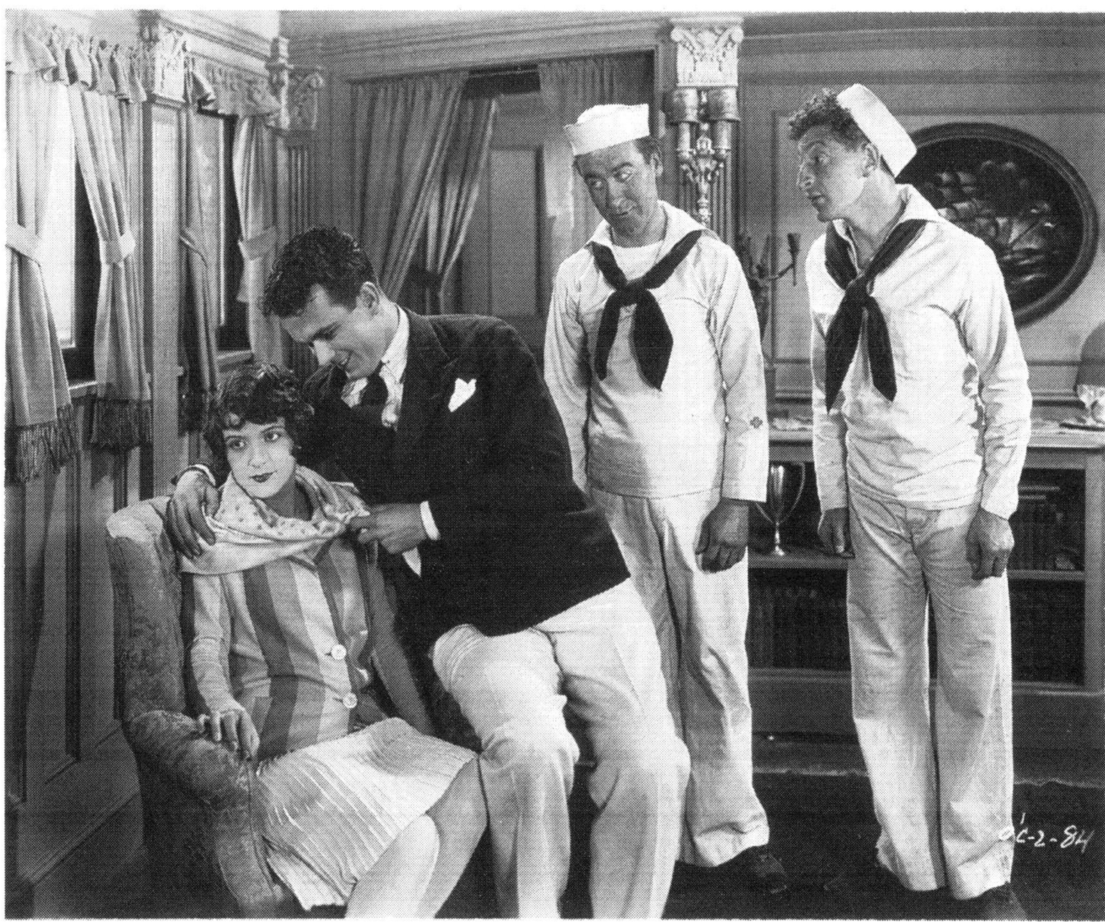

Why *Sailors Go Wrong* scene still: Sally, Nick Stuart, Ted McNamara and Sammy Cohen

THE NEWS PARADE

Sally's second feature of 1928 was *The News Parade.* It was directed by David Butler, again co-starred Nick Stuart and was released May 29, 1928.

The only surviving copy of *The News Parade* was found in the 1990s, hidden beneath the floor of a chicken coop on a farm in the Czech Republic. Beginning in 1938, just before World War II, when Hitler's government took over large parts of Czechoslovakia, much effort was made by the Czechs to prevent the Germans from confiscating their films. The Germans had already begun confiscating Czech art works and other cultural property. Someone, believing that *The News Parade* was worth preserving, hid the film under the floorboards of a chicken coop of a farm, assuming that the Germans would never find it there. This person was correct, because, many years later, after the hiding spot had been totally forgotten and the chicken coop was being torn down, the film was found and was still in good condition. It was turned over to the Czech film archives, officially known as Národní Filmový Archiv. Unfortunately, the film has its intertitles in Czech not in English. Sally's name is listed in the actors' credits as "Sally Phippsova." As is, it was shown at the 17th Pordenone Silent Film Festival in Italy in 1998.

The News Parade required several months of location shooting, first in New York City, then Lake Placid in upstate New York, then Palm Beach, Florida, and finally Havana, Cuba. Sally was allowed to take her mother Edithe Beutler along as chaperone. The cast and company arrived by train at Pennsylvania Station in New York City on January 30, 1928 to begin the New York City location shots.

In *The News Parade*, Nick, a newsreel photographer, becomes enamored with the daughter of a tobacco magnate. The daughter, played by Sally, is travelling with her father as they visit his business interests in various localities. In order to stay close to Sally, the photographer, keeping well out of sight of her father, follows the magnate and Sally as they travel. During an attempted kidnapping of Sally in Havana, Nick saves her from the kidnappers. At the end of the film, the father gives Nick permission to marry Sally.

***The News Parade* scene still, with Nick Stuart and Sally**

Even before *The News Parade* opened in May 1928, Fox studio planned a sequel. A photo of Sally appeared in the New York City *Morning Telegraph*, April 24, 1928, with the following caption:

Sally Phipps, who will follow the newsreel escapades in a picture to be titled "Chasing Trough Europe," which is to be a sequel or rather follow up of "The News Parade."

While Sally was in New York filming *The News Parade*, the famous New York City restaurant Sardi's, located at 234 West 44th Street, where Broadway openings were always celebrated, had Sally's caricature drawn by Alex Gard, its in-house caricaturist. The exaggerated image was hung in Sardi's gallery of celebrity caricatures. Sally autographed it: "My 'Gard' what a likeness! Sally Phipps." Sally's caricature is now in the New York Public Library's Billy Rose Theater Collection.

Sardi's Restaurant's 1928 caricature of Sally, by Alex Gard

EDITHE COMMENTS ABOUT SALLY AS MOVIE STAR

When Edithe was on location as chaperone for her 16-year-old daughter Sally, she was interviewed by W. H. R. in a column called "Star Gazing," about how she dealt with Sally's new status as a movie star. The column appeared in the *Daily Star* (Brooklyn, New York), March 29, 1928 and was headlined "Mother Aids Sally." It includes two head shots of Edithe and Sally. Under one, the caption says: "Movie mothers should guide and not interfere with their daughters in their climb to movie fame, according to Mrs. Edith Phipps [sic], mother of the new star Sally Phipps." Another caption points out that, "Sally, though already a big name in the films, is just sixteen." The column then continues with the following:

Sally and Edithe, New York City, late January 1928

More than one promising screen beauty has lost a career because of motherly interference that annoyed directors, press agents, and producers, and around the studio, mamas (as distinguished from mothers, who are characters put in photoplays to wring tears from sentimental audiences) have the reputation of being abominations.

Such a reputation, Mrs. Edith Phipps is trying her best to elude. Mrs. Phipps is in New York as chaperone on her daughter, Sally, who at sixteen is playing leading roles in pictures and is well on the road to stardom. Sally is doing "The New Parade" here.

"I realize that I am only background now. It's a position mothers of boys and girls in the limelight have to learn," she told me.

"Frankly, I am bewildered by my totally new existence. A short time ago, or so it seems, I was rushing Sally off to high school, worrying about her new party frock, worrying about her grades, and hoping the little dress I made for her would not appear to be too low in the neck.

"My life was wrapped in the existence of a sedate, domesticated housewife until the day Sally came home with her own problems as a featured movie player. There are many of these you may imagine. Overnight, my life was changed into a background for Sally. I ceased to have a life and problems of my own. I'm sort of a lady in waiting to her now.

"I know that the average film player's mother is commonly regarded as a pest in the studios. During production, I never go on a set. I would only be in the way. I never made demands for Sally from the executives, knowing that they'd look upon me as just another grasping mother.

"But all these things can't change me in one way; she may be to the world a worldly actress, but to me she is just a naïve girl, who is ill at ease when interviewed and who really needs a mother fluttering around her."

Sally's climb to screen prominence was short and swift. She was still attending high school when selected through a screen test, for the leading role in "The High School Hero."

WALLACE SULLIVAN

During her several trips through New York City while working on the film, Sally was wooed by a local newspaperman, Wallace Sullivan (1902-1991), who was nine years older than she and who wrote a daily column called "Broadway" for New York's *Morning Telegraph*. Mention of Sally first appeared in Wallace Sullivan's column on Friday, March 2, 1928, when she returned to town after the film company finished its location shooting in Lake Placid, but before it was ready to move on to Palm Beach and Havana. Sally appeared again in his Saturday and Sunday, March 3 and 4 columns. His Wednesday, March 7, column was extremely long and was totally about her. Sullivan was quite smitten with Sally. He took her to Broadway shows and popular nightspots and introduced her to many show business celebrities. In his column, he bragged about how he kept Sally out until late in the morning, buttering up Sally's mother to get her permission for this.

Wallace Sullivan was born in Chicago in 1902 into an Irish family. According to various magazine and newspaper articles, he had blond hair, blue eyes, and was five feet eight inches tall. The stories also say that he was very handsome, charming, and had a real way with the ladies. His physical description could also fit Sally's father, Albert Bogdon.

Sullivan was already working as a reporter for the *Chicago Herald and Examiner* in 1924. He was, in fact, among the reporters who covered the famous Leopold and Loeb murder trial that year. In 1928, Sullivan started his "Broadway" column for the *Morning Telegraph*, reporting on the latest gossip and happenings in the New York City theaters and nightclubs. Sullivan also told Sally he was working on a law degree. In later years, he became a successful screenwriter. One of his biggest screenwriting hits was the 1936 MGM feature film *Libeled Lady*, starring Jean Harlow, Myrna Loy, William Powell, and Spencer Tracy. It has both a journalistic and legalistic angle. He continued to write screenplays well into the 1950s.

PUBLICITY OF THE ROMANCE

The romance caused some consternation at Fox studio. The publicity was certainly good for the studio, except that Sally was still only sixteen. On the other hand, any kind of romantic entanglement that their stars had could always be dangerous to their future careers. In a *Roxy Theatre Weekly Review*, dated "Week beginning March 24, 1928," there is an article by Harry N. Blair entitled "Thou Shalt Not – Divorce! Marry! Fall In Love! Be Bobbed! Grow Obese! Lose Flesh! – Cinema Commandments." The article includes, among other photos, one of Sally with the caption "Who Can't Let a Heart Affair Interfere With Work? – Sally Phipps." The article goes on to discuss how movie studios have historically prevented their actresses from falling in love or marrying. One section of the article describes Sally's current situation:

> **A distinct case of "flirtations barred" is that of Sally Phipps, of "A High School Hero," who is to masculine youth as a flame to a moth.**
>
> **While it isn't set forth in cold type in her contract with her Fox discoverers, it is clearly understood that she must not fall in love. The verbal agreement between this lively young actress and her employers is that she must conscientiously avoid the distractions of a love affair during the term of her indenture.**
>
> **And little Miss Phipps, a preferred brunette, had a hard pull of it in keeping faith when the merry-go–round of the movies kept her in Gotham for a few weeks last month. A fatally handsome young reporter appeared as an interviewer and remained as wooer. Fortunately for the sanctity of verbal understandings, a hurried location trip to Florida yanked the eighteen-year-old girl out of reach of a tempestuous suitor.**

SALLY GETS ENGAGED

Wallace Sullivan may not have known that Sally was still only sixteen years old, for he proposed marriage to her, and, being a romantic teenage girl, she accepted. He knew she was leaving town for Palm Beach any day, and he did not want to take the chance of losing her.

Their engagement was announced in *Variety* on March 14, 1928, and in many other newspapers in the weeks that followed. On March 31, 1928, the following appeared in the *Staten Island Advance* in the "Star Gazing by C.K." column:

> **Sally Phipps is engaged to wed Wallace Sullivan after a whirlwind courtship, which began when Sullivan, a New York reporter, went around to interview her.**

Another newspaper article from the New York area, dated April 29, 1928, even reported a planned transatlantic flight:

> **The couple expect the denouement of their romance to be reached on the flight across when they marry either in Paris or Berlin.**

This is a little less than a year after Charles Lindbergh's record-breaking flight from New York to Paris. Transatlantic flight was still in its infancy.

Newspaper articles and other publicity about the engagement continued to appear in April and May. In June, the nature of the engagement took on a "spin." The engagement was now called a "companionate engagement." As described in the *Boston Post* on June 3, 1928:

> **Enter the 'companionate engagement.' Sally Phipps and Wallace Sullivan, writer on the *New York Morning Telegraph*, call theirs that. Each has given the other a signed agreement to remain true for one year. If then they still care for each other, they will marry.**

Elaborate coverage of the entire story appeared in the movie magazine, *Screen Secrets*, September 1928, "Her Companionate Engagement; Sally Phipps has a new idea about love. Will it become the rage in Hollywood?" by Ruth M. Tildesley. In the article, Sally admits to having been originally swept off her feet by Wallace Sullivan and to having made a hasty decision to marry him. Coming to her senses, she claims to have come up with the idea of the companionate engagement for practical reasons:

> **You see, I had come back to Hollywood to make pictures, and he had to stay there and write about night clubs while he studied to be a lawyer. He'll be admitted to the bar when he's finished his course and then he can come out here and practice, if he can get some clients to let him. ... So we decided that we'd be engaged for a year and if we still cared at the end of that time we'd get married. According to the terms of our engagement, we are supposed to**

> **write at least twice a week – more if we feel like it, but not less – and we are both free to go around with other people. Of course, it wouldn't be possible for us to play lone wolves in our business and staying home would be sure to wreck the match in two weeks. Besides, this way we can find out if there is somebody else for us. … I haven't a ring. We thought that would make it old-fashioned and we're both modern.**
> **In describing how she decided on a companionate engagement, she says:**
> **You know how terribly romantic moonlight makes you feel … or hearing music on the water, or sitting on the observation platform of a train going over the mountains? Whenever you're away from familiar places and you meet someone interesting, you're liable to lose your sense of proportion. Lots of girls rush out and get married the minute the man looks a little willing, and pretty soon they're married going around saying: "Well, I must have been crazy!" So when it happened to me, I thought I'd better give myself a chance, and it seemed to me this was a grand idea."**

The author then gives the readers a physical description of Wallace Sullivan, who is:

> **… some two or three inches taller than Sally [who is five feet two inches]. His hair is blond and his eyes are blue – he is Irish through and through – and oh what a way with the ladies!**

Sally continues:

> **Girls are just mad about him … Some of them have tried to commit suicide over him – because they couldn't get him, you know… He's simply frightfully brilliant, too. He wrote a book on the Loeb and Leopold case. I'll have to read it.**
>
> **Five months have passed already …He's still writing to me. I s'pose he's taking other girls out to see the night life of New York, but he says they don't mean anything to him.**
>
> **I'm going around with other boys. I go a lot with one boy. But I couldn't find out who I truly care about unless I get to know more than one man, now could I?**
>
> **If we're still mad about each other at the end of the year, he will come out here and we'll have a wedding. We'll know by that time, so we won't need a companionate marriage.**
>
> **I think I'm going to New York soon for another picture. If I do – I don't know – I wouldn't care to say positively – but we might not wait for the end of the year.**

There are three pictures with the article, one large headshot and two full-body shots, one standing and another reclining.

By the middle of September 1928, Sally decided to end her official engagement to Wallace Sullivan. The following announcement appeared in the *Buffalo Courier-Express*, September 13, 1928:

> **A companionate engagement which was sealed with a ring – a long distance telephone ring from New York to Hollywood – has become unsealed by a postage stamp. The Hollywood part of the romantic understanding, Miss Sally Phipps announced the termination of her understanding with Wallace Sullivan of New York. They met while Miss Sally was making scenes for a film in New York and, when Sally had to come back to the coast, the pair bargained to try a companionate betrothal of a year. "But the distance spoiled it all," Sally averred, "and we decided we would just remain good friends."**

NONE BUT THE BRAVE

By May 1928, Sally had returned to Hollywood. At the end of May, when *The News Parade* went into release, she had already started work on her last film of 1928. As it turned out, it was the last feature film in which she was cast as the leading lady.

None But The Brave was directed by Albert Ray and released on August 5, 1928. Charles Morton, a handsome and athletic young man who was relatively new to films, was her leading man, a change from her usual co-star Nick Stuart. Morton plays a lifeguard, while Sally plays a concessionaire. The film features a beauty contest in two-strip Technicolor. As was the usual case in a number of her films, she was only required to look pretty, and *Variety* reported on September 5, 1928: "Sally Phipps hasn't a lot to do."

None But The Brave **scene still, with Sally, Billy Butts, and Charles Morton**

KLIEG EYE

It was while working on *None But The Brave* that Sally developed a condition called "klieg eye," an irritation caused by the intensely bright light of the powerful carbon-arc lamps used in silent film production. (The etymology of the term "klieg" comes from "Kliegl," the name of the brothers who invented the lamps.) In Sally's memoirs, the only reference to her condition was that she "got klieg eye" and "after that, [I] was ready for a vacation." Her eye condition very likely came about filming the Technicolor insert scene in the picture, in which she is featured in a beauty contest. At that time, Technicolor film required a great deal of light for its relatively slow exposure time, and it was necessary to augment the already intense light produced by the usual carbon arc lamps with even more arc lamps. Sally was one of the many silent film performers who would develop a light sensitivity that he/she would have to live with for the rest of his/her life. That's why, during the day, Sally always wore dark glasses, even indoors, depending on the harshness of the lighting.

This "vacation," which she took initially to recover from "klieg eye," would eventually turn into a nine-month period in which she did not appear in any new films. Her subsequent film, *Joy Street,* did not come out until May 12, 1929.

SALLY'S POPULARITY AT THE BOX OFFICE

Aubrey Solomon, in his book *The Fox Film Corporation, 1915-1935: A History And Filmography* (Jefferson, NC: McFarland, 2011), refers to Sally Phipps five times. In Chapter 8, entitled "The Golden Age of Fox Films," he cites the year 1928 and writes:

> **...a star like Sally Phipps could start out the year being a moneymaker and then drop off in popularity.**

What did her fans think? Were they still there? Mark Larkin, in his article "What Happens To Fan Mail," *Photoplay*, August 1928, revealed some interesting comments about her fans:

> **Little Sally Phipps' letters come mostly from girls and college lads. Her severest criticisms relate to her lingerie pictures – fans were shocked at her "undress."**

Was Fox's pin-up exploitation of Sally's youth, beauty, and sex appeal possibly hurting her at the box office?

After her tremendous popular success in *High School Hero,* her subsequent films were not well received by the critics. Her youth-oriented films were not doing very well at the box office. New contract players were being given the chances at stardom that Sally had been given. Several films that were announced in mid-1928 for her to appear in were eventually cancelled or were turned over to other contract actresses to complete. However, Fox still had her in mind for more films.

THE TALKIES!

Everything in Hollywood was changing. Most significantly, silent films were being replaced by talkies. Fear of the microphone and whether one's voice would register well with it were concerns for all the silent performers. Sally was caught in the middle of the nightmare that all of Hollywood was going through in late 1928 and early 1929.

Even a family member suggested that the quality of her voice may have been a problem. Her first cousin, Jack E. Jones, who grew up in Miami, Florida, recalled in his published memoirs, *No Rocking Chair Yet* (Meridianville, AL: NightSky Publishing, 2005):

> **After Fox came out with the first talking movies, [Sally] lost her job. This was about 1929. They said Sally just wasn't up to "talkies." Her voice was not good enough for movies (so they said)."**

Regardless of what her cousin Jack said in his book, Fox did offer her a role in a talkie, which was a three-reel comedy short, made in mid-1929 called *Detectives Wanted.*

SALLY'S ILL-FATED NEWSPAPER STORY FILM

In 1928, Fox planned *two* silent feature films with newspaper story lines. *Speakeasy* was the first to be announced, in late May 1928. The leading female role was to go to Fox's new contract player, Lois Moran. By the time the film went into production, it was converted to a talkie and the female lead went to another new contract player, Lola Lane. The story involves a female reporter assigned to a story about a prizefighter who hangs out in a speakeasy.

The other newspaper film, the one in which Sally was involved, was to remain a silent film but one to be enhanced with Movietone sound effects. The film was first announced in *Exhibitors Herald and Moving Picture World*, October 6, 1928, with the working title *Calamity*:

> **Newmeyer's "Calamity" Superfeature Fox Film**
>
> **Fred Newmeyer's first picture at Fox will be "Calamity" under the supervision of Luther Reed. It is reported to be a superfeature which will cost well up in five figures. Movietone effects throughout.**

On October 15, 1928, *Exhibitors Daily Review* reported:

> **NEWMEYER GATHERS CAST**
>
> **Sally Phipps, Robert Elliott, Frank Albertson, and Francis McDonald have been chosen by Director Fred Newmeyer to play the leading roles in the newspaper story he is to produce for Fox Films. The picture has not yet been titled.**

The story is about a reporter who plays a major part in breaking up a bootlegging ring. The studio executives took a few weeks to agree on a new working title. Having eliminated *Calamity*, they decided on *Scarehead*, referring to frightening large-type newspaper headlines. Another considered (and sometimes publicized) title was *Headlines*.

After filming began, a group of British journalists came to visit the Fox studios, and Sally's participation in the visit was reported in the *Los Angeles Times*, November 8, 1928:

> **Stars and directors at the Fox Studio chuckled when Sir Charles [Igglesden] and Ralph D. Blumenfeld of the London Daily Express and president of the Institute of Journalists, were led into an interview on a Movietone set by Sally Phipps, playing the part of a society editor in a newspaper picture being made on the set.**

At Fox, the excitement among the executives about the upcoming film was so intense that J. Harrison Edwards in the *Exhibitors Daily Review*, November 23, 1928, wrote a feature article about the goings on, "Fox Row Goes Journalistic; 25 Ex-Newspapermen on Prod. Staff – Sheehan and Publicity Dept. to Appear In 'Scarehead,'":

> **It's a time-honored saying in journalism circles that once a newspaper man gets the printer's ink in his blood, he never gets it entirely out.**
>
> **Fox is making a newspaper story under the title of "Scarehead," directed by Fred Newmeyer, written by J. Clarkson Miller and supervised by Luther Reed – all seasoned newspapermen. They thought they represented quite a goodly proportion of journalistic talent on the Fox lot. But their activities have brought graduates from Park Row and other printing press hotbeds swarming from all sorts of nooks and corners.**
>
> **Winfield Sheehan, vice president and general manager of Fox Films; Malcolm Stuart Boylan, editorial supervisor and head title writer; Chandler Sprague, scenario editor; Freddie Schader [and 21 more] and the entire publicity staff, will be seen in the picture.**
>
> **The average director feels he is kept hopping by having one supervisor to stand at his elbow. Just figure how fast Newmeyer and his assistants are bound to keep moving, with such an array of experts willing -- nay, eager -- to give suggestions.**

Within two weeks of this visit, the following startling headline appeared in *Motion Picture News*, December 8, 1928:

> **... Newmeyer, Reed Are Reported Out At Fox. (Hollywood, Dec.5.)**

The article said that "Newmeyer was working on a newspaper story [*Scarehead*]," that "Luther Reed supervised that story," and that it was "now reported as being temporarily shelved," with another film "being rushed to replace it on the Fox release schedule." Why? A follow-up article two days later points the finger at Luther Reed. *Exhibitors Daily Review*, December 10, 1928 said:

> **REED RESIGNS**
> **Luther Reed, who recently completed his work on "Headlines" [i.e. *Scarehead*], a newspaper story for Fox, asked Winnie Sheehan for his release as production supervisor and got it. It seems that this picture, Reed's first for Fox, did not satisfy Mr. Sheehan.**

Exhibitors Herald and Moving Picture World, on December 15, 1928, referred to *Scarehead*, after its filming was completed, as "one of the most pretentious newspaper dramas ever produced."

By February 1929, the situation changed. *Syracuse Herald*, on Febrary 3 reported:

> **Ben Stoloff has been assigned by Fox to remake "Scarehead," made originally in silent form by Fred Newmeyer.**

On February 16, *Motion Picture News* reported:

> **Fox Execs Shake Dust Off "Scarehead" For Fixing**
> **Hollywood, Feb. 13. – Fox executives have taken down "Scarehead" from the shelf and are now trying to doctor it up. The picture was originally called "Calamity" and its shelving was said to be responsible for Luther Reed, supervisor, and Fred Newmeyer, director, leaving Fox. It is a newspaper story, and production heads are submitting it to newly signed writers on the lot who used to be newspapermen themselves for "fixing."**

Scarehead did finally get made. After the script was "reworked" as a talkie, it was even given a new title, *Protection*. Dorothy Burgess was assigned as the new leading lady, and the film was released in May 1929. By that time, Sally was already involved with other Fox film work.

1928 MOVIE MAGAZINES

Sally gave a number of interviews to movie magazines in 1928, some of which were revealing.

Photoplay published an un-signed piece in April 1928 entitled, "A Summary of Sally," with a headshot and a full bathing beauty shot. The article emphasized a frequently referred to fact, that Sally put aside her study of law to become a movie actress:

> **Really a narrowly averted tragedy because of once almost going highbrow. This induced by an overdose of study at the San Francisco High School. Actually believed for a while she wanted to become a lawyer or a doctor or something very professional.**

The caption under her bathing beauty picture reads:

> **Sally had aspired to a sign tacked up on the old homestead bearing her name followed by M.D. or Attorney-At-Law. But a visit to Hollywood persuaded her that beauty is more valuable than brains and that a shingle on the head is worth two on the front door.**

Another tidbit in the article was that she drove her own car. In her memoirs, she writes, "I had a turquoise Chrysler." A photo of her driving it, a 1926 Chrysler roadster, was in her personal files. She used it to drive to work to the Fox studio, and years later often bragged to her son Robert about the luxury of having her own car.

Sally driving her turquoise 1926 Chrysler roadster

Motion Picture Classic, October 1928, published "Kute, Kool and Kalm; Twenty Years From Now Sally Phipps Might Take Pictures Seriously," by Dorothy Manners, including a headshot and a lounging pose with Sally holding a beach umbrella. Since she was currently in a rather skeptical attitude about Hollywood, considering how her current career was going, Sally says:

> **They're mostly politics, anyway ... Somebody's mother, or brother or sister or friend is always around to be taken care of. Or else a company sinks so much money in a star that they have to keep plugging her in all the good parts that come up to get their investment's worth out of her. ... I studied to be a lawyer ... and I'm just as interested in the contracts and the production**

end of the business as I am in my own career. ... Oh, I suppose my interest in law was more or less inherited. My father was a lawyer and I grew up listening to the fine points of various law cases that he handled. When we left San Francisco to come down to Los Angeles to live, I enrolled in the law classes at high school just out of habit.

Sally Eilers [*a Fox starlet*] and I went to school together. We used to have a lot of fun. But I couldn't get over Sally's enthusiasm about the movies. For my part, I simply wasn't interested in the movies at all. When I see all the pretty girls standing around the gate over here at Fox just dying to get in pictures, I realize what a lucky girl I've been. I never did a day's extra work in my life. One day I came over to the studio to see Frank work--...Borzage ...We had known him in Seattle. Well, Frank asked me to make a test and I did and then they offered me a contract. That's how I got in pictures.

I think pictures are a woman's game. I absolutely believe that. There's no other profession in which a girl can make so much money and have such nice things for herself, such as cars and clothes and flattery and attention. But the main reason I am glad I am in them is the happiness I can bring to other people.

Sally then pointed to the large stack of fan mail on the floor. Sally also stated her preference for comedy over the "darker and gloomier dramatic situations:

'Sally Phipps, of course, is a typical comedy name. My real name is Byrnece Beutler but Mr. Sheehan [Winfield Sheehan, Fox producer] re-named me Phipps when he signed the contract because it sounded more pert and flappery. When I go into drama, it will be a rather hard name to live down.'

As for her concern about the dramatic adaptability of her name, she states:

'I'm not worrying about them. Pictures haven't gotten into my blood so much that I couldn't give them up. I could fool 'em and get married.'

In *Motion Picture* magazine, September 1928, there is an article about her frequent co-star, Nick Stuart, "Join the Movies and See the World! Nick Stuart Did – and Has – and How!" by Dorothy Manners:

'It's almost all settled that Sally Phipps and I are going to Europe to make a picture, sort of a sequel to "The News Parade" called "Touring Through Europe"'

Touring Through Europe was never produced, although, as early as April 1928, Fox announced that they would make it. A sequel to *The News Parade* did indeed get made but not with Sally Phipps and not titled *Touring Through Europe.* The film was called *Chasing Through Europe*, and it was released in August 1929, almost a year after the Nick Stuart article said it was scheduled. Nick Stuart starred, but the female star was Sue Carol not Sally. Why Sue Carol instead of Sally Phipps?

SUE CAROL

Sue Carol, whose real name is Evelyn Lederer, was born in 1906 in Chicago into a wealthy family. She went into films in 1927, working at several different studios before settling at Fox as a contract player. Like Sally, she was one of the Wampas Baby Stars, but for the year following Sally -- 1928. Unfortunately for Sally, Sue closely resembled Sally -- both her face and figure -- although she was not as beautiful as Sally. In her son Robert's collection, there is a Fox postcard labeled Sally Phipps, but it is really of Sue Carol, demonstrating the confusion that occurred even in the Fox marketing department.

Other information about one tangential connection between Sally and Sue Carol comes from a film historian, who prefers anonymity. According to the historian, while Sally was recovering from "klieg eye," she was selected to appear in a film called *The Air Circus*, which was to star Louise Dresser as the mother of one of the aviators, played by David Rollins, a new young actor at Fox. Sally was to be his aviatrix girlfriend. The historian said that Louise Dresser took a dislike to Sally and asked for Sue Carol to replace her. Sally never recounted this story and may not even have known about it. However, she did tell her son Robert that she always considered Sue Carol a kind of rival, for film parts as well as for Nick Stuart as her co-star.

Sally and Nick Stuart were co-stars in seven consecutive two-reel comedies and features between June 1927 and May 1928. Although the sequence was broken with her last starring feature, when she was paired with Charles Morton, she continued to feel that Nick was her logical co-star.

However, as early as 1927, Sally sensed that Sue Carol had already set her sights on Nick Stuart, both romantically and professionally. Sue latched onto Nick soon after her arrival at Fox, and an item from a gossip column from *Photoplay*, November 1927, is quite revealing:

> **Sue Carol, Douglas MacLean's leading lady, may have several of Chicago's millions tucked up her sleeve, but she isn't depending upon her shekels to help hold her boy-friend.**
>
> **Of course, nineteen-year-old Sue trusted twenty-year-old Nick Stuart. But while he was playing the lead in "The High School Hero" opposite Sally Phipps, she just wasn't taking any chances. Especially since Sally had just broken her engagement to a non-professional youngster. So Sue hied herself daily to the Fox lot and watched every wee bit of the filming. No, she didn't use any alibis, either.**

Almost a year later, a feature article about Nick Stuart from *Liberty* magazine, July 7, 1928, (accompanied by a beautiful pose of Sally wearing beach attire and sporting a bamboo parasol) made a major announcement about the Stuart-Carol relationship:

> **Right now he is reported engaged to Sue Carol, the young Hollywood flapper who has a million on her own name.**

Then in early 1929, Nick was cast for the first time with Sue Carol in the silent feature *Girls Gone Wild*. The film was originally intended for Sally, as reported in an article in the *Springfield Weekly Republican*, February 21, 1929:

> **Lew Seiler has rounded out his fourth week of camera work on his ... 30th Fox Film production, "Girls Gone Wild," co-featuring Nick Stuart and Sally Phipps, supported by Roy D'Arcy, Lumsdem Hare, William Russell, Hedda Hopper and others.**

But, *Girls Gone Wild* was released without Sally in the cast on March 24, 1929. The aforementioned *Chasing Through Europe* was released in August of 1929, co-starring the engaged couple. In November 1929, it was discovered that Nick and Sue had been secretly married since July 1929.

HOLLYWOOD INFLUENZA EPIDEMIC

In late 1928/early 1929, America again experienced a major national influenza epidemic, and Sally did not escape it. Although not as potent as the 1918-1919 one, the deadliest in American history, this later one still resulted in a significant number of deaths. Newspaper reports even commented on the epidemic's effect on Hollywood. The *Chicago Daily Tribune*, November 28, 1928, declared in an article headlined: "502 New Cases of Flu Reported in Los Angeles," including Sally Phipps:

> **The motion picture colony in Hollywood has been particularly hard hit . . . Clara Bow today was reported as gradually improving from the disease. Hoot Gibson was stricken today.**
>
> **Other film notables under physicians' treatment for flu include: Mary Philbin and Olga Baclanova, Monte Blue, Richard Barthelmess, Mrs. Barthelmess (formerly Mrs. Jessica Sargent), Lois Wilson, Sally Phipps, Loretta Young, Ruth Taylor, Jean Arthur, Yola D'Avril, John Gilbert, Buster Keaton, William Haines, Edward Sedgwick, director; Fred Murnau, director; Fred Newmeyer, director.**

UNHAPPY WITH STEPFATHER BEUTLER

Another important factor in Sally's life at the time was how unhappy she was at home. She was still living with her mother Edithe, Edithe's second husband, Albert Beutler, and her younger brother, Lane. Sally and Lane disliked Albert from the start, and the enmity grew over the years.

In Sally's memoirs, she mentioned trying to escape from the pressures of filmmaking. She wrote, "I tried to get away. I took a trip to SF [San Francisco] but studio sent for me & step father drove me back." Even though her act of rebellion may have been wrong in itself, being driven back home by a stepfather whom she disliked intensely must have been painful and humiliating. In another section of the memoirs, when referring to travelling on location for *The News Parade*, she adds: "Mother would go. I was glad. I was fed up with Beutler & excruciatingly unhappy at home." In addition, things were not going well in her career, and she made a life-changing decision.

SALLY'S EMANCIPATION COURT CASE

Disturbing reports started to appear in the California newspapers in early March 1929 about her volatile domestic situation. One of the earliest was on the front page of the *Modesto News Herald* on March 9, "Court Asked To Name Guardian For Wampas Star; Sally Phipps Charges Her Stepfather With Cruel Treatment:"

> **Los Angeles, March 8.--Sally Phipps, Wampas Baby moving picture star, to-day appealed to Superior Court for the appointment of a guardian, charging her stepfather, A. S. Beutler, with dissipating her earnings and cruel treatment. Roger Marchetti, an attorney, was appointed temporary guardian.**
>
> **Miss Phipps, who said she was 17 years old and was earning $225 a week, stated that she had supported her mother and herself for four years and had been the principal support of her stepfather since his marriage to her mother in 1922.**
>
> **The actress said Beutler frequently told her he "would be glad to see you get out" of their home and that he had caused her to suffer nervous breakdowns.**

On March 11, 1929, in the *San Jose News*, another article appeared, entitled: "Cruel Stepfather Is Assailed by Actress":

> **Los Angeles, March 11 (UP). – Sally Phipps, motion picture actress, has asked that she be freed from the custody of her mother, that her stepfather be forced to give an accounting of her money and that Roger Marchetti be appointed her guardian.**
>
> **Miss Phipps explained that her stepfather, Albert S. Beutler, was cruel, although she helped support him, and said that he had her mother completely subdued. The actress declared that her present home life was unbearable.**
>
> **Miss Phipps now is 17 and has been working since she was 13, she said.**

Variety printed an article on March 13, 1929 entitled: "Sally Phipps Says Parents Misuse Money; Suing":

> **Sally Phipps, 17, has filed suit in Superior Court asking to have a guardian appointed. Miss Phipps alleges that her mother, Mrs. Edith [*sic*] Beutler, and stepfather have misused the money that she earned. She further asserts her stepfather mistreated and slandered her, injuring her position at the Fox studio, where she is employed.**

> **She asks that Attorney Roger Marchetti, at present her guardian ad litem, be made guardian of her estate and that her name be changed legally from Byrnece Beutler to Sally Phipps. Attorney Russell Kuhn represents Miss Phipps.**

On March 29, 1929, several newspapers reported the following short announcement:

> **Sally Phipps, screen star, had Roger Marchetti, an attorney, appointed as her guardian to supervise the spending of her $8,000 a year salary. She testified she had disagreed with her stepfather about financial affairs.**

The *Los Angeles Times* had a much fuller story on March 29, 1929: "Guardian Named For Actress; Attorney Will Pull Girl Out of Debt":

> **Because Sally Phipps, 17-year-old motion-picture actress, couldn't keep books, she appeared in Superior Judge Guerin's court yesterday and had an attorney appointed her guardian.**
>
> **Although Miss Phipps is paid a salary of $200 a week, she is $1000 in debt and said she just didn't see how she could pay off. Because of a disagreement with her step-father, Miss Phipps declared her domestic affairs became tangled, and she said she wanted the attorney, Roger Marchetti, to handle her affairs rather than her parents.**
>
> **So Judge Guerin ordered Attorney Marchetti to collect her pay check, give her $125 a week a week and apply the other $75 to creditors' claims and her attorney's fees.**

According to Sally's memoirs, after her court emancipation became finalized in early April 1929, she moved out of her parents' house and temporarily into the home of her best friend, Dorothy Day, who lived in Beverly Hills. Roger Marchetti became Sally's financial guardian, and Dorothy's mother, Emma Day (1884-1932), agreed to become Sally's family guardian. A photograph of the three together ran with the above story, Marchetti wagging his finger at Sally with Emma standing by protectively.

JOY STREET

When *Joy Street*, a silent feature film starring Lois Moran and Nick Stuart, was released on May 12, 1929, Sally played only the supporting role of Mabel and was the eighth name billed. This was a definite drop in status from what she was used to. However, publicity stills continued to pose her with her former co-star, Nick Stuart.

Joy Street **scene still, with Nick Stuart, Sally, and unidentified woman**

ROLE CUT FROM *FOX MOVIETONE FOLLIES OF 1929*

Sally remembered being part of the production of the lost film *Fox Movietone Follies of 1929*, recording a song as a specialty act. She thought the title of the song was something like "Don't Be That Way" or "Don't Be Like That." The film is sometimes referred to as *William Fox Movietone Follies of 1929*. It was to be Fox studio's contribution to the Hollywood craze for all-talking, all-singing, all-dancing musicals. It was released on May 25, 1929, after many changes and a production schedule of more than six months. Although it was originally planned as a plotless review, it ended up as a backstage melodrama, full of musical numbers, but with many of the previously filmed specialty acts eliminated.

A *New York Times* article, dated March 3, listed Sally as a performer:

> **The first "Fox Movietone Follies," a screen musical revue, the first of an annual series, is being completed under the direction of Marcel Silver and has a cast of stage and screen luminaries including Gertrude Lawrence, Bobby Clark and Paul McCullough, Robert Benchley, Charles (Chick) Sale, Sylvia Field, Helen Twelvetrees, Lois Moran, Nick Stuart, Sue Carol, David Rollins, Marjorie Beebe, and Sally Phipps.**

However, her name did not appear in the final credits. Hers was one of the many specialty acts cut from the film.

Evidence of the many cuts is in the following quotes. The first comes from *The First Hollywood Musicals: A Critical Filmography Of 171 Features, 1927 Through 1932*, by Edward M. Bradley. (Jefferson, NC: McFarland, 1996), p. 41-42:

> **The initial idea was to present *Movietone Follies* as a plotless revue, the first of a series (which explains the "1929" in the title). The company considered it something of an experiment, and the filming was shrouded in mystery. Each director on the lot was to film a scene; each director would provide the story and gags, as well as select his personnel from the list of contract players. But this method proved too unwieldy. By March of 1929, it was decided to weave a love story throughout the film and supplement it with the musical numbers. By this time, the film's budget was already about $850,000. A Frenchman named Marcel Silver was assigned to direct, but he soon was replaced by David Butler (1894-1979), a character actor who was just beginning a 40-year career as a director.**
>
> **Silver began the project by filming a series of elaborate musical numbers, but nothing else, which – as Butler recalled nearly 50 years later -- alarmed Fox production head Winfield Sheehan enough to put in a call for reinforcements.**
>
> **Buddy [De Sylva] phoned me and said, "We've got a meeting tonight at 8 o'clock in Sheehan's office." So we went in: De Sylva, Brown, Henderson and myself. Sheehan said, "You've got to save us. We've got 10 numbers. If we can get any kind of a story – Dave, you can direct it fast – we'll save some of this money that I've spent." We said we'd look at these numbers the next day, which we did. We sat down that night and the next day and came up with the story of the *Fox Follies of 1929*. ... I shot the story in five days and five nights. We used some of the numbers, but we threw out six of them.**

The second quote comes from *A Song In the Dark; The Birth Of The Musical Film*, 2nd ed., by Richard Barrios (New York: Oxford University Press, 2010), p. 93-94:

> **...it had started out in 1928, as another candidate for "the screen's first musical comedy," shot in great secrecy and at interminable length ... [with] the pervasive aura of tension on the set, much of it likely due to the uncertainty of its creators' intention. As completed, it was a plotless procession of unrelated sequences with little style, less consistency, and no reason for being. Fox writers quickly devised a plot to stuff around and between the songs, and director David Butler shot it in March. It was – surprise - another backstage story ... [where] the show becomes a hit with an assist from a rather meager array of Fox talent. To make room for so masterfully contrived a story, many of Marcel Silver's revue scenes were excised... By early May, when it was all pasted together, the cost had ascended ... [and] Fox hyped it ferociously, but ... the critics and the exhibitors felt let down.**

THE ONE WOMAN IDEA

In her second silent feature film released in June 1929, Sally was billed merely as one of three "lady passengers on the boat." It was called *The One Woman Idea*, and starred Rod La Rocque and Marceline Day.

DETECTIVES WANTED

Her last film for Fox, the third in 1929, was her first talking picture, and one in which she received billing and spoke some lines. It was a three-reel comedy short called *Detectives Wanted*, starring the comedy team of Bobby Clark and Paul McCullough. It was directed by Norman Taurog, began filming in late May 1929, and was released on August 1, 1929. The brief *Variety* review makes no mention of Sally, but she undoubtedly played some kind of attractive ingénue, her standard role.

She was obviously preparing for more roles in talkies and perhaps musicals, as a March 17, 1929 *Los Angeles Times* article indicates:

> **Sally Phipps, Fox picture star and 1927 Wampas Baby star, is now studying voice with Felix Hughes, well-known Los Angeles vocal teacher, and brother of Rupert Hughes.**

In addition to being the brother of author and playwright Rupert Hughes, Felix was the uncle of the famous aviator and filmmaker Howard Hughes.

Howard Hughes was currently in Hollywood working on *Hell's Angels*, which he began filming as a silent in 1927, later converted to a talkie, and finally premiered in May 1930. Sally told her son Robert that Howard Hughes had promised her a contract after she left Fox. She said she stayed around Hollywood for several months in late 1929 waiting for the offer, which never materialized. He probably had made the same offer to many other attractive starlets.

OFFICIAL APPEARANCES – PARTIES

The studio continued to keep her busy. There were the usual appearances at parties, premieres, and contests, some officially studio related, some purely social, but certainly connected to her status as a movie star. She was frequently written up in the social columns of the *Los Angeles Times*, attending parties given by "The Breakfast Club" and "The Thalians," the latter comprised of young Hollywood actors and actresses. She was alone (April 7, December 29), with a male date (December 8), and sometimes even as hostess (April 21.)

Among the premieres and openings in which Fox showcased her was the inauguration of its new Fox Theater in San Francisco on June 28, 1929, and at the opening of a three-act comedy in Los Angeles called *This Is College*, which had its gala on July 15.

Two *Los Angeles Times* articles mention other society events Sally attended. One, on December 8, 1929, describes a party held at the home of director James Cruze and actress Betty Compson on their estate called Flintridge. Sally was listed as attending with date Milton Bren, a Hollywood screenwriter. The other party, reported on December 29, was an engagement party for actress Blanche Sweet and producer William Hawks at the Chateau Elysée. Sally's name was prominent on the elite guest list.

LAKE ARROWHEAD

Sally, in her memoirs, mentions going to Lake Arrowhead on vacation. She rented a house that Greta Garbo once stayed in. Her mother visited her while she was there. Sally remained on good terms with Edithe. It was her stepfather with whom she had problems. Two *Los Angeles Times* articles record events about her at Lake Arrowhead. One, dated June 23, reports a dancing contest where Sally awarded the winners a silver loving cup. Another article, dated September 15, reports on Sally's success at rainbow trout fishing.

SALLY LEAVES FOX

Soon after her stay at Lake Arrowhead, Sally's association with Fox ended. She was informed that the option on her Fox contract had been dropped, meaning that she was fired. (Fox dropped Sue Carol's option around the same time.)

Sally reclining in her Fox studio dressing room

She then had to clear out her bungalow dressing room on the Fox lot. In *Photoplay*, May 1929, in an article about movie stars' dressing rooms, there is a photo of Sally lounging on her couch in the dressing room that she was soon to leave. The article says:

> **Sally Phipps had a dressing room done in pamico cloth in green and English prints. The cushions are made from quaintly printed old calicos and challis. The chair cover is calico.**

In another article, "They Got What They Wanted, But --," written by Samuel Richard Mook, *Picture Play*, December 1929, Sally's situation after leaving Fox is described:

> **Sally Phipps got a contract from Fox and featured leads in a number of pictures, among them "Cradle Snatchers," "The High-School Hero," and "The News Parade," all with Nick Stuart, and "None But The Brave," opposite Charles Morton. She is one of the few real beauties in Hollywood, but when her contract expired, the option was not taken up.**
>
> **I could learn no reason for this at the studio, executives explaining that in cases of this sort they prefer to let the player make his or her own announcement to save them embarrassment.**

Chapter 3
Florida – New York – Philadelphia -- London

SALLY MOVES TO FLORIDA

In January 1930, at loose ends after her contract was not renewed, Sally took the train to Miami, Florida, and moved in with her favorite aunt, Billie Jones.

Aunt Billie Jones and Sally in Florida (1930)

Sally's mother, Edithe, always kept in touch with her biological family after she was adopted. Billie Jones was her older sister, born Ida Alberta Green in Sacramento in 1890, two years before Edithe. The family story was that Billie was nicknamed after the famous actress Billie Burke. In 1914, she married Harold Grover Jones, a Navy man whom she met in California and who now practiced law in Miami. They had three children -- Harold, Jack, and Dorothy, who were about 13, 11 and 7 when Sally arrived in Miami.

Billie knew the Green family history, and Sally was interested in hearing all about it.

THE GREEN ANCESTORS

As mentioned previously, Edithe's biological father, Sally's grandfather, was Louis Bassett Green. He was born into a wealthy family in Quincy, Illinois, on April 8, 1855. Edithe's biological mother, Emily, was born in August 1864. Louis and Emily were married in 1867 and had three children – Harold, Ida, and Edithe -- before Emily died of typhoid fever in 1892, 7½ months after Edithe was born.

Louis Bassett Green, young man (1870s)

Emily Alberta Weaver Green (1880s)

Louis' father, Ephraim S. Green, defines the expression "doing a land office business": The government offered free land to veterans of the American Revolution and then again after the War of 1812. There was a considerable amount of new territory ready for the taking. Land agents were needed to process the various warrants and patents for land ownership, and Green found his niche by opening a "land office" in Quincy where he moved from Pennsylvania in the 1840s. He also purchased hundreds of acres of land for himself in the sparsely populated Calhoun County, Illinois. Ephraim passed away in 1868, two years shy of his 60th year.

Ephraim S. Green (1860s)

Louis's mother, whose maiden name was Maria M. Bassett, was from a New Hampshire seafaring family. She was born in Philadelphia, July 26, 1815. A newspaper article, published in the *Burlington Hawk-Eye*, July 23, 1911, commemorating her upcoming 96th birthday, said she:

> **. . . was once a wealthy and popular woman of Pittsburgh, and of Quincy, Ill., who in the generosity of her heart, dissipated practically all of her wealth to give the wounded soldiers of the Civil War comfort and renewed health.**
> **. . . Among Mrs. Green's cherished possessions is a miniature of herself, when a young and beautiful woman, painted in Philadelphia by Rembrandt Peale, founder of the Philadelphia Museum, and considered an unusually beautiful work of art. It was exhibited in Burlington [Iowa] a number of years ago, during the time that Mrs. Green was a resident of Quincy.**

The location of the miniature is unknown, but Billie Jones inherited a large unsigned oil portrait of Maria, painted probably some time in the 1840s and possibly also by Rembrandt Peale. Maria died in May 1913 at the age of 97, outliving her husband by 45 years.

Maria M. Bassett Green (1860s)

JACK E. JONES

Billie's son Jack published several family memoirs, and, in his aforementioned *No Rocking Chair Yet*, he again writes about his first cousin Sally:

> **The Fox Studio required its starlets to keep up their education; so it was, when she was eighteen years old, she came to stay at our house while she attended Miami Senior High School. One day a big Cadillac touring car came through town bringing her to our house in Grove Park. I had fallen in love with her on that visit during the train trip when I was little. I still was madly in love with Sally Phipps.**
>
> **George Smathers had an eye on Sally. He was the senior class president of our school, later a big US Senator. After graduating from the University of Florida, George was a US Senator for years.**
>
> **Jack Beckwith, who later became a dentist, was Captain of the football team and he also had an eye on Sally. My cousin brought the two guys to our house. They would slip me 10 to 50 cents to leave the room and forget my baby sitter, Sally Phipps, the movie star.**

When Billie found out about the goings on, she decided that it was not the healthiest situation for Jack, and politely asked Sally to leave.

Jack E. Jones – at summer camp (late 1930s)

Sally did leave, but in her memoirs, she says that it was because the Jones family could no longer afford to keep her after the "banks failed" in the Depression.

In late May 1930, Sally left by ship for New York City, looking forward to a possible new career on the legitimate stage -- on Broadway, she hoped.

SALLY IN NEW YORK IN *ONCE IN A LIFETIME*

Sally, again, was in the right place at the right time. Soon after she arrived in New York in June 1930, she was cast as the movie-struck ingénue in *Once In A Lifetime.* This was a Broadway satire about Hollywood, written by George S. Kaufman (1889-1961) and Moss Hart (1904-1961) and produced by Sam Harris.

In an early press release written in the form of an interview with Sally and published in the *Philadelphia Inquirer*, September 7, under the headline "She Just Couldn't Find Usual Early Bad Luck," Sally is quoted as saying:

> **In all the interviews with young actresses which I have ever read, the young ladies seem to love to dwell upon their early hardships. Nothing would please me better than to tell about how I starved in a three-dollar-a-week room and made the weary rounds of the theatrical offices for weeks on end, to be finally rewarded with an offer of thirty dollars a week to play a French maid with two lines to speak in a company booked to play a whole season**

of one-night stands in the tall grass, but unfortunately nothing like that happened to me.

Sam Harris' clever press agent, John Peter Toohey, had Sally continue, telling how she went about hunting for theatrical work when she first arrived in New York:

> **I came to New York a few weeks ago determined to go on the stage. I'd been in the movies, you know, and I'd played ingénue leads in a few Fox films – notably "High School Hero" and "The News Parade." However, that didn't help me at all. I wasn't up in the Clara Bow class, and I found that people in New York didn't know much about me. Someone told me that I should get an agent, but I thought I'd try to go on my own first.**
>
> **I read the theatrical notes in daily papers and saw that Crosby Gage was going to do a new play with an all feminine cast. So I looked up his address in the telephone book and called on him. We had a little talk and he gave me the play to read, suggesting that he'd like to have me play a certain part. I read the play, didn't like the part and turned it down. I guess that was pretty nervy of me. According to formula, I should have gone down on my knees and thanked Providence for an opportunity like that.**
>
> **Then I read that Sam Harris was going to do a play about the movies, and so I made my second call on him. He'd never heard of me. Neither had Mr. Kaufman, who was doing the casting, but they seemed to think I'd do, and so they gave me the part, and here I am. They tell me that's something of a record – calling on only two managers and being offered my first part by both of them. I wouldn't know about that. I suppose it is.**

Incidentally, the first play that Sally turned down, "Blind Mice" by Vera Caspary and Winifred Lenihan, opened in October 1930 and closed after only 14 performances.

When *Once In A Lifetime* opened on September 24, 1930, at Broadway's Music Box Theatre on 45th Street, it received ecstatic reviews. *The New York Times* raved about the leading players but did not single out Sally. However, Arthur Pollock of the *Brooklyn Daily Eagle* said: "Sally Phipps makes just the right kind of heroine." Harry N. Blair of *Film Daily* said: "Sally portrays a goofy movie ingénue with convincing cleverness." The comedy was a hit and ran for 406 performances. It starred Hugh O'Connell, Jean Dixon, Grant Mills, and Spring Byington. In the program, Sally was billed sixth. George S. Kaufman, in addition to directing the play, also played the part of a frustrated writer who was hired by a movie studio.

The play was a hilarious satire of Hollywood. It revolved around three members of a failed vaudeville act who decide to pass themselves off as vocal coaches during the time when talking films were replacing silent films. Sally played Susan Walker, a Hollywood hopeful, who meets the trio on the train to California and becomes romantically involved with one of them. The joke of the play is that even though the trio know nothing about voice coaching, Sally and her boyfriend become the biggest successes in Hollywood.

THE MUSIC BOX

SAM H. HARRIS AND IRVING BERLIN,
MANAGERS

PROGRAM · PUBLISHED · BY · THE · NEW · YORK · THEATRE · PROGRAM · CORPORATION

FIRE NOTICE: Look around now and choose the nearest exit to your seat. In case of fire, walk (not run) to that exit. Do not try to beat your neighbor to the street.
JOHN J. DORMAN, Fire Commissioner.

BEGINNING
WEDNESDAY EVENING,
SEPTEMBER 24, 1930

MATINEES
THURSDAY AND
SATURDAY

SAM H. HARRIS

PRESENTS

"ONCE IN A LIFETIME"

A NEW COMEDY

BY MOSS HART AND GEORGE S. KAUFMAN

Settings by Cirker and Robbins
Staged by George S. Kaufman

CAST

GEORGE LEWIS	Played by	HUGH O'CONNELL
MAY DANIELS	" "	JEAN DIXON
JERRY HYLAND	" "	GRANT MILLS
THE PORTER	" "	OSCAR POLK
HELEN HOBART	" "	SPRING BYINGTON
SUSAN WALKER	" "	SALLY PHIPPS
CIGARETTE GIRL	" "	CLARA WARING
COAT CHECK GIRL	" "	OTIS SCHAEFER
PHYLLIS FONTAINE	" "	JANET CURRIE

Once In A Lifetime **program**

Once In A Lifetime **scene still: Sally, Charles Halton, Hugh O'Connell, and unidentified**

Once In A Lifetime **scene still, with Frances Brandt and Sally**

Once In A Lifetime **scene still: Hugh O'Connell, Sally, Granville Bates, Edward Loud**

For Sally, *Once In A Lifetime* was a life-altering experience in more ways than one. She was finally free of any family domination, since Albert and Edithe Beutler were far away in California. She had gracefully survived her tenure at Fox films and had now become an immediate success on the legitimate stage, a medium that always appealed to her and one she was growing to love. She even told one newspaper columnist, "Every [performance] night seems like a party to me." Now that she had a steady theatrical paycheck, she was able to move into a Sutton Place apartment at 320 East 57th Street, the former residence of Natacha Rambova, the last wife of Rudolf Valentino.

Sally enjoyed the free time she had between performances. She had time to visit friends and to pal around with her best friend, Dorothy Day, who arrived in New York City just as the play opened. But she was not completely idle, for she pursued her interests in art and also took acting classes, as evidenced by an article in *Film Daily*:

> **Sally Phipps, former Fox ingénue and now appearing on Broadway in "Once in a Lifetime," her first stage vehicle, is spending her spare time in study at the Dramatic Art Institute.**

According to a newspaper interview in November 1930, Sally turned down several movie offers because of her commitment to *Once In A Lifetime.* However, because she had spare time during the day, she decided to work on short films that would not interfere with her performances in the theater.

Only five weeks after she opened in *Once In a Lifetime*, she agreed to appear in a short film, as reported in *Film Daily*, October 29, 1930:

> **SALLY PHIPPS FOR SHORT**
> **Sally Phipps, now appearing in the stage hit, "Once in a Lifetime," has been signed for the ingénue lead in "Her Story," a two reel drama to be made by Broadway Talking Pictures at the Audio Cinema Studios. Wyndham Standing, Roy D'Arcy and Louise Carter also are in the cast.**

There is no record of this film's existence in any of the major sources, so it is very likely that, although Sally was signed, the film was never completed. In February 1931, she was offered another part, this time in a Vitaphone comedy short, *Where Men Are Men*, which she did complete in Vitaphone's nearby Brooklyn studio.

Also, while in Philadelphia during the September out-of-town tryout of *Once In A Lifetime*, she met Benedict Gimbel, Jr., one of the wealthy brothers of the famous Gimbel Brothers department store chain. During the run of the play in New York, he persistently courted her.

ONCE IN A LIFETIME – HISTORY

Once In A Lifetime had a long history before Sally joined the company. It was written in 1929 by Moss Hart. Later that year, Hart brought in George S. Kaufman to collaborate on rewrites. There were two unsuccessful out-of-town tryouts before a final rewrite and re-casting of certain parts, including a couple of the lead roles and the part that Sally eventually got.

Hart's autobiography, *Act One* (New York: Random House, 1959), discusses *Once In A Lifetime*, but covers the time period before the final cast was chosen. Sally is not mentioned in the book, but she is the focus of a photo that appeared with an article by Moss Hart in *Life* magazine, August 24, 1959. In the photo, she is speaking determinedly to three men, including actor Charles Halton and the play's leading man Hugh O'Connell. The caption reads: "Once In A Lifetime: First of Hart's six biggest successes, the play with Sally Phipps, was a 1930 satire on Hollywood." In April 2014, a play based on Moss Hart's book, *Act One*, opened on Broadway with the same title as the book.

In 1930, Sally's stage work was covered in *Theatre Magazine*. The December 1930 issue published an illustrated script condensation of *Once In A Lifetime*. In the article, several scenes from the play are pictured, most with Sally prominently shown. She is in an 11-member cast shot. She is also in two shots in connection with a wedding in the play, one in a close-up with her leading man, another while the wedding is being performed.

Sally also showed up in several newspaper feature articles near the end of the year. One was an interview given to Gilbert Swan for his syndicated column "In New York," which appeared in a number of papers throughout the country. The following *Cumberland Evening Times* version appeared on November 5, 1930:

> **And returning to my desk, found a note from one of the cutest of them all – Sally Phipps.**
>
> **So to take tea with Sally, and found her dwelling quietly and simply in a charming apartment over by the swanky Sutton Place and learned that she had chosen to drop somewhat out of the social whirl while making a serious effort to win her way as a stage figure.**
>
> **And if ever there was an amusing ironic situation, here it is; for Sally rose from a school girl to film stardom. And, when the talking pictures had been launched for a year or so, she grew ambitious to grow as an actress of the speaking stage.**
>
> **She had been visiting with an aunt in Florida, while keeping in touch with Broadway stage conditions. One day she heard that she could have an audience with Producer Harris. She didn't know whether it was Jed or Sam Harris. Having spent most of her time in filmdom, she had never had occasion to care much which might be which. So, quite by accident, she drifted into the office of Sam Harris.**
>
> **It so happened that Sam Harris was casting for his highly successful satire on Hollywood, "Once In A Lifetime."**
>
> **And today you'll find Miss Sally Phipps, late of the movies, appearing on the stage as one of the doll-faced, naïve morons who clutter up the cinema town. Rather amusing – eh, what! – that a girl who found success there should be playing a role which kids the life out of many of her sisterhood.**

Be all that as it may, Sally is intent upon perfecting herself as an actress who can be heard as well as seen. And such applause has she drawn from the critics. Meanwhile, two highly flattering Hollywood contracts have been thrust under her nose. But she isn't ready yet. When Sally returns – if she does within the next year or so – she wants to take a lot of theater experience with her.

A smart gal – this Sally Phipps. And if I recall, she played one of my favorite parts in "The High School Hero."

And talking the "old days" over with this cute red-haired youngster, I learned that she had come from Marin County, California, and once commuted to the Tamalpais High School. The funny part of it was, I happened to be a resident of this neighborhood at the time and rode on the same train that she took daily.

If I'd only known then what I know now!

Another article appeared in her former hometown newspaper, the *Oakland Tribune*, December 21, 1930, headlined "California Girl Enacts Bride Role in Comedy Kidding Screen Colony," by syndicated columnist Marguerite Tazelaar:

New York, Dec. 20. – Susan Walker, if you have been to see "Once in a Lifetime," is the same pretty, wide-eyed, baby-voiced girl off stage as she is in her bridal costume saying "I do" to the racing-form parson at the Music Box [Theatre]. She is not, of course, "beautiful AND dumb," as Messrs. Hart and Kaufman have drawn her so brilliantly; she is, rather beautiful and young.

For Sally Phipps, who acts Susan Walker, impresses you chiefly as a friendly little girl, who has had more or less, Cinderella luck – except that her lovely clothes have not turned back into rags.

She was born in San Francisco 21 years ago, and her true name is Byrnece Beutler. Scarcely five years ago, she was in her third year of high school in Los Angeles, when Frank Borzage, a friend of her family's, asked her if she wouldn't like to take a screen test at the Fox studios, where he was directing.

The result was that in a few weeks she found herself, at 15, a full- fledged screen actress with a three years' contract in her pocket. At the same time she continued studying with a private tutor at her family's insistence.

At the completion of her contract, she thought she would rather go to college than be a "movie" star, so went to live with an aunt in Florida, where she entered the University of Miami. Up to date, her chief pictures had been "High School Hero," "The News Parade," "None But The Brave," "Why Sailors Go Wrong," "Joy Street" and "The One Woman Idea." Now she was deliberately trading her stardom for education.

However, this fall, she felt an urge to come to New York. One morning, during her visit, she walked into the Sam Harris office, where to her surprise, she was greeted with the words, "Don't go. You're the answer to a producer's prayer." And presto: she was changed from Sally Phipps into Susan Walker.

She has never acted on the legitimate stage before, but she hopes to keep right on acting on it – she loves the real people out front, the color, life and gaiety of the stage.

"Every night seems like a party to me . . . No, I wasn't a bit scared on the opening night . . . I think acting in pictures is fine training for the stage."

Tell me, Miss Phipps, are the "movies" as bad as they're painted in "Once in a Lifetime?" the young star was meanly asked.

"Well, I don't know that I should say this, for I think 'Once in a Lifetime' is such a grand show, but I never found them so – so burlesqued – though it is true that playwrights have to sit around like that without doing anything."

The thing she wants to do more than anything else, after wanting "Once in a Lifetime" to have a long, long run, is to go to Europe, where she has never been . . . . And she does not want to become a type actress . . . . And she misses her mother (now in Los Angeles) woefully.

Picture Play, January 1931, in an article entitled "Over The Teacups," by The Bystander, included an over-the-shoulder facial photo of Sally as well as some career information:

"That's nothing, though, to the luck Sally Phipps fell into. She walked right into 'Once in a Lifetime.' the biggest hit of the year."

I thought I'd seen that girl somewhere. Of course, there is this to be said for my failing memory. "Once in a Lifetime" keeps you in such gales of laughter from the time you go into the theater, that you might be forgiven for not recognizing your own sister if she made a late entrance. It is a diabolically clever satire on Hollywood and, compared to its barbed shafts, "Queer People" is a eulogy of the film colony. The play has made such a hit that three more satires on Hollywood are scheduled to be produced before the winter is over.

"Where has Sally Phipps been hiding all this?" I asked, finally giving up the struggle of trying to remember where I had seen her before.

"Oh, she made a lot of those juvenile comedies with Nick Stuart for Fox," Fanny told me. "You wouldn't go to them, if I remember rightly. You were having an attack of being very sophisticated and passing up everything short of Lubitsch. But you missed a lot of amusement, particularly in 'The High School Hero.'

"Finally, she got sort of fed up with Hollywood and pictures."

If you have the sort of disposition I have, you are already singing, "Or maybe they got fed up with her."

"And she went to Florida to visit her aunt for several months. She had a grand time just playing around, and then she went to Southampton. One day when she came in town, she had some idle time on her hands, and what did she do but go to Sam Harris's office and apply for a job! She'd always had a vague idea of going on the stage sometime if she got the chance, and it

seemed like a good time to do something about it. She's just that casual. And she is undoubtedly the luckiest girl I've ever known. She walked into that office the very day they were looking for someone just like her. So there she is all set in a play that is sure to run for a year. And Mr. Harris is so pleased with her work that he's planning to put her in a musical next year. And she probably will do some short films while she's working in the play.

It's really the greatest relief to meet someone who is gay and untroubled and unselfconscious. She's perfectly willing to trust everything to luck; it's treated her well so far. It got her into pictures; she just wandered past Frank Borzage, you know, and he decided to make a test of her. She has awfully good features. Youthful, and sweet, and sort of doll-like.

"She's taken an apartment in East Fifty-Seventh Street, and she adores having most of her afternoons free so that she can have people in for tea. The only trouble with her sudden success is that it didn't give her time to see very many of the New York shows. Now she can only see the plays that have Wednesday matinées."

In the third to the last paragraph, there is the statement:

And Mr. Harris is so pleased with her work that he's planning to put her in a musical next year.

This is in reference to the famous musical, *Of Thee I Sing*, which was in the planning stages while "Once In A Lifetime" was enjoying its run during the 1930-1931 Broadway season. *Of Thee I Sing* opened in December 1931. Sam Harris produced it. George and Ira Gershwin wrote the music and lyrics, and George Kaufman and Morrie Ryskin wrote the play. Sally was asked to play the singing role of Mary Turner, the love interest in the musical. When Sally turned down the role due to personal events in her life, the film actress, Lois Moran, who was a friend of Sally's and who had long coveted the role, got the job. Coincidently, Lois and Sally had appeared together in one of Sally's last feature films, *Joy Street.* Lois Moran was wonderful in the role, and the musical play ran over 440 performances.

Screenland, February 1931, published an article by Rosa Reilly headlined, "Is the Stage the Port of Missing Screen Stars," with a head shot of Sally. The caption reads:

Sally Phipps knocked the Big Town dead in the successful New York stage play "Once in a Lifetime."

In the text of the article there is the comment:

Sally Phipps is appearing – and doing very well – in "Once in a Lifetime," the stage sensation that burlesques Hollywood.

At another point in the text there is the following:

> **Sally Phipps has no cause for anxiety since she's made a hit in the stage play, "Once in a Lifetime." She works at odd times, too, in the Paramount Long Island Studio.**

Here, the author was mistakenly confusing the Paramount Long Island Studio with the Warner Brother's Vitaphone Studio in Brooklyn, where Sally actually worked.

Sally's final movie magazine appearance was in *Film Fun*, May 1932, in an article entitled "You, Too, Can have A Body Beautiful," by Sonya Ann Yetsofa, as told to Edward Sammis. Sally's photo, which fills one-third of the page, portrays her standing in a niche and ostensibly nude from head to toe, except for a metallic-swirl-patterned veil, which she holds across her body. It is one of her most famous (and now collectible) "pin-up" photos. The metallic swirls on the veil are strategically positioned to barely cover her nipples and privates. The caption reads:

> **There's no excuse for going around looking like a ten-dollar blimp in a windstorm, says Sonya. Let's all get beautiful white bodies like Sally Phipps and delight our friends!**

This same "pin-up" photo also appeared on postcards that Fox sold in the European market.

WHERE MEN ARE MEN – 1931 VITAPHONE COMEDY SHORT

In early 1931, Sally appeared in a Vitaphone two-reel comedy short called *Where Men Are Men.* It was filmed in the Vitaphone Studio on Avenue M in Brooklyn. (This studio was purchased by Warner Brothers in 1925 from the old Vitagraph Film Company, specifically for the purpose of making talking pictures.) The comedy starred comedian Joe Penner (later widely known for his tag line "Wanna Buy a Duck?") and was directed by Alf Goulding. Sally received no billing for her small but significant part as Joe Penner's cowgirl girlfriend, Nancy Carter (as evidenced by the copy viewed at the Library of Congress). Sally appears in several scenes with Penner, including the final hilarious surprise boy-gets-girl fadeout. In the film, Sally looks adorable as a cowgirl, has a pleasant speaking voice, and proves again to be a delightful comedienne.

The first mention of her gig at Vitaphone was in the Brooklyn *Standard Union* newspaper, February 5, 1931:

> **Sally Phipps Talkie.**
>
> **Sally Phipps, ingénue of "Once In a Lifetime" at the Music Box Theatre, starts work to-day at the Warner Studio in Brooklyn on a short called "Where Men Are Men."**
>
> **Previous to her engagement in the Moss Hart-George Kaufman smash hit, Miss Phipps was featured in many Fox films.**

Film Daily also recorded Sally's connection with this film production. On February 8, 1931, the following appeared:

> **Sally Phipps With Vitaphone.**
> **Sally Phipps, who is now playing a prominent role in the Broadway stage production, "Once In A Lifetime," has been signed for the leading feminine role in a forthcoming Vitaphone comedy, opposite Joe Penner.**

On February 22, a follow-up to the previous *Film Daily* article appeared:

> **Joe Penner, Vitaphone's lisping comedian, goes wild and wooly in his latest comedy short, "Where Men Are Men," just completed at the Warner studio. Sally Phipps, stage and screen player, heads the supporting cast. Alf Goulding directed.**

Although, according to *Film Daily*, the film was made in February 1931, the earliest newspaper reference found for a screening of it is in the July 23 *Cleveland Plain Dealer*. Reviews did not appear in the trade papers until September. Unfortunately for Sally, none of the reviews in *Variety*, *Film Daily*, or *Motion Picture Herald* mention her or the character she plays. On the other hand, she was now experiencing a different kind of attention in her personal life – a new boyfriend and fiancé.

BENEDICT GIMBEL, JR.

Benedict Gimbel, Jr. (1899-1971), whom Sally referred to as "Ben," met her during the *Once In A Lifetime* out-of-town tryout in Philadelphia in September 1930. He was one of the many "stage-door johnnies" who lined up after performances to meet Sally, probably offering the usual late night supper followed by an after-hour nightclub crawl. Although Ben was one of the Gimbel brothers who owned the famous chain of department stores, he was much more interested in show business and with mingling with celebrities than in participating in the family business. Around the time he met Sally, he was preparing to take over as head of the store's subsidiary radio station, which he felt was the closest he could get to being in show business. The station was named WIP-WFAN, and he became president of it some time in early 1931.

SALLY MARRIES BEN – JUNE 5, 1931

In her memoirs, Sally does not give any details about how her romance with Ben began or progressed during the time she was performing in *Once In A Lifetime* in 1930 and 1931. However, as early as April 7, 1931, in the *Glenn Falls Post-Star* New York newspaper, in Walter Winchell's "On Broadway" column, the following appeared:

Benedict Gimbel and Sally ("Once in a Lifetime") Phipps will ankle up an alter in June.

She left the play on May 25, 1931, and her role was taken over by Jane Buchanan, an actress who held a small part in the play. Sally married Ben in Philadelphia on June 5, 1931.

Ben was twelve years older than Sally, and he wanted a Jewish marriage, which required Sally to convert to Judaism. The conversion process was handled by Rabbi Louis Wolsey of Congregation Rodeph Sholom (Rodeph Shalom), a reform synagogue in Philadelphia, and Sally took the name "Ruth" for the conversion. The marriage ceremony was also performed by Rabbi Wolsey in Philadelphia in Ben's mother's apartment at 250 South 17th Street. Sally's mother, Edithe, and her Aunt Billie both attended the ceremony -- Edithe coming from California, Billie from Florida. The married couple then went on a honeymoon cruise to Nassau, the Bahamas.

Benedict Gimbel, Jr. and Sally on honeymoon sail to Nassau, Bahamas (June 1931)

SALLY IN PHILADELPHIA

When they returned, Sally and Ben moved into their new apartment at 1530 Locust Street (now called The Versailles) in Center City Philadelphia.

1530 Locust Street, Philadelphia (today)

Although it was the middle of the Depression, Sally was living in a beautiful apartment with a butler, a maid, and several servants, and she could pick out gowns by the dozens.

Sally at the Philmont Country Club orphans picnic, Philadelphia (July 1931)

However, feeling more and more out of place with conservative Philadelphia society life, Sally returned to her hobby of painting, got her own art studio, and even took continuing education courses at the nearby University of Pennsylvania.

SALLY LEAVES BEN

Things went well for about a year, but Sally became increasingly uncomfortable with what she considered Ben's "rough treatment" of the servants, most of whom were black. Then, in May 1932, the butler informed Sally that Ben was "fooling around." Sally consulted a lawyer and moved out of their apartment into the local Warburton Hotel for a month. On June 23, she filed for divorce in Philadelphia. The divorce suit hit the papers on June 24, but no grounds were disclosed.

In July, Sally moved back to New York City, into a hotel on Gramercy Park. Ben followed her soon after, checked into a room next door to hers, and began pleading reconciliation. By August, Sally gave in to Ben and moved back in with him in Philadelphia. However, during the short time she was in New York before the reconciliation, she was offered a part in a production of the play *The Barretts of Wimpole Street*. She turned it down because of her decision to return to Ben and go back to Philadelphia.

Ten months later, Sally discovered more of Ben's indiscretions and, in June 1933, moved out. This time, she decided to leave Ben permanently. She went back to New York City, where she looked for work, found nothing, and finally gave up, but kept on with her lessons. She studied voice with the famous Metropolitan Opera singer Madame Frances Alda (1879-1952), attended soft shoe dancing classes with Dan Drake, and took courses at the American Academy of Dramatic Arts. She also met new people from the occult world, a world she was always attracted to. Amador Botello, a famous theosophist and professional psychologist, convinced her to become a vegetarian, while George Wehner, a well-known spiritualist medium and music composer, became a good friend.

In late November 1933, a possible networking opportunity presented itself. Sally heard through various sources that the Île De France ocean liner was sailing from New York City to Europe on November 25 with several producers on board. Full of hope, Sally renewed her passport and booked passage in first class. Two days before she was to leave, the following article appeared in the November 23rd *New York Times*:

> **B. Gimbel Jr. Seeks Divorce.**
>
> **Special to the New York Times.**
>
> **PHILADELPHIA, Nov. 22.—Benedict Gimbel Jr. of this city filed suit for divorce today against the former Sally Phipps, movie actress, whom he married June 5, 1931. Mrs. Gimbel, whose right name before her marriage was Byrnece Beutler, started a divorce suit in June, 1932, but a reconciliation was effected later.**

Sally ignored the divorce filing and boarded the ship on Saturday, November 25th at Pier 15 for the six-day crossing.

Sally on board the Île De France (November 1933)

During the voyage, she met and became friendly with the famous ballet dancer Serge Lifar (1905-1986), who was then considered the successor to Nijinsky. He had been a principal dancer with Serge Diaghilev's Ballet Russes and was currently the ballet master of the Paris Opera.

Unfortunately, after no movie offers came from the ocean crossing, Sally disembarked in Plymouth, England, on Friday, December 1 and headed for London, assuming that she could get some kind of work there. She decided to stay in London until her one-year visa expired near the end of November 1934.

SALLY IN LONDON

When Sally arrived in London, she first lived at the American Women's Club of London, a membership organization set up to help American female expatriates settle into their new living and employment situations. Sally had trouble finding a job. The Depression had hit England badly, and jobs were scarce and preference was given to English nationals. She took acting courses at the Royal Academy of Dramatic Art, and participated in courses in Shakespeare repertory at the Old Vic Theatre. She remembered playing "Ariel" in *The Tempest* in a class workshop. During this time, she said she got a film offer from Paris but turned it down. She also met the film producer Alexander Korda, but no offers resulted.

In April 1934, Dorothy Day, her best friend, arrived in London, and they rented an apartment together in Hampstead Heath. Sally started to study shorthand and also took some business courses that resulted in secretarial positions at the British Psychic Institute and at the British College of Psychic Science. She first worked with the author Paul Brunton (1898-1981), while he was in the process of writing his book, *A Search In Secret India*, which was published in 1935. Sally also involved Dorothy in the Brunton project. Later Sally was employed by the famous British psychic and medium, Kathleen Barkel. Barkel was impressed with Sally's work and asked Sally to move into her house and become her private secretary, which Sally agreed to do.

Along the way, Sally also became acquainted with prominent members of the United Lodge of Theosophists, the London branch of the international organization, founded by Helena Petrovna Blavatsky (1831-1891). Its mission was to introduce the various oriental philosophies and religions to the western world.

Chapter 4
New York – Also Hawaii And India

SALLY RETURNS TO NEW YORK

With her English visa due to expire, Sally booked passage back to America. She purchased a third-class ticket on Holland America Line's S.S. Volendam, leaving Southampton on Saturday, November 24, 1934, and arriving in New York City on Tuesday, December 4. On the passenger list, Sally has her name spelled "Sallie" with an "ie" instead of the usual "y," a spelling she adopted while living in London.

Sally's best friend, Dorothy Day, however, chose to stay in London a full year and continue to work. She did not return to America until May 1935.

When Sally arrived back in New York, she found an apartment and again began looking for work.

According to Sally's memoirs, in early 1935 she was "active" in The Group Theatre, a New York City theatre collective, founded in 1931 by Harold Clurman, Cheryl Crawford, and Lee Strasberg. In the early months of 1935, it produced the wildly successful *Waiting For Lefty* by Clifford Odets, first Off-Broadway and then later on Broadway. Since Sally's name was not in either of the *Lefty* cast lists, her work with the company must have been something other than in an acting capacity.

SALLY IN BROADWAY COMEDY *KNOCK ON WOOD*

A few months later, Sally was offered a part in an upcoming Broadway show, *Knock On Wood*, a comedy about Hollywood by playwright Allen Rivkin. Rehearsals began on May 6, 1935, under the direction of John Hayden. Like *Once In A Lifetime*, it was a Hollywood lampoon. In this case, all the action took place in an agent's office. The play starred James Rennie, Lee Patrick, Albert Van Dekker (Albert Dekker), Bruce MacFarlane, and Sally, billed with the new spelling of her name "Sallie Phipps." She played a naive young actress from Tennessee named "Lurline Marlowe" who longs to get into the movies. The *New York Times*, on May 26, published a publicity picture of James Rennie and Sally, with the following caption:

> **Two Players From "Knock On Wood," which Is Expected Tuesday Evening At The Cort Theatre. They Are James Rennie and Sallie Phipps.**

The play opened on May 28 at the Cort Theatre, but the reviews were devastating. Brooks Atkinson said in the *New York Times*, May 29:

> **The casting is undiscriminating, the direction lacks purpose, and the script is an aimless, synthetic affair.**

Sally, however, got a positive mention in one newspaper article, "The Reporter At The Play," by George L. Cassidy, *New York Post*, May 29. It included the following audience member comment:

> **Then, too, it was so well acted – Rennie was good as ever and I liked Sallie Phipps.**

Unfortunately, *Knock On Wood* lasted only 11 performances, and Sally was again out of a job.

CORT THEATRE

DIRECTION 138 WEST 48th STREET THEATRE CO., INC.

FIRE NOTICE: The exit, indicated by a red light and sign, nearest to the seat you occupy, is the shortest route to the street.
In the event of fire or other emergency please do not run—WALK TO THAT EXIT.
JOHN J. McELLIGOTT, Fire Chief and Commissioner

THE · PLAYBILL · PUBLISHED · BY · THE · NEW · YORK · THEATRE · PROGRAM · CORPORATION

BEGINNING TUESDAY EVENING, MAY 28, 1935

MATINEES WEDNESDAY AND SATURDAY

KNOCKWOOD INC.

Offers

KNOCK ON WOOD

A New Comedy
By
ALLEN RIVKIN
with

JAMES RENNIE

Staged by John Hayden
Setting by Watson Barratt

CAST
(In order of their appearance)

CHRISTIAN HUGO	Played by	BRUCE MACFARLANE
JAKE	" "	RICHARD TABER
PAT MORAN	" "	LEE PATRICK
EDITH	Played by	BEVERLY PARKER
HARRY	" "	WALTER WILSON
NICK HUGO	" "	JAMES RENNIE
MORT CHANDLER	" "	CALVIN THOMAS
LURLEEN MARLOWE	" "	SALLIE PHIPPS
JOAN WEXLEY	" "	BEATRICE SWANSON
STUART SCHUYLER	" "	ALBERT VAN DEKKER
FRANCIS Z. BARRINGTON	" "	TOM MORRISON
THE MAJOR	" "	NICHOLAS JOY
FINK WILSON	" "	JAMES SPOTTSWOOD
GARY "SLUG" GREEN	" "	DONALD BLACK
POTTS JACKSON	" "	HORACE MACMAHON
ELMER McGURK	" "	CHARLES COMORODA
JOHN GREYLOCK	" "	WILLIAM DAVID
TWO HOODLUMS	" "	ROBERT GRAY HARRY SETON

ALL THE CHARACTERS IN THIS PLAY ARE FICTITIOUS—EXCEPT—THOSE YOU RECOGNIZE.

***Knock On Wood* program**

***Knock On Wood* photo with Lee Patrick, James Rennie, and Sally**

SALLY'S DIVORCE FROM GIMBEL

Soon after *Knock On Wood* closed, Sally received final divorce papers from Ben Gimbel. As previously mentioned, Ben had filed suit before she left for Europe, and after a year and seven months, the divorce became final on June 24, 1935. The *New York Times*, June 25, 1935, reported the following:

> **GIMBEL DIVORCE GRANTED**
> **Benedict Jr. Gets Decree From Sally Phipps in Philadelphia**
> **Special to THE NEW YORK TIMES.**
>
> **PHILADELPHIA, June 24.—Benedict Gimbel Jr., of this city, obtained a final divorce decree in Common Pleas Court today from Sally Phipps Gimbel, whom he married June 5, 1931.**
>
> **The suit was filed in November 1933, and testimony was heard by W. Logan McCoy, a master, whose report recommending the divorce was approved by the court about two weeks ago. The papers were impounded.**
>
> **Mrs. Gimbels's real name was Byrnece Beutler. A native of California, she took academic degrees in art and law, entered the movies as Sally Phipps in 1926, and three years later was named a Wampas Baby Star.**

Ben's cause for action, as recorded in the document, was "desertion." Sally received a very small settlement, leaving her in a bad financial situation.

Ben Gimbel wasted no time in getting married again. On June 25, the day after the divorce became final, he married Margaret Sweney, a former Gimbel Brothers department store employee.

In the months after the divorce, Sally was unable to find another job in the theater and had to move into a smaller furnished apartment. Having sold her furniture, she lived off the proceeds while she continued to look for work.

SALLY IN JAMES HENDRICKSON-CLAIRE BRUCE COMPANY

In January 1936, Sally got an acting job with the James Hendrickson-Claire Bruce Company. This was a touring company of professional actors who brought Shakespeare plays into college, university, and high school theaters and auditoriums throughout the East Coast. The company travelled from place to place in their own bus. James Hendrickson and Claire Bruce, a married couple, owned and administered the company, and played all the lead roles. Sally remembered appearing in minor roles in *Macbeth*, *Hamlet*, *Julius Caesar*, and *The Merchant Of Venice.*

Sally posing outdoors with a fellow Shakespearean actor

In June 1936, Sally's employment with the theatrical company was interrupted by an invitation from Edithe to visit her in Hawaii, where Edithe was now living. The invitation suggested a stay for at least two months. Of course, Sally already knew about Edithe's new work situation and the story behind her settling in Hawaii.

Edithe had gotten laid off from her job at Warner Brothers-First National studio in late 1934, and soon after she was hired by Eastman Kodak Company as a colorist of aerial photographs. This required her to move to Hawaii. And, having become increasingly unhappy with Albert Beutler, she decided to go there without him and eventually got a divorce.

Edithe, late 1934

Now that she was free of Albert Beutler, she planned to make Hawaii a place to reconsolidate her family. In 1931, her son Lane graduated from Fairfax High School, the same school that Sally had attended, and was now working. In 1933, he married his high school sweetheart, Elinor Erickson, another Fairfax graduate. Edithe plotted to eventually have them come to Hawaii and live near her.

Lane Beutler

EDITHE IN HAWAII

Edithe's new job required her to be based in Honolulu, Hawaii, and secondarily in Manila, the Philippines. She was hired to work with a husband and wife team of aerial photographers who were also employed by Eastman Kodak. Edithe's job was to apply color to their photographs. She accompanied them on their flights so she could accurately reproduce the colors of the landscapes. Edithe always emphasized the importance of accurate color, for this is vital for distinguishing nuances in terrain, foliage, buildings, and other constructions.

Edithe had already built a reputation as a master colorist of black-and-white photographs by enhancing portraits and Hollywood scene stills in color. She was now putting her skills to work on enormous wall-sized blow-ups of aerial sites.

Edithe coloring an aerial photo (late 1930s)

These photographs may have been for the United States government, which probably used the work for mapping and other potential military purposes. Japan was becoming increasingly aggressive in exactly the same areas in the Pacific and Southeast Asia that Edithe's photo team was covering. Edithe worked with this team until the summer of 1939, when illness required her to take a medical leave.

Before starting her new job, Edithe had made an exploratory visit to Honolulu, arriving on January 10, 1935. On this trip, she met her new colleagues and searched for a place to live. She found a house not far from downtown Honolulu, in an area called Nuuanu Valley. The address was 50 Bates Street, and the house was situated on beautiful grounds, full of coconut trees and lush greenery. In addition to her aerial photographic coloring work, Edithe was promised a franchise for a future Kodak processing store, which she could open whenever and wherever she wanted. She then returned to Los Angeles, and after finally settling her affairs, went back to Hawaii on March 22.

Edithe then invited Lane and his new wife Elinor to join her, and they loved the idea. They arrived in Honolulu on April 11, 1935 and moved into Edithe's new house in Nuuanu Valley. Lane and Elinor stayed in Hawaii for two years before returning to Los Angeles in 1937.

SALLY VISITS MOTHER IN HAWAII

A year later, in June 1936, when Sally got her invitation to visit, she was thrilled for the opportunity for many reasons. First of all, she was missing her family very much. It was already five years since she had seen Edithe -- at her wedding with Gimbel in June 1931. Also, she was looking forward to seeing her brother and his wife Elinor. And then, the two-month stay in the tropical environment, which Sally loved, would serve as a wonderful respite from her grueling theatrical trouping.

Sally gave her notice to the James Hendrickson-Claire Bruce Company and booked passage for Honolulu on Matson Line's passenger ship S.S. Malolo, which left from Los Angeles on June 26. She arrived in Los Angeles by bus with enough time to make several visits with old friends before boarding the ship. She arrived in Honolulu on July 2. A few days earlier, her best friend Dorothy Day arrived in Honolulu. Sally must have arranged a reunion with her, for, according to passenger ship manifests, they arrived and left Honolulu within days of each other.

Edithe, Lane, and Elinor all welcomed Sally at the Honolulu dock with a multitude of flower leis, the usual Hawaiian welcome. Thanks to Edithe's connection with Eastman Kodak, there are many photographs recording Sally's visit, all posed on the grounds of Edithe's new property in Nuuanu Valley. One group of photographs shows her after her arrival at the house, still profusely covered with leis. Another group shows her dressed in Japanese style, in kimono and slippers. A third group comprises scene stills from "The Play," a short silent home movie filmed like a hokey melodrama, written jointly by Edithe, Sally, Lane, and Elinor. Directed by and starring Sally, the plot line had to do with a wacky South Sea Island princess and some stolen pearls. The family had great fun filming this piece of nonsense, all on the verdant, photogenic grounds of Edithe's property.

Edithe's immediate family was always big on nicknames, and Sally now learned a few new ones. Edithe always liked to be called "Lovey." And now, Elinor liked to be called "Puddy" (short for "tapioca pudding"), a name of endearment her husband Lane had recently invented. During Sally's stay, Edithe began calling Sally "Frangipani," another name for the local plumeria flower. Sally's son Robert remembers the use of these nicknames until the end of their lives.

Sally and Edithe in Hawaii in 1936

Elinor and Sally in Hawaii in 1936

SALLY RETURNS TO NEW YORK

Sally left Hawaii in September and returned to New York City by passenger steamship. The trip took almost a month. She left Honolulu on September 10 aboard Dollar Line's S.S. President Cleveland, which made stops in San Francisco and Los Angeles, then passed through the Panama Canal, made another stop in Havana, and finally docked in Jersey City at Pier 12 on October 5.

As she passed through San Francisco, *Variety* found out about her return to New York, and she was written up in their September 30 issue:

SALLY PHIPPS RESUMING BROADWAY CAREER ----

San Francisco, Sept. 29. --- Sally Phipps, Broadway ingénue and former film player with Fox, announced yesterday that she intends shortly to go to New York, where she will resume her theatrical career.

Miss Phipps, who was the ingénue in 'Once in a Lifetime,' arrived here last week from Honolulu, where she passed a vacation with her parents.

Sally had high hopes for resuming her theatrical career. However, she arrived in New York City practically broke, and theatrical work, or any kind of work, was not easy to find. She relied on old friends for a while, even approaching former colleagues from The Group Theatre for help.

For lodging, she was fortunate to find a small room at the top of an apartment building down the street from Carnegie Hall at 140 West 57th Street, between Sixth and Seventh Avenues.

140 West 57th Street, New York City

Sally's apartment was described, in a June 1938 newspaper article by the famous gossip columnist Earl Wilson in the *New York Post*, as:

> **a penthouse cubicle on the seventeenth floor . . . eight feet long and six feet wide . . . a one-flight walk-up after she left the elevator.**

The article mentions a sun terrace, but there was no mention of a bathroom. Sally's son Robert, curious about this unusual apartment, visited 140 West 57th Street in early July 2012 and met with the building's superintendent, Felix Despiau. Mr. Despiau, with great hospitality and kindness, agreed to give him a tour of the building. When Mr. Despiau was told about the one-flight walk-up from the top floor of the building, he immediately recognized Sally's former apartment as the one he uses today as his office. The room's dimensions are actually about double those given in newspaper article, roughly 8½ by 12 feet, with one large window. There is a bathroom a short way down the hall, and a door that leads out to the roof. Sally sunbathed on the roof, as if it were her terrace. In fact, New Yorkers like to refer to such a roof as a "tar beach." Sally mentioned using this terrace often and enjoyed it tremendously. She paid $20 a month for rent and was able to manage pretty well with the apartment's peculiarities. She kept it for several years.

SALLY IN THE FEDERAL THEATRE PROJECT

The federally funded Works Progress Administration (WPA) was a godsend for Sally. It was founded in 1935 to create civil service jobs for the unemployed, as part of President Franklin D. Roosevelt's New Deal program. Sally submitted her application in October 1936 for the WPA Federal Theatre Project, but she had to wait until December to become eligible for employment. There was a two-year residency requirement, and she had not returned from her year in England until December 1934.

When December finally came, she began her work with the Federal Theatre Project, which had offices at 1697 Broadway, between West 53rd and West 54th Streets in New York City. "1697 Broadway," as it was commonly called then, is a 13-story, brown-brick and terra-cotta office building completed in 1927. In 1936, it was also the home of CBS radio, and Sally frequently referred to it as the "radio building on Broadway." The ground floor theater, built as part of the office building, was originally named Hammerstein's Theater. In 1936, it became part of the CBS radio broadcasting studios. Today, it is known as the Ed Sullivan Theater, the former home of *The Ed Sullivan Show* and most recently *The Late Show With David Letterman*, soon to be taken over by Stephen Colbert.

Hallie Flanagan Davis (1890-1969), a theater professor from Vassar, headed the Project. Ms. Davis used Sally well. She at times employed Sally as her secretarial assistant, sometimes assigned her to clerical positions in the Project's Research Department, and frequently gave her performance assignments in the Project's Radio Division.

Sally's boss in the Research Department was Harriet B. Meyer (1910-1988), whose title was Director of Research. In this Department, Sally eventually became Assistant to the Director and was also given responsibilities as a Junior Supervisor of Research. According to Sally, "We outlined work for all the 500 collators of the Eastern Region who were engaged in research on various subjects falling within the scope of the Project." Sally and Harriet Meyer remained close friends for many decades after their working relationship.

Sally was also kept busy performing in the Federal Theatre Project's Radio Division. During her two and a half years with the Project, she was involved with two major radio broadcasting series. One was a Jules Verne (1828-1905) series of dramatic programs, in three parts, which was broadcast between October 1937 and June 1938. *A Journey To The Center Of The Earth* ran from October 1937 through early February 1938. *Mysterious Island* ran from mid-February through March 1938. *From The Earth To The Moon* ran from April through June 1938. The other program was a documentary dramatic series based on the books of Paul De Kruif (1890-1971), entitled *Men Against Death*. This focused on the lives of scientific and medical trailblazers, such as Lister and Pasteur, and ran from July 1938 through April 1939.

The *New York Times*, October 10, 1937, listed Sally in the cast of characters for one part of the Jules Verne series:

> **JULES VERNE'S FANTASY, "Journey to the Center of the Earth," divided into eight half-hour weekly dramatic episodes, is begun today by the Federal Theatre Players. Ashley Buck, writer, directs: WHN, 5 P.M.**
> **The cast:**
> **Professor Van Hardwigg -- Philip White**
> **Harry, his nephew -- Robert Crozier**
> **Mme. Dupre -- June Bradley**
> **Gretchen -- Sally Phipps**
> **Hans -- Jack Raymond**

Seven months later, a photograph appeared in the newspaper, *The Canton Repertory*, May 4, 1938, in the column "On The Air And In Radio Studios." It showed Sally and Ms. Bradley, from the waist up, standing in a soundproof studio, in front of a microphone, reading from their scripts.

TAKE PART IN 'JULES VERNE' BROADCASTS

ACTRESSES on the WPA'S popular "Jules Verne" series on the air are Sally Phipps, left, and June Bradley, pictured during a broadcast.

Sally on radio, with June Bradley

An accident with a ten-ton truck warranted a photograph and short article in the *San Francisco Examiner* on June 14, 1938, entitled "Truck Not Enough To Halt Her Career:"

> **New York.--Miss Sally Phipps, radio actress and production assistant with the Federal Theatre's Radio Division, pictured during a rehearsal for a broadcast of the Federal Project today, June 14th. Miss Phipps, former star of the screen and stage is staging a theatrical comeback. This was imperiled several weeks ago when Sally was struck by a ten-ton truck. Her knee was badly injured.**

Sally in 1938 photo from *San Francisco Examiner* article

The long version of the previously referred to article by Earl Wilson appeared one week later in the *New York Post*, June 21, 1938. It tells a fuller story:

WAMPUS EX-BABY LIVES ON WPA $23 – AND LIKES IT

Sally Phipps, Who Earned $500 Per Week in Hollywood,
Finds Artistic Outlet in the Simple Life.
Screen's Ex-Sizzling Baby Now Demure Working Girl.

By EARL WILSON

Miss Sally Phipps, whose multitudinous curves and misbehaving hazel [sic] eyes earned her $500 a week when she was a Wampas Baby Star in Hollywood in 1927, is on WPA now and enjoying it mightily, thanks.

Sweet Sally has been discovered pummeling a typewriter up at the offices of the Federal Theatre Project's Radio Division at Fifty-Third Street and Broadway.

For this and other chores – not including brightening up the office, which she does gratis – Miss Phipps receives $23.86 a week, not even a flyspeck on her 1927 pay.

$5 FOR PENTHOUSE CUBICLE

Upon this sum, however, the new Sally Phipps luxuriates.

Five of her large and tremendously important dollars go every week for a penthouse cubicle on the seventeenth floor of 140 West Fifty-Seventh Street. Eight feet long and six feet wide [sic], it's as roomy as a cell at Sing Sing.

Now, no gentlemen may call upon Miss Phipps in this retreat. "An ascetic like me never has any visitors," Miss Phipps, who is twenty-seven now but still has her curves and beauty but not her baby-face, says concerning the no-gentlemen-need-drop-around-evenings rule.

"Why," she adds, giving her pile of auburn hair a toss, "I've become a student, a philosopher. I'm even learning to read Sanskrit."

(Reporter's Note: With due apologies to Sanskrit as a fireside companion, our opinion is that no gentlemen are permitted to call upon Miss Phipps because Miss Phipps and a gentleman, even one gentleman, could not get into her cell at the same time without busting the sides out of the building.)

TRAFFIC'S HEAVY

You'll probably have to push away several gents to get to her. With a lady of her voltage in the vicinity, naturally a lot of guys have discovered they have some work which has to be done in the same office at the very same minute. It's very important work which can't be done anywhere else at any other time, apparently.

So you invite Sally down to the Bryant Hotel bar and mighty, mighty proud of yourself you are, too, when you note the other swains glaring at you jealously.

"Tea," says Sally, firmly, to the waitress.

Well, she won't take a cigarette, either; and you note that her nails don't glisten with polish, and that in other ways also the sizzling baby star of the vamp days is now very prim and demure. She even whips out a Chinese fan (or maybe it was Japanese) and sets up a little breeze, at which the manager rushes over, like for a riot call. "That's an insult to our air conditioning," he says, grinning, and finally traffic like this gets so heavy around our table that we decide we've got to go to Sally's penthouse room for some privacy.

UH -- SHORTS

Sally pilots the reporter and photographer up a one-flight walk-up after she leaves the elevator; then she puts us out on the roof while she hops into some white shorts. She comes onto the roof by way of the window, the shorts detracting nothing from her figure.

"See the movie star's makeup kit?" she coos, pointing through the open window.

We observe a jar of cold cream, a jar of finishing cream, some empty vials which once contained nail polish and not much else – an extremely modest layout for a beauty. But on a shelf below this we see a few copies of the *The Hound and Horn*, the old poetry magazine cherished by intellectuals, and a copy of the modernized translation of the *Bible*.

Miss Phipps is soon discovered lying full length on a deck chair with the sun beating down upon her already tanned legs, and begins telling the story of how she came from stardom to WPA.

"I was fourteen and going to Fairfax High School in Los Angeles when it began," she says. "Sally Eilers was there, too. I wanted to be a lawyer and was trying to get ready for law school. Before I knew it, I had been given a screen test and was offered a stock contract -- $75 a week."

BERNICE TO SALLY

Her name was Bernice Beutler then, and she never supposed it would be anything else; in fact, why should it?

"But one day, Winnie Sheehan called me into the casting office at Fox, and they gave me a new contract at $150 a week – it was a voluminous thing – and they said 'Sign here. Your name will be Sally Phipps from now on.'"

The 1938 Sally Phipps now pauses to recall some of the details of that funny old contract they gave her – seems that one of its quaint provisions was that her salary was to he hiked $50 a week for every six months.

"So how much did you make in the movies, Miss Phipps?"

Sally borrows the reporter's pencil to do some calculating and finally decides her Hollywood earnings must have reached $40,000.

"Gee," she says, coming as close to a swear word as she does during the interview, "I never realized I made that much money! That's a lot of money, isn't it?"

JUST CHICKEN FEED

The photographer and reporter say "N-a-w, that's not much money!" in unison.

"Well, I didn't believe money should be piled up and frozen in a bank. I believed in spending it. I always had chauffeurs and servants and rode in cabs when my chauffer wasn't around. At eighteen I was a featured player in 'High School Hero,' and was a Wampas Baby Star, and decided to go to Florida for a rest. I put what money I had left in a Florida bank.

"Well" – Sally spread her hands out, palms up – "that bank failed."

PHOTOGRAPHER (excitedly) – "Didn't those banks pay back some of that money?"

SALLY – "Not that bank!"

Sally swept into New York soon after that tragedy, landed a $200-a-week job in "Once in a Lifetime," the play kidding the Hollywood she had just left; lived a showgirl's life for a while with Ginger Rogers in Central Park West, and quickly got a second opportunity to display her indifference to wealth. This time she married a wealthy Philadelphia merchant and became a dashing society matron.

"I would order a dozen gowns at a time," she remembers. "I would say, "'I'll take twelve of those, please.'"

SALLY THE STENOG

Soon there followed a friendly divorce action and, in this instance, Sally perhaps set a precedent for showgirls who marry millionaires – she did not even ask a huge cash settlement.

Gadding around Europe while waiting for the divorce, she took a couple of secretarial jobs which were to fit her – though she didn't know it at the time – to do typing in her present $23.86 berth.

I got back here in December, 1934, and went on the road with the James Henderson [i.e. Hendrickson] Shakespeare Repertory Company. We played mining towns where the people, the most primitive I have ever seen, had never seen a play in their lives. We had no footlights, only candles. The boys put their feet up on the stage. We barnstormed in ice and snow, and all the time I was getting letters from my mother, a commercial painter, asking me to join her in Honolulu.

"'It's always summer here,' her letter said."

Sally saved $50 to make the cross country trip, was presented with passage money by a girlfriend, stayed in Hawaii two months, and came back here in October, 1936, with $20.

LOTS OF TIPS

"The Chinese on the ship all came forward when we landed and said 'Don't you remember me? I did such and such a thing.' And so I handed out most of my money in tips."

Enter the WPA now –

"I got a room on Nineteenth Street for $5 or something. I used to wake up and realize I didn't have a penny. The landlady was very kind and

wouldn't ask me for the rent for three or four weeks. But although the period was trying, it fortified me with great faith.

"Always somebody would seem to know I was hungry and ask me to lunch. I was like the monks who started on a pilgrimage without funds."

She applied for a WPA job almost at once, was told she would have to go on home relief to be eligible, and then found that under the two-year residence requirements of the State she would not be eligible until December, 1936, more than two months away.

Dinner invitations became more and more welcome . . .

And since that time, more than a year and a half, Miss Sally Phipps the Wampas Baby Star of 1927, has been working faithfully at her WPA job, in comparative anonymity. The Radio Division is proud to have one of her decorativeness and talent gradually upped to a job which amounts to assistant production manager, although she is frequently called back to do stenography and typewriter-pounding in emergencies. And, of course, now and then the broadcasts.

STUDIES TELEVISION

Sally is now enrolled at New York University, where she is studying television, hopeful that this new art will bring her back to the public's attention.

"I think I will be successful in this because of my complexion. It requires a sort of darkish person.

"It will transform the country, and I predict it will break after the World's Fair," she says.

The Sanskrit that Sally boasts of studying is taught her by Swami Boddananda of the Vedanta Society at 34 West Seventy-First Street. "As a student of metaphysics," she says, "I'd like to study some of the manuscripts in their original forms. This language is also valuable in studying and developing the voice. I'm taking courses in voice on the Federal Music Project. Oh, I was serious when I told you I've become a student." Very vague about the name of her philosophy at the moment, Sally says, "I take care of every moment as it comes along. I don't have any personal life. Instead of going to dances, I go to lectures. I think every possession is a care as well as a joy, whether it's polo ponies or what. That about expresses it."

A big Mack truck plowed into Sally as she was standing near a trolley line at Forty-Second Street and Broadway the other day and gave her a chance to demonstrate one more time that she can sniff at gold.

She refused to sue, and declined to take any compensation, save for $30 damage to her coat. All sorts of people wanted to know why she didn't go to the hospital for a while, and then ask for $10,000 for an alleged broken leg.

Instead, she told the truck driver, "Don't worry about me. I'm all right."

The truck driver belligerently demanded that she be examined on the spot.

"You can't trick me!" he roared.

Wampas Ex-Baby Lives on WPA $23—and Likes It

Sally Phipps, Who Earned $500 Per Week in Hollywood, Finds Artistic Outlet in the Simple Life

By EARL WILSON

Miss Sally Phipps, whose multitudinous curves and misbehaving hazel eyes earned her $500 a week when she was a Wampas Baby Star in Hollywood in 1927, is on WPA now and enjoying it mightily, thanks.

Sweet Sally has been discovered pummeling a typewriter up at the offices of the Federal Theatre Project's Radio Division at Fifty-third Street and Broadway.

For this and other chores—not including brightening up the office, which she does gratis—Miss Phipps receives $23.88 a week, not even a flyspeck on her 1927 pay.

$5 for Penthouse Cubicle

Upon this sum, however, the new Sally Phipps luxuriates.

Five of her large and tremendously important dollars go every week for a penthouse cubicle on the seventeenth floor of 140 West Fifty-seventh Street. Eight feet long and six feet wide, it's as roomy as a cell at Sing Sing.

Now, no gentlemen may call upon Miss Phipps in this retreat.

"An ascetic like me never has any visitors," Miss Phipps, who is twenty-seven now but still has her curves and her beauty but not her baby-face, says concerning the no-gentlemen-need-drop-around-evenings rule.

"Why," she adds, giving her pile of auburn hair a toss, "I've become a student, a philosopher. I'm even learning to read Sanskrit."

(Reporter's Note: With due apologies to Sanskrit as a fireside companion, our opinion is that no gentlemen are permitted to call upon Miss Phipps because Miss Phipps and a gentleman, even one gentleman, could not get into her cell at the same time without busting the sides out of the building.)

Anyway, Sally Phipps today is a Cinderella In Reverse as she herself will tell you if you ascend to her office.

Traffic's Heavy

You'll probably have to push away several gents to get to her. With a lady of her voltage in the vicinity, naturally a lot of guys have discovered they have some work which has to be done in the same office at the very same minute. It's very important work which can't be done anywhere else at any other time, apparently.

So you invite Sally down to the Bryant Hotel bar and mighty, mighty proud of yourself you are, too, when you note the other swains glaring at you jealously.

"Tea," says Sally, firmly, to the waitress.

Well, she won't take a cigarette, either; and you note that her nails don't glisten with polish, and that in other ways also the sizzling baby star of the vamp days is now very prim and demure. She even whips out a Chinese fan (or maybe it was Japanese) and sets up a little breeze, at which the manager rushes over, like for a riot call.

"That's an insult to our air conditioning," he says, grinning, and finally traffic like this gets so heavy around our table that we decide we've got to go to Sally's penthouse room for some privacy.

Uh—Shorts

Sally pilots the reporter and photographer up a one-flight walk-up after she leaves the elevator; then she puts us out on the roof while she hops into some white shorts. She comes onto the roof by way of the window, the shorts detracting nothing from her figure.

"See the movie star's makeup kit!" she coos, pointing through the open window.

We observe a jar of cold cream, a jar of finishing cream, some empty vials which once contained nail polish and not much else—an extremely modest layout for a beauty. But on a shelf below this we see a few copies of The Hound and Horn, the old poetry magazine cherished by intellectuals, and a copy of a modernized translation of the Bible.

Miss Phipps is soon discovered lying full length on a deck chair, with the sun beating down upon her already tanned legs, and begins telling the story of how she came from stardom to WPA.

"I was fourteen and going to Fairfax High School in Los Angeles when it began," she says. "Sally Eilers was there, too. I wanted to be a lawyer and was trying to get ready for law school. Before I knew it I had been given a screen test and was offered a stock contract—$75 a week."

Bernice to Sally

Her name was Bernice Beutler then and she never supposed it would be anything else; in fact, why should it?

"But one day Winnie Sheehan called me into the casting office at Fox and they gave me a new contract at $150 a week—it was a voluminous thing—and they said 'Sign here. Your name will be Sally Phipps from now on.'"

The 1938 Sally Phipps now pauses to recall some of the details of that funny old contract they gave her—seems that one of its quaint provisions was that her salary was to be hiked $50 a week for every six months.

"So how much did you make in the movies, Miss Phipps?"

Sally borrows the reporter's pencil to do some calculating and finally decides her Hollywood earnings must have reached $40,000.

"Gee," she says, coming as close to a swear word as she does during the interview, "I never realized I made that much money! That's a lot of money, isn't it?"

Just Chicken Feed

The photographer and reporter say "N-a-w, that's not much money!" in unison.

"Well, I didn't believe money should be piled up and frozen in a bank. I believed in spending it. I always had chauffeurs and servants and rode in cabs when my chauffeur wasn't around. At eighteen I was a featured player in 'High School Hero,' and was a Wampus Baby Star, and decided to go to Florida for a rest. I put what money I had left in a Florida bank.

"Well"—Sally spread her hands out, palms up—"that bank failed."

PHOTOGRAPHER (excitedly)—"Didn't those banks pay back some of that money?"

SALLY—"Not that bank!"

Sally swept into New York soon after that tragedy, landed a $200-a-week job in "Once in a Lifetime," the play kidding the Hollywood she had just left; lived a showgirl's life for a while with Ginger Rogers in Central Park West, and quickly got a second opportunity to display her indifference to wealth. This time she married a wealthy Philadelphia merchant and became a dashing society matron.

"I would order a dozen gowns at a time," she remembers. "I would say, 'I'll take twelve of those, please.'"

Sally the Stenog

Soon there followed a friendly divorce action and in this instance Sally perhaps set a precedent for showgirls who marry millionaires—she did not even ask a huge cash settlement.

Gadding around Europe while waiting for the divorce, she took a couple of secretarial jobs which were to fit her—though she didn't know it at the time—to do typing in her present $23.88 berth.

"I got back here in December, 1934, and went on the road with the James Henderson Shakespeare Repertory Company. We played mining towns where the people, the most primitive I have ever seen, had never seen a play in their lives. We had no footlights, only candles. The boys put their feet up on the stage. We barnstormed in ice and snow, and all the time I was getting letters from my mother, a commercial painter, asking me to join her in Honolulu.

"'It's always summer here,' her letters said."

Sally saved [illegible] to make the cross-country trip, was presented with passage money by a girl friend, stayed in Hawaii two months, and came back here in October, 1936, with $30.

Lots of Tips

"The Chinese on the ship all came forward when we landed and said 'Don't you remember me? I did such and such a thing,' and so I handed out most of my money in tips."

Enter the WPA now—

"I got a room on Nineteenth Street for $5 or something. I used to wake up and realize I didn't have a penny. The landlady was very kind and wouldn't ask me for the rent for three or four weeks. But although the period was trying, it fortified me with great faith.

"Always somebody would seem to know I was hungry and ask me to lunch. I was like the monks who started out on a pilgrimage without funds."

Screen's Ex-Sizzling Baby Now Demure Working Girl

She applied for a WPA job almost at once, was told she would have to go on home relief to be eligible, and then found that under the two-year residence requirements of the State she would not be eligible until December, 1936, more than two months away.

Dinner invitations became more and more welcome . . .

And since that time, more than a year and a half, Miss Sally Phipps, the Wampas Baby Star of 1927, has been working faithfully at her WPA job, in comparative anonymity. The Radio Division is proud to have one of her decorativeness and talent in its offices, and she has been gradually upped to a job which amounts to assistant production manager, although she is frequently called back to do stenography and typewriter-pounding in emergencies. And, of course, now and then the broadcasts.

Studies Television

Sally is now enrolled at New York University, where she is studying television, hopeful that this new art will bring her back to the public's attention.

"I think I will be successful in this because of my complexion. It requires a sort of darkish person.

"It will transform the country and I predict it will break after the World's Fair," she says.

The Sanskrit that Sally boasts of studying is taught her by Swami Boddananda of the Vedanta Society at 34 West Seventy-first Street. "As a student of metaphysics," she says, "I'd like to study some of the manuscripts in their original forms. This language is also valuable in studying and developing the voice. I'm taking courses in voice on the Federal Music Project. Oh, I was serious when I told you I've become a student."

Very vague about the name of her philosophy at the moment, Sally says, "I take care of every moment as it comes along. I don't have any personal life. Instead of going to dances, I go to lectures. I think every possession is a care as well as a joy, whether it's polo ponies or what. That about expresses it."

A big Mack truck plowed into Sally as she was standing near a trolley line at Forty-second Street and Broadway the other day and gave her a chance to demonstrate one more time that she can sniff at gold.

She refused to sue, and declined to take any compensation, save for $36 damage to her coat. All sorts of people wanted to know why she didn't go to a hospital for a while, and then ask for $19,000 for an alleged broken leg.

Instead, she told the truck driver, "Don't worry about me. I'm all right."

The truck driver belligerently demanded that she be examined on the spot.

"You can't trick me!" he roared.

Sally Phipps — Post Photos by Calvacca

Miss Phipps easily reaches the roof from her penthouse.

Princeton Honors Moore As Thrice N. J. Governor

Mild Applause Greets Conferring of Degree—Two Honor Grads Hazed as Foes

2 Women Try Deadly Trip Through the Grand Canyon

None of Their Sex Has Ever Survived Attempt—Four Men in Party

Earl Wilson 1938 newspaper article

Five days later, the *New York Journal and American*, June 26, 1938, had a similar story:

EX-FILM STARLET, EX-RICH WIFE, HAPPY IN $23 JOB

Sally Phipps Turns To Philosophy. – Motors and Money Mean Nothing Now.

By GEROLD FRANK

It's hard to know where to begin the amazing tale of Sally Phipps, a demure, hazel-eyed bit of loveliness who once made $500 a week as a Baby Wampas star and now "pulls down" – to her intense joy – exactly $23.86 a week in the WPA Theatre.

She is one of the strangest characters in the throbbing life drama of our New York. One in-between step in her career was a wealthy marriage.

She earns her $23.86 between incredible sorties in the direction of psychic research, readings in Sanskrit, hours devoted to Buddhism, Theosophy and the Principles of the Vedanta Society and – when she still has time – lessons in television dramatic technique.

Even Max Shohet, the doughty publicity representative of the WPA Theatre's Radio Division, where Miss Phipps is currently making life ecstatic for everyone around her, waves his hands in despair.

"I'm telling you," he says darkly. "She's like a character out of 'Alice–in-Wonderland.' Don't say I'm not warning you."

Three minutes later, Miss Phipps floated into the room, settled upon a chair, and fixing me with a wide and apparently innocent eye, opened her cupid-bow lips to announce in a clear, childlike voice:

"Have you ever thought about reality? What is reality? Is it the reality beyond what is? Or is it the superstructure upon what we think is reality? I mean, from the cosmic view?"

"See," said Mr. Shohet, and he swallowed once or twice. "Sit around and listen. You'll be pinching yourself to see whether you're really here."

HAD CARS, MONEY; NOW WANTS NOTHING

Sally sighed.

"He says that," she observed, with the sort of sweetly-sad smile Gandhi might bestow on a bewildered disciple, "because of my metaphysics. My belief in the unimportance of the supposedly important. Because I'm perfectly satisfied and don't want anything in the world."

"Nothing? How about a trip to Europe, for instance?"

"Oh, no," says Sally. "I've been to Europe."

"How about a luxurious car?"

"No," says Sally. "I've had a luxurious car. Now, I haven't. So what?"

"Well, then, how about money?"

"Money, money, money!" exclaims Sally. "I've had money. I've had a lot of it. Now I have hardly any. But what's the difference? I live, I do what I want. After all, you can only wear one dress at a time. You can only sleep in one bed at a time. You can only eat one meal at a time.

"It's all a matter of the philosophy you live by – a sort of psychic net you create which bolsters you up just as a net supports a circus acrobat if something unexpected happens to him."

Miss Phipps, you gather quickly, gives her philosophy a daily workout. It's something that helps a girl who, just turned the ripe old age of 27, finds herself living in a $5 a week cubby hole on 57th Street, near Carnegie Hall, and using the subway after living in a Hollywood mansion and riding about in a purple and gold Rolls-Royce.

That was back in 1927 when the newspaper hailed Sally as "a Fox Films prodigy, a second Clara Bow – sweet, cute, svelte, saucy" – and her charms swept even the high seas until the Chinese Chamber of Commerce, moved to complete unrestraint, voted her the most popular American film star in China, and sent her enough silk pajamas to clothe Hollywood itself.

Since then a lot of things have happened to Sally. Still "sweet, cute svelte, saucy," her red hair neatly fixed in a provocative little bun at the nape of her neck, still in appearance resembling a large, animated Dresden doll, Sally has wandered from Honolulu to New York, proving to herself that her philosophy has a solid foundation.

"I made $40,000 in Hollywood before I was 19," Sally said. "And I lost everything I had when a bank crashed. "And I have come to this conclusion: each of us at one time or another in our lives must decide whether things happen by chance or for a reason. I've decided it's for a reason – that there is orderliness and logic in the universe.

CAN'T LOOK AROUND THE CORNER AHEAD

"That means that everything has a value. You may not know it at the time. In my case, Hollywood was just one phase of my life. My work now is another. At one, I made a lot of money. At the other, I don't. But each has its place. And I'm not prepared to say now which has been the most important in my life. How can I? I can't look around the corner ahead of me."

Sally wasn't 20 when she came to New York, broke. She landed a job on the Broadway stage as the original ingénue in "Once in a Lifetime." Her roommate then was a girl who since has returned to Hollywood – Ginger Rogers.

When she was 20, Sally married a very rich merchant. For a few years she was plunged into an altogether different sort of life. It was in part a social life, but also she began university studies and worked hard at them – particularly philosophy – and this led her into the occult. She took life in her stride. She took her ensuing divorce the same way. She neither asked for nor got any large settlement, she says. She went to Europe. She was introduced to London society. She returned to New York.

She toured through the United States in Shakespeare repertoire. Her mother, a painter, lived in Honolulu. Nothing hesitant, Sally went there. Then she returned to New York to start all over again.

"I was awfully hungry for a while. But I figured, what was the use of brooding over anything? It didn't help. And I'd be wasting time brooding that I might otherwise use to help myself to do something concrete."

Then the WPA position bobbed up, and now Sally is going to play the lead role in a series of WPA radio dramatizations of Paul de Kruif's books. Meanwhile, she cheerfully does all kinds of office work at the Theatre Project, and likes it -- with no extra money for the office work.

"It's all a matter of faith and fear," says Sally. "You must have faith that all things happen for a purpose. There are ordered laws in the universe.

HAD MONEY, BUT MISSED SOMETHING

"You must have faith that each moment is sufficient unto itself. It's no good to make too many plans. We don't know what will happen. There is no use being discouraged. After all, it's human to know that your ambitions are always a little ahead of your achievements. Life wouldn't be worthwhile if there weren't any striving.

But fear is terrible. It does no good to fear that you'll lose your job next week or next year, or that you won't have food next week or next year. What good is fear going to do? And the ironic part is that fear is destructive. It takes something away from your powers to fight.

"When I had money, I had responsibilities. I'd sit up suddenly at night and try to understand what I was doing. I was going through all the motions of living, but I was missing something. I wasn't complete. I wanted to read and meet ordinary people and follow cultural pursuits and have a chance to think.

"But now," says Sally, "I really feel alive. I wake up in the morning and while I dress I listen to the symphonic music over WQXR. With all my money in Hollywood I never had time for that. I attend all sorts of classes.

"I'm really alive and learning more about the process of life. It's all life – the wheeling of the stars in the universe, or Benny Goodman's swing.

"People sometimes tell me," says Sally, speaking slowly, "that they wonder how I feel, having gone through this cycle that most persons don't go through, if they ever do, until they're much older – from anonymity to fame back to anonymity again.

"Well, I say it's not a cycle. It's a spiral – ever onward, ever upward."

THEN—

Sally Phipps as she appeared as a Wampas star in Hollywood where she earned $40,000 before she was 19.

Ex-Film Starlet, Ex-Rich Wife, Happy in $23 Job

Sally Phipps Turns to Philosophy

By GEROLD FRANK

IT'S HARD to know where to begin the amazing tale of Sally Phipps, a demure, hazel-eyed bit of loveliness who once made $500 a week as a Baby Wampas star and now "pulls down"—to her intense joy—exactly $23.86 a week in the WPA Theatre.

She is one of the strangest characters in the throbbing life drama of our New York. One in-between step in her career was a wealthy marriage.

She earns her $23.86 between incredible sorties in the direction of psychic research, readings in Sanskrit, hours devoted to Buddhism, Theosophy and the principles of the Vedanta Society and—when she still has time—lessons in television dramatic technique.

Even Max Shohet, the doughty publicity representative of the WPA Theatre's radio division, where Miss Phipps is currently making life ecstatic for everyone around her, waves his hands in despair.

"I'm telling you," he says darkly, "She's like a character out of 'Alice-in-Wonderland.' Don't say I'm not warning you."

Three minutes later, Miss Phipps floated into the room, settled upon a chair, and, fixing me with a wide and apparently innocent eye, opened her cupid-bow lips to announce in a clear, childlike voice:

"Have you ever thought about reality? What is reality? Is it the reality beyond what is? Or is it the superstructure upon what we think is reality? I mean, from the cosmic view?"

"See," said Mr. Shohet, and he swallowed once or twice. "Sit around and listen. You'll be pinching yourself to see whether you're really here."

Had Cars, Money; Now Wants Nothing

Sally sighed.

"He says that," she observed, with the sort of sweetly-sad smile Gandhi might bestow on a bewildered disciple, "because of my metaphysics. My belief in the unimportance of the supposedly important. Because I'm perfectly satisfied and don't want anything in the world."

"Nothing? How about a trip to Europe, for instance?"

"Oh, no," says Sally. "I've been to Europe."

"How about a luxurious car?"

"No," says Sally. "I've had a luxurious car. Now I haven't. So what?"

"Well, then, how about money?"

"Money, money, money!" exclaims Sally. "I've had money. I've had a lot of it. Now I have hardly any. But what's the difference? I live, I do what I want. After all, you can only wear one dress at a time. You can only sleep in one bed at a time. You can only eat one meal at a time.

"It's all a matter of the philosophy you live by—a sort of psychic net you create which bolsters you up just as a net supports a circus acrobat if something unexpected happens to him."

Miss Phipps, you gather quickly, gives her philosophy a daily workout. It's something that helps a girl who just turned the ripe old age of 27, finds herself living in a $5 a week cubby hole on 57th st., near Carnegie Hall and using the subway after living in a Hollywood mansion and riding about in a purple and gold Rolls-Royce.

That was back in 1927 when the newspapers hailed Sally as "a Fox Films prodigy, a second Clara Bow—sweet, cute, svelte, saucy"—and her charms swept even the high seas until the Chinese Chamber of Commerce, moved to complete unrestraint, voted her the most popular American film star in China, and sent her enough silk pajamas to clothe Hollywood itself.

Since then a lot of things have happened to Sally. Still "sweet, cute, svelte, saucy," her red hair neatly fixed in a provocative little bun at the nape of her neck, still in appearance resembling a large, animated Dresden doll, Sally has wandered from Honolulu to New York, proving to herself that her philosophy has a solid foundation.

"I made $48,000 in Hollywood before I was 19," Sally said. "And I lost everything I had when a bank crashed. And I have come to this conclusion: each of us at one time or another in our lives must decide whether things happen by chance or for a reason. I've decided it's for a reason—that there is orderliness and logic in the universe.

Can't Look Around the Corner Ahead

"That means that everything has a value. You may not know it at the time. In my case, Hollywood was just one phase of my life. My work now is another. At one I made a lot of money. At the other I don't. But each has its place. And I'm not prepared to say now which has been the most important in my life. How can I? I can't look around the corner ahead of me."

Sally wasn't 20 when she came to New York, broke. She landed a job on the Broadway stage as the original ingenue in "Once in a Lifetime." Her roommate then was a girl who since has returned to Hollywood—Ginger Rogers.

When she was 20, Sally married a very rich merchant. For a few years she was plunged into an altogether different sort of life. It was in part a social life, but also she began university studies and worked hard at them—particularly philosophy—and this led her into the occult. She took life in her stride. She took her ensuing divorce the same way. She neither asked for nor got any large settlement, she says. She went to Europe. She was introduced to London society. She returned to New York.

She toured through the United States in Shakespeare repertoire. Her mother, a painter, lived in Honolulu. Nothing hesitant, Sally went there. Then she returned to New York to start all over again.

"I was awfully hungry for a while. But I figured, what was the use of brooding over anything? It didn't help. And I'd be wasting time brooding that I might otherwise use to help myself to do something concrete."

Then the WPA position bobbed up and now Sally is going to play the lead role in a series of WPA radio dramatizations of Paul de Kruif's books. Meanwhile, she cheerfully does all kinds of office work at the theatre project, and likes it—with no extra money for the office work.

"It's all a matter of faith and fear," says Sally. "You must have faith that all things happen for a purpose. There are ordered laws in the universe.

Had Money, but Missed Something

"You must have faith that each moment is sufficient unto itself. It's no good to make too many plans. We don't know what will happen. There is no use being discouraged. After all, it's human to know that your ambitions are always a little ahead of your achievements. Life wouldn't be worth while if there weren't any striving.

"But fear is terrible. It does no good to fear that you'll lose your job next week or next year, or that you won't have food next week or next year. What good is

Motors and Money Mean Nothing Now

fear going to do? And the ironic part is that fear is destructive. It takes something away from your powers to fight!

"When I had money, I had responsibilities. I'd sit up suddenly at night and try to understand what I was doing. I was going through all the motions of living, but I was missing something. I wasn't complete. I wanted to read and meet ordinary people and follow cultural pursuits and have a chance to think.

"But now," said Sally, "I really feel alive. I wake up in the morning and while I dress I listen to the symphonic music over WQXR. With all my money in Hollywood I never had time for that. I attend all sorts of classes.

"I'm really alive and learning more about the process of life. It's all [illegible]—the wheeling of the stars in the universe, or Benny Goodman's swing.

"People sometimes tell me," says Sally, speaking slowly, "that they wonder how I feel, having gone through this cycle that most persons don't go through, if they ever do, until they're much older — from anonymity to fame back to anonymity again.

"Well, I say it's not a cycle. It's a spiral—ever onward, ever upward!"

—NOW

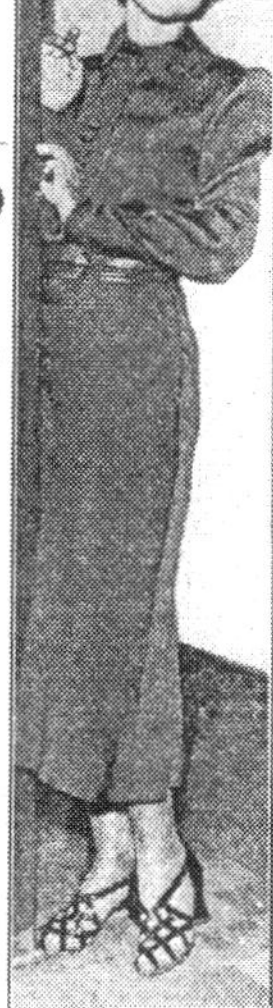

As Sally Phipps appears today at 27, rehearsing for lead in WPA Theatre radio play and also doing office work for $23.86 a week!

Gerold Frank 1938 newspaper article

Sally stayed with the Federal Theatre Project until its funding was cancelled on June 30, 1939. The Project was closed down largely because of Congressional objections to what some considered the left-wing content of many of its theatrical productions.

However, Sally was already planning on leaving. She knew that Edithe was in India as part of her Eastman Kodak work. Edithe had been working in the Orient for several years and was going back and forth to her home in Honolulu.

Edithe (right) in India, with two friends, all wearing saris

Sally now received word that Edithe was in a hospital in Calcutta recovering from an operation. Edithe explained later that she was having some "female bodily problems," and needed an operation, most likely a hysterectomy. The surgery had gone badly, and Sally was told that Edithe was not recovering well. There was an intimation in the message that Edithe's life was in danger. Sally was urged to come to India, and she unhesitatingly went.

SALLY LEAVES NEW YORK FOR INDIA

She renewed her passport on May 15, 1939 and gave her termination notice at work. A WPA Form 403 – Notice of Termination of Employment dated June 16, 1939 was found in Sally's personal files. The effective date was given as "close of business" on Friday, June 30, 1939, giving the reason "Leaving the United States of America."

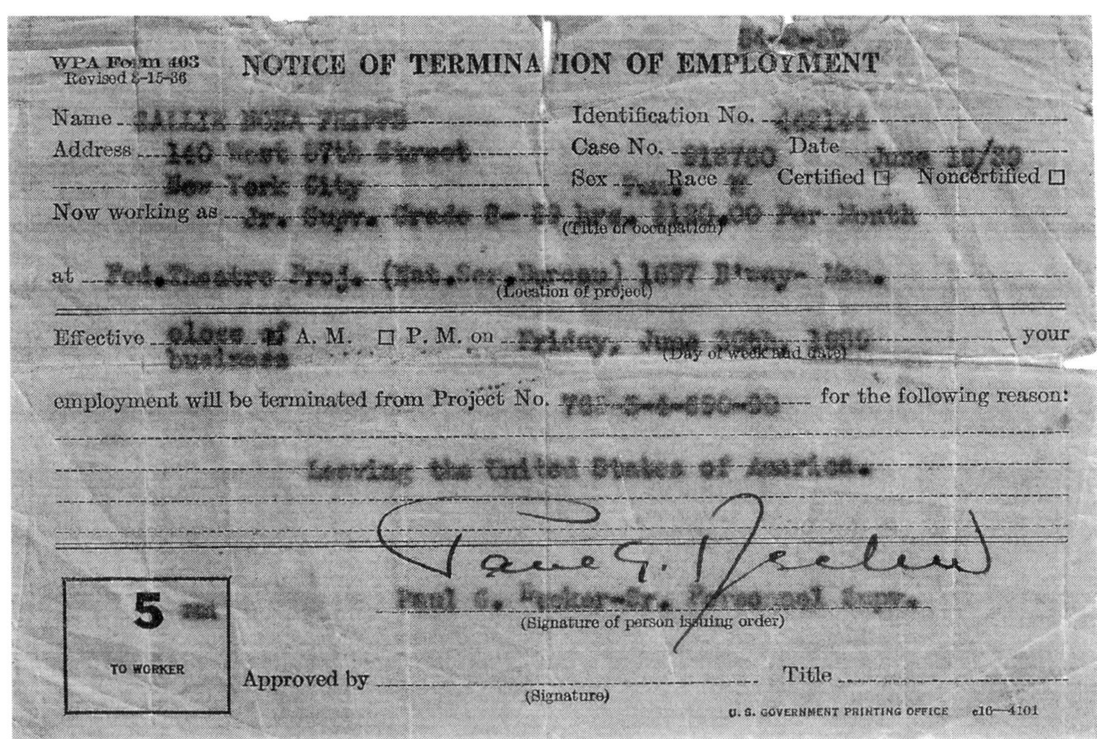

WPA Form 403
Revised 8-15-36

NOTICE OF TERMINATION OF EMPLOYMENT

Name [illegible] Identification No. [illegible]
Address 140 [illegible] Case No. [illegible] Date [illegible]
New York City Sex [illegible] Race [illegible] Certified ☐ Noncertified ☐
Now working as Jr. Supr. [illegible] Per Month
(Title of occupation)
at Fed. Theatre Proj. [illegible]
(Location of project)
Effective close of business ☐ A. M. ☐ P. M. on [illegible] your
(Day of week and date)
employment will be terminated from Project No. [illegible] for the following reason:

Leaving the United States of America.

[illegible]
(Signature of person issuing order)

5
TO WORKER

Approved by ______ Title ______
(Signature)

U. S. GOVERNMENT PRINTING OFFICE c16—4101

Sally's Federal Theatre Project employment termination notice

The notice, a 4 x 6 inch pink paper copy of a multi-copy form, shows that Sally is using her new spelling, "Sallie," and has added the middle name "Nona," (who knows why?). It also gives her home address, identification and case numbers, rank, working hours, monthly pay, and work address as of her last month of work.

Name: Sallie Nona Phipps
Address: 140 West 57th Street
New York City
Identification Number: 442144
Case Number: 918760

Now working as: Jr. Supv. – Grade 8 – 39 hrs. - $120.00 Per Month
At: Fed. Theatre Proj. (Nat. Ser. Bureau) – 1697 B'Way – Man.
Signature of person issuing order: Paul G. Decker, Sr. Personnel Supv.

She withdrew her savings from her bank and booked passage on a ship sailing from New York to Karachi, India (today Pakistan). In her sketchy memoirs, she says that the first port stop was four weeks later in Port Said passing through the Suez Canal. There were more stops in Jedda and Aden. To add to her concerns, on September 1, 1939, while she was at sea, World War II began in Europe with Germany's invasion of Poland.

SALLY IN INDIA

She got off the ship sometime in October in Karachi, one of the main seaports of then British India. She travelled across India by train to Calcutta, where she found Edithe still in the hospital. The first thing Sally did was to move Edithe to a better hospital. In the new one, the examining doctors discovered that a sponge had been left inside Edithe during her surgery. After a new operation was performed to remove it, Edithe recovered quickly.

By November, Edithe was able to leave India and get back to her secondary base in Manila. In Manila, she was told by Eastman Kodak that, because of the developing war in Europe and the encroaching aggression by the Japanese in the Far East, her coloring work was discontinued. She then returned to Honolulu, arriving on December 1, 1939.

After Sally rescued Edithe, she decided to stay in India. As early as 1937, in a letter to a friend, she wrote of her desire to spend time in India. Now that she was there, she felt completely at home. It seemed to her that much of her life had been a kind of preparation for India – her interests in astrology, numerology, the occult, Hindu and Buddhist religions, vegetarianism, and more recently her studies in the Sanskrit language. Also, her whole philosophical attitude toward life was much more in harmony with India. Sally once told her son Robert that some Indian friends endearingly called her "Sally Phipps-losophy." She loved the Indians, and the Indians loved her. She made many friends there, some lasting her lifetime, and she wanted to stay as long as she could. Her visa allowed her to remain an entire year, so she decided to stay until it expired in October 1940.

In India, according to her memoirs, Sally did not seem to have any problem finding work. While she was in Calcutta, she taught dramatic art at the exclusive Bani Mandar Girls School. She also found secretarial work in two organizations - the India Research Institute under Satis Chandra Veal and the broadcasting station, All India Radio (AIR), a British Broadcasting Corporation (BBC) subsidiary. Besides handling the radio station's correspondence at AIR, she was also given some directing, producing, writing, and sometimes even performing assignments, in such radio shows as "The Story Of Shah Jehan," "Taj Mahal," "King Ashoka," "Gautama Buddha," and other historical scripts and even some social comedies. She also travelled with a team of broadcasters to the home of the Nobel Laureate

Rabindranath Tagore (1861-1941) to record and broadcast a program of his personal talks in English. Tagore's home was in the small town of Santiniketan, or "The Abode of Peace," about 120 miles north of Calcutta.

Sally was able to travel to other parts of India during her year there, and photographs of some destinations survive. One, undated, shows her in a bathing suit and smiling radiantly, "Taken today – Poona Gymkhana Club." A second photograph is labeled, "Observatory Hill, Darjeeling, just after birthday," indicating it was taken after May 25, 1940. Sally stands on a hilltop dressed in light-colored riding clothes, jodhpurs and riding boots. A third photograph shows Sally in another mountainous location, labeled, "14,000 feet in the Himalayas, the Frozen Lakes, Gulmarg – Kashmir – July [1940] – snow?"

Sally in India, 1939, Poona

Sally in India, 1940, Darjeeling

Sally in India, 1940, Gulmarg, Kashmir

EDITHE BACK IN HAWAII

While Sally was in India, Edithe was back in Honolulu taking advantage of a business perk that she was promised years earlier by Kodak -- a franchise to establish her own Eastman Kodak film processing business. She opened her first "Color Art Shop" at 129 South Hotel Street in downtown Honolulu in 1940.

Edithe's Color Art Shop on Hotel Street, Honolulu

The shop provided film processing services, as well as the coloring of black and white photographs. She soon opened another shop just outside of downtown Honolulu, and later another "Color Art Shop" in Waikiki, the fashionable beach resort area of Honolulu. Edithe also purchased an additional house at 342 Lewers Road (today Lewers Street), a short walk from her Waikiki store.

Edithe's Waikiki house

In addition, in 1944, she and a local photographer, Frank S. Warren, created a book entitled, *Trees and Flowers Of The Hawaiian Islands*, published by the Outdoor Circle of Hawaii and comprising 32 5x7-inch color plates. She and Warren shared the photography work, but the color artistry is all Edithe's.

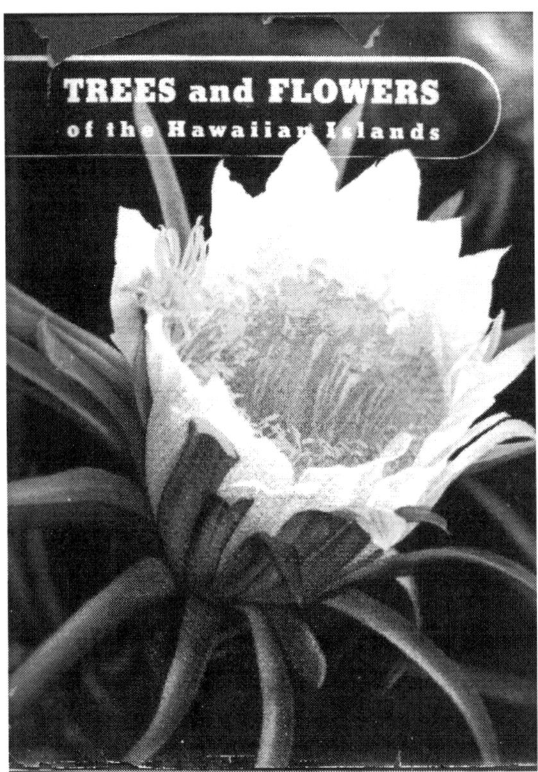

Edithe's book

SALLY RETURNS TO NEW YORK

In spite of the love affair Sally was having with India, it all had to come to an end because her visa was expiring. She said her goodbyes and began her long trip back to New York. She left India from Bombay on a Japanese passenger ship, which passed through Ceylon and Singapore and then arrived in Shanghai in early January 1941. There she changed to an American ship, the S.S. President Pierce, which sailed on January 8 for San Francisco. This ship made a short stop in Honolulu, where she was able to visit with Edithe for a few days.

Sally in Hawaii, 1941, passing through

The ship then crossed the Pacific, docking in San Francisco some time in late January. There she disembarked and stayed for a few days with her Aunt Lulah Kramer, who was one of Edithe's half-sisters, born Lulah Marie Green. Then she headed across the country for New York, confident that she could again make a go of it there. When she arrived in New York City, she realized, because of the routes she had taken getting to and from India, that she had completely circumnavigated the globe.

Chapter 5
New York, Mexico, Iowa, Hawaii

SALLY BACK IN NEW YORK

Sally's penthouse studio apartment at 140 West 57th Street was fortunately still available for rent when she arrived, and she was able to move right back into her favorite low-rent apartment with the wonderful terrace.

In no time she got some publicity about her Indian adventure, especially because she claimed to have secret information about the approaching war. *The New York World-Telegram*, on February 18, 1941, was the first to write about her:

ONE-TIME CINEMA STAR RETURNS HERE WITH SECRET TACTICS OF THREE NATIONS.
Sallie Phipps Talked to British, Chinese and Japanese.

BY ALLAN KELLER

The very beautiful Sallie Nona Phipps, onetime cinema star now turned military strategist, is back in the city from a round-the-world tour during which she was fortunate enough to learn the secret tactics of the British Far Eastern forces, the Japanese army clique and the Chinese guerilla bands.

Before divulging these secrets, the World-Telegram considered long and earnestly the result of such publication and finally decided to throw back the veil of secrecy in the hope that, if both sides knew the other's plans, stalemate might be achieved and further bloodshed be unnecessary.

Miss Phipps, who would not say whether her curvaceous charm helped her to break through official guards, said the British were expecting the war to spread to many new fronts, far the from the British Isles.

PASS TO KHYBER PASS

"I found that out before I had been in India a week," confided the glamorous strategist. "At Poona – the army headquarters, you know – they talked of nothing else. That's why I was so lucky to get a pass allowing me to enter the Khyber Pass."

That frontier spot, scene of invasion for three thousand years, is now a vital link in the British Empire's far-flung outposts, one where Russian influence is growing and where Soviet troops might start their push to the south if Britain falls.

"What did you see in the Pass?" Miss Phipps was asked.

"Well," said the former film star, looking as intent as any general studying his terrain maps, "there was barbed wire all along the border and a big barricade across the trail through the Pass. They wouldn't let me go any

further. More than that, I had to be inside the camp at Peshawar by 7 p.m., the officers said, or they wouldn't be responsible. They said the hill tribesmen did the most hideous things to any white woman they found outside the encampment. Gee, was I scared!"

SAW ITALIANS IN INDIA

Miss Phipps went on to tell of the large number of Italian prisoners who were arriving in India from the battlefields at Sidi Barrani and Solum.

"I could have learned how they felt about being Hitler's pawns, but the wounded were so sick and the prisoners so sad I didn't want to embarrass them," she said.

With India behind her, the actress visited Singapore, key defense point in the Orient for the British Empire. Rumors have been current that Japan is about to push southward and attack this fortress and that the United States might use it as a naval base in cooperation with the British fleet.

"I was in Singapore for several days, and you could just sense the way the English were rushing preparations for defense," said the actress.

"I don't know what they were hiding, but you could see camouflage along the shore as your ship came into the harbor. It was all green, you know, just like the jungle. And there were big warships in the port, too, destroyers, and minesweepers."

An officer on a Japanese passenger liner let the cat out of the bag about the plans of the Nipponese army.

THE GODS WILL DECIDE

"You see that red ball in the center of our white flag," he explained to Miss Phipps. "Well, that's Japan. When the old gods of Japan tell us to expand we use another flag with red shafts extending from the red circle. Whatever we decide to do will be determined by the Shinto gods, not by the actions of friend or foe."

Miss Phipps said Shanghai was a dismal city, where all the Occidentals danced and drank all night to forget the sense of doom that hung over the international settlement.

"Everyone has an unhealthy pallor," she said, squirming in her chair and making a face. "They say the people on 52nd St. look the same way."

Miss Phipps went around the world because her mother was seriously ill in Karachi [sic], India, and once she had gone that far one way she decided to return the rest of the way by completing the circumnavigation of the globe. Not much more than a decade ago, she was a Wampas Baby Star in Hollywood, earning $500 a week. She gave up the films to marry a Philadelphia merchant. The depression found her earning $23.36 a week as an actress in the Federal Theatre Project.

After her year and a half abroad, she said she was happy to get home.

"It's amazing how many changes have come in the world in just that short time," she added. "Why, the gear shift lever is on the steering wheel post now."

One-Time Cinema Star Returns Here With Secret Tactics of Three Nations

Sallie Phipps Talked To British, Chinese And Japanese

By ALLAN KELLER.
World-Telegram Staff Writer.

The very beautiful Sallie Nona Phipps, onetime cinema star now turned military strategist, is back in the city from a round-the-world tour during which she was fortunate enough to learn the secret tactics of the British Far Eastern forces, the Japanese army clique and the Chinese guerrilla bands.

Before divulging these secrets the World-Telegram considered long and earnestly the result of such publication and finally decided to throw back the veil of secrecy in the hope that if both sides knew the other's plans stalemate might be achieved and further bloodshed be unnecessary.

Miss Phipps, who would not say whether her curvaceous charm helped her to break through official guards, said the British were expecting the war to spread to many new fronts, far from the British Isles.

Pass to Khyber Pass.

"I found that out before I had been in India a week," confided the glamorous strategist. "At Poona—the army headquarters, you know—they talked of nothing else. That's why I was so lucky to get a pass allowing me to enter the Khyber Pass."

That frontier spot, scene of invasion for three thousand years, is now a vital link in the British Empire's far-flung outposts, one where Russian influence is growing and where Soviet troops might start their push to the south if Britain falls.

"What did you see in the Pass?" Miss Phipps was asked.

"Well," said the former film star, looking as intent as any general studying his terrain maps, "there was barbed wire all along the border and a big barricade across the trail through the Pass. They wouldn't let me go any further. More than that, I had to be inside the camp at Peshawar by 7 p. m., the officers said, or they wouldn't be responsible. They said the hill tribesmen did the most hideous things to any white woman they found outside the encampment. Gee, was I scared!"

Saw Italians in India.

Miss Phipps went on to tell of the large number of Italian prisoners who were arriving in India from the battlefields at Sidi Barrani and Solum.

"I could have learned how they felt about being Hitler's pawns, but the wounded were so sick and the prisoners so sad I didn't want to embarrass them," she said.

With India behind her the actress visited Singapore, key defense point in the Orient for the British Empire. Rumors have been current that Japan is about to push southward and attack this fortress and that the United States might use it as a naval base in co-operation with the British fleet.

"I was in Singapore for several days, and you could just sense the way the English were rushing preparations for defense," said the actress.

"I don't know what they were hiding, but you could see camouflage along the shore as your ship came into the harbor. It was all green, you know, just like the jungle. And there were big warships in the port, too, destroyers and minesweepers."

An officer on a Japanese passenger liner let the cat out of the bag about the plans of the Nipponese army.

The Gods Will Decide.

"You see that red ball in the center of our white flag," he explained to Miss Phipps. "Well, that's Japan. When the old gods of Japan tell us to expand we use another flag with red shafts extending from the red circle. Whatever we decide to do will be determined by the Shinto gods, not by the actions of friend or foe."

Miss Phipps said Shanghai was a dismal city, where all the Occidentals danced and drank all night to forget the sense of doom that hung over the international settlement.

"Everyone has an unhealthy pallor," she said, squirming in her chair and making a face. "They say the people on 52nd St. look the same way."

Miss Phipps went around the world because her mother was seriously ill in Karachi, India, and once she had gone that far one way she decided to return the rest of the way by completing the circumnavigation of the globe. Not much more than a decade ago she was a Wampas Baby Star in Hollywood, earning $500 a week. She gave up the films to marry a Philadelphia merchant. The depression found her earning $23.36 a week as an actress in the Federal Theater Project.

After her year and a half abroad she said she was happy to get home.

"It's amazing how many changes have come in the world in just that short time," she said. "Why the gear shift lever is on the steering wheel post now."

World-Telegram Photo by Palumbo.
Sallie Nona Phipps.

Allan Keller article

Another columnist, Regine Kurlander, at the *Cleveland Plain Dealer*, saw the above article and wrote her response to it in the February 21 issue:

YOU CAN BE GLAMOUROUS, ETC.
BY REGINE KURLANDER
OPEN SEASON

Well, well and well. The open season for the masculine ribbing of incipient Mata Haris has begun. I thought it would, sooner or later. For aside from every woman secretly imagining herself a reincarnation of Cleopatra . . . there probably never lived a femme (since Judith lopped off Holofernes' noodle), however myopic, who hasn't fancied herself besting the enemy. And that, not with prosaic bayonet, machine gun, or aerial bombs . . . or even by waving a flag out of a window, achieving the w. k. "Who touches a hair on yon gray head" . . . but by luring some so-and-so general with her seductiveness to where he tells her all – or else.

And, whereas, many a woman skilled in intelligence work has rendered her country service by knowing her strategic way around . . . there still remain uncounted millions who don't know their ears from their elbows in this highly specialized and hazardous calling. Nevertheless, a lot of them are already beginning to bleat that they have all the tactics memorized and are ready to push into Der Fuehrer's perch in the mountains of Berchtesgaden.

Now, I see a piece in a N. Y. news sheet, written by a colleague with his tongue in his cheek, anent a "glamorous young strategist," named Sallie Phipps, a Wampas Baby Star, just before her self-imposed stint as a spy, "with make-up by Perc Westmore."

MISS PHIPPS

Miss Phipps, (whose last job in the States was as actress with a federal project, earning $23.36 per week) says the reporter, has just returned from a round-the-world tour during which "she was fortunate enough to learn the secret tactics of the British Far Eastern forces, the Japanese Army clique, and the Chinese guerilla bands." He goes on to say that before divulging these secrets, the paper for which he works "considered long and earnestly the result of such publication and finally decided to throw back the veil of secrecy in the hope that if both sides knew the other's plans, stalemate might be achieved and further bloodshed would be unnecessary."

Poor Miss Phipps was so taken in by this sympathetic young wag, that she admitted "an officer on a Japanese passenger liner let the cat out of the bag about the plans of the Nipponese Amy." She also confided that the officer had admitted the army is entirely advised by the old Shinto gods of Japan and not, as is currently supposed, by the actions of friend or foe.

Whereupon, I am simply suggesting that if any military men full of Scotch offer you information, which they maintain Gen. Marshall or President Roosevelt doesn't know about . . . don't rush off to the nearest newspaper with your findings. Because, if you do, you are likely to be given the run around by those owl-faced gentlemen who sit behind desks and have a diabolical genius for soberly saying: "Thank you very much . . . we certainly will look into that."

And furthermore, don't get the romantic notion that the world is simply panting to see you doing the dance of Siva or even the rhumba while major generals gaze raptly into your big blue eyes and hand over the papers without a murmur.

About the most you can expect to achieve in the business of spying, by spending a week-end in Tokyo or a fortnight in Shanghai, as Sallie did on her way to see her sick mother in Karachi, India . . . is to get a pass allowing you to enter Khyber Pass. And, like Miss Phipps, all you will be able to report is that "there was barbed wire all along the border and I had to be inside the camp at Peshawar by 7 p.m."

Once in a long while, a woman does appear whose sense of adventure and military genius merge into tremendous effectivity. And then she is intrepid where most males would blanch and wilt with fear. But when this does occur

. . . there is usually something wrong with her glands. And if you can't do the dance of the seven veils before a board composed of Petain, Hitler, Churchill, Stalin and Roosevelt . . . spying wouldn't be much fun anyway.
Would it?

Sally again started looking for employment. She hoped to return to radio work and immediately began auditioning. When nothing materialized right away, she looked for work in other places. She modeled for art classes. She served as hostess and cashier for one of the many branches of the Nell Kirby Restaurant chain.

Her longest employment was at the George Maillard Kesslere Portrait Photography Studio, where she was given various jobs, mainly in promotion and publicity. George Maillard Kesslere (1894-1979) was one of New York City's most important portrait photographers for the entertainment world. He had two studio locations, 11 West 46th Street and 44 East 50th Street. Knowing that Sally had been a famous actress, Kesslere was delighted to have her as one of his employees. He also enjoyed photographing Sally and provided her with a number of publicity photos for her audition portfolio.

A Kesslere head shot, hand colored

Sally had many friends to look up when she returned. One of these was George Wehner, whom she met in June 1933, just after she had left Ben Gimbel and moved back to New York. She had not seen Wehner since she left for India, so she telephoned to let him know she was back. She didn't know at the time that this phone call was going to change her life.

GEORGE WEHNER

George Wehner (1890-1970) was a colorful character. He was a composer, actor, writer, painter, and spiritualist. In the early 1920s, Wehner was writing popular songs, and he asserted that all or most of his music was channeled from his spirit guide, a Native American Indian named White Cloud. According to Wehner, White Cloud began appearing and singing songs to him when he was a little boy. The musically precocious Wehner said he was easily able to transcribe the songs and music. His interest in spiritualism grew. He became a professional medium and developed a large circle of clients. He became celebrated after he met the movie costume designer Natacha Rambova, Rudolph Valentino's wife, and began leading regular weekly séances for her and her friends. He traveled with Rambova and her entourage to Europe in 1926. She was estranged from her famous husband, and Wehner achieved much more publicity after predicting Valentino's death. Later, after Valentino actually died, Wehner conducted a series of séances during which Rambova believed she was communicating with Valentino's departed spirit.

In the 1930s, Wehner stopped working as a medium and returned to musical composition. White Cloud continued to provide him with increasingly complex music.

When Sally phoned him in February 1941, Wehner was working on his latest musical composition, a piano concerto. The previous year, he had hired a local New York City arranger, composer, copyist, and instrumentalist named Alfred Marion Harned. Harned's assignment was to write out the orchestral parts for Wehner's new concerto -- for 27 instruments of a symphony orchestra.

Alfred Harned at work, ca. 1941

Wehner asked Harned to move into his residence at 156 West 56th Street, so that they could work together intensively without interruption. There is a massive amount of work involved in orchestrating a concerto, and he wanted to be closely involved with Harned in the creative process.

Wehner's home was situated directly across the street from the stage door of Carnegie Hall. Alexis (or Alex) Rotov, a professional ballet dancer whom Wehner had befriended, also lived in the same residence. Rotov was barely over five feet tall and, because of his diminutive height, concentrated on comedic and satiric characterizations in his performances. Wehner and Rotov, both homosexual, shared the same address for many years and may have been lovers. Harned, having been in show business practically all his life, was totally unfazed by the bohemian living arrangement.

SALLY MEETS ALFRED HARNED

On the particular day that Sally phoned Wehner, both Wehner and Rotov were out, but Harned was in the house working on the concerto. He answered the phone and took Sally's "I'm back" message. Within a few days, Wehner invited Sally to attend one of the séances he held in his house. Sally met Harned at the event, and they were immediately attracted to each other. They found that they had much in common spiritually and in their life experiences. Also, coincidentally and conveniently, they lived only a block apart.

They began dating. Their first date was to see Walt Disney's *Fantasia* at the Broadway Theatre. *Fantasia* had opened the previous November and was doing sensational business due to its unique popularization of classical music. Needless to say, both Alfred and Sally were serious classical music lovers. They also spent much time taking romantic walks in nearby Central Park to get to know each other better.

Sally learned that Alfred came to New York in 1931 as a band musician, even though his true passion was arranging and orchestrating. At one time he played in Al Skinner's orchestra, and Al's brother Frank was a music arranger in New York City. Al offered to introduce Alfred to Frank. Through this introduction, Alfred studied with Frank in New York and worked with him later on a book about orchestra scoring. Alfred was proud of his collaboration with Frank Skinner on the book, *Frank Skinner's New Methods Of Orchestra Scoring* (New York: Robbins Music Corporation, 1935).

However, when the book was published, Alfred's name was left out. Alfred believed that he had done most of the work on the book, and he felt robbed of credit for his hard work. Alfred was a kind, gentle, and deeply spiritual man who was extremely diligent and conscientious when it came to any kind of musical output. However, he was not professionally aggressive. Although he was deeply hurt, he let the whole situation go.

Frank Skinner's 1935 book

During this period, he also befriended fellow musician Red Nichols, whose orchestra was playing as the pit band for the then-current George and Ira Gershwin Broadway hit musical *Girl Crazy*. The show starred Ethel Merman and Ginger Rogers, opened in October 1930, and ran through June 1931. (Ginger Rogers had been a good friend of Sally's during her *Once In A Lifetime* days.) Benny Goodman, Gene Krupa, Glenn Miller, Jimmy Dorsey, and Jack Teagarden were all members of Red Nichols' orchestra. When the cast recording was planned and the regular guitarist could not make the recording date, Alfred was asked to fill in as guitarist during the recording session. Alfred's friendship and contact with these fellow musicians was invaluable over the years as he pursued his arranging and orchestrating career. All these men ended up with their own bands and constantly needed orchestration assistance, which Alfred was always available to provide.

The famous bandleader, Artie Shaw, was also a good friend. Alfred roomed with him for a while before moving in with George Wehner. Alfred found Shaw to be one of the most intellectual people he ever met and a true spiritual mentor.

ALFRED HARNED'S FAMILY

Sally learned more about Alfred and his family. Alfred Marion Harned was born in the small town of Grand Junction, Iowa, on December 27, 1903. His parents were Francis John Harned (1863-1934) and Anna Amelia Bowers (1868-1930). He was the youngest of five siblings, four boys and a girl.

Frank J. Harned

Anna Amelia Bowers Harned

It was the Harned family tradition to refer to their sons by their middle name. Therefore, Alfred was "Marion" to his family in Iowa, to his school, to his townspeople, to his professional colleagues in New York, even to Sally, but, in his later years, he preferred to use his first name, Alfred.

There was an almost eighteen-year difference between Alfred and his older brother Walter Max Harned ("Max"). But, Daniel Dwight Harned ("Dwight"), another brother, was senior to him by only 21 months, and Alfred said they did everything together. They were not only close in age but also close in their intense interest in music. Music had always been an important part of Harned family life. Even though Max became a dentist, he played the violin like a virtuoso. Ezma, his sister, who married a local lawyer, was an excellent pianist. Francis Paul ("Paul"), his other brother, who became a lawyer, may also have played a musical instrument, but the Harned history is silent on this. It was Dwight and Alfred who were to become professional musicians.

Dwight and Alfred's musical training began at a young age with piano lessons. When Dwight began to "hog" the piano, Alfred turned to the more accessible stringed instruments, such as the banjo and the ukulele. By their teenage years, they were already getting gigs, Dwight on the piano and Alfred on the banjo. After a while, they became so busy, together and separately, that they frequently missed much time in school.

Their parents, Frank and Anna Harned, gave their young sons free reign to pursue their musical careers. It is astonishing to hear that Alfred was allowed to join an itinerant musical troupe as a banjo player during the summer of 1919 when he was only 15. The troupe was headed by a married couple, Rolly Coy and his wife, and they traveled all the way to Nevada by car, returning in late December, just before Alfred's 16th birthday. He had missed the entire first semester of his sophomore year of high school.

Both boys constantly placed their musical gigs at a higher priority than their formal education. They formed their own Harned Brothers Orchestra during their last semester of high school, in the first half of 1923.

Harned Brothers Orchestra, 1923 (Alfred far right)

Besides performing local gigs, they also had great success with a national radio broadcast that was heard as far away as Canada. When they finally graduated, at the same time, from Jefferson High School in mid-1923, Alfred at 19½ and Dwight at 21 were much older than their fellow classmates. They both took courses at Drake University, but they followed a similar pattern, attending classes only between gigs. As a result, neither got a college degree. This became a problem for Alfred professionally, particularly for his future career as a music teacher. Although the brothers kept in touch, eventually each brother went his own way.

In early 1925, Alfred joined Dart's Troubadours, a jazz band headed by bandleader Kermit Dart. All seven men in the band were in their twenties, handsome, and sexy. The group played for dances or sometimes worked as a vaudeville act between movie theater screenings. In 1926, the group allied itself with other vaudeville performers, resulting in the creation of a brand new act, billed as "The Transfield Sisters And Their Voyagers, With Dart's Troubadours, and Eugenie La Blanc." The Transfield sisters were specialty singers, while Engenie La Blanc served as a novelty dancer. This act usually headlined on the bill, playing all the major vaudeville circuits – Keith, Orpheum, and Pantages – and toured throughout the country.

Alfred, all by himself, was always the first to appear on stage. This is the how and why: The act commenced with The Troubadour musicians walking on stage, one at a time, playing their respective musical instruments. When they were all assembled, the singing and dancing members of the act joined them on stage. The first musician had to have the biggest, warmest, and most welcoming smile – a smile that could be seen all the way to the last row of the theater. Every band member knew that had to be Alfred, for no one had a better smile. So he always walked on stage first, strumming his banjo and smiling winningly.

Alfred's vaudeville bookings were sometimes in theaters where Sally's films were showing. He was on stage. She was on the screen. Yet they did not meet in person for 14 years.

As the years passed, Alfred became more and more interested in the technical side of music -- arranging, orchestrating, and composing. When he played with a new band or orchestra, he would often ask if he could participate in the musical chart arrangements.

In early 1929, Alfred moved back with his parents (now living in Des Moines), feeling the need to concentrate on the academic study of musical arranging and orchestrating. Not officially matriculating with the local Drake University music department, he instead studied privately with Franz Kuschan (1891-1937), a professor of music theory and cello at Drake, in hopes of getting academic credit from him for the study. This study required Alfred to learn to play a classical stringed instrument. Since cello was Professor's Kuschan's specialty, Alfred took up the cello and loved it. However, within a year, a job opportunity presented itself to Alfred, and Alfred moved on.

Alfred had been working successfully in New York as an arranger and orchestrator for almost a decade when he met Sally. It did not take long for them to make permanent plans.

Vaudeville act – postcard

Vaudeville act – entire cast (Harned second front left)

SALLY ELOPES WITH ALFRED TO MEXICO

Alfred's handwritten memoirs continue the story:

In June 1941, Sally Phipps and I eloped to Mexico City. [We] were married and visited many towns for their fiestas with Alonzo Mischado [sic], an artist for Savilla [sic] Moving Picture Studio. [I] studied music with Julian Carillo.

Why Mexico? For years, Sally's best friend Dorothy Day regaled Sally with wonderful tales of Mexico and living in Coyoacán, the artist colony suburb of Mexico City, with her husband Jean Charlot (1898-1979), a prominent painter. Dorothy had recently married Charlot. He was born in France of French and Mexican ancestry and emigrated to Mexico in the early 1920s. He soon became a member of the "Mexican Mural Renaissance" under the leadership of Diego Rivera. Dorothy first met Charlot in Mexico in 1931 but did not marry him until 1939.

During their trip to Mexico, Sally and Alfred made a number of stops and took many photographs.

Alfred and Sally en route to Mexico

After they settled themselves in Coyoacán, they got married, at noon on August 18, 1941. The marriage license lists several Spanish-named witnesses who were possibly friends or neighbors living in or near their Coyoacán apartment building at Aguayo, No. 26.

Alfred and Sally on their wedding day

The address is only five blocks away from Frida Kahlo's Blue House (La Casa Azul) at Londres, No. 247, today a famous museum. This is the house that Kahlo grew up in, and also where she spent her married life with Diego Rivera. Rivera and Kahlo were living in Coyoacán during the same time that Sally and Alfred were living there. Given Sally's film and Broadway star status, Alfred's accomplishments as a musician, Sally's connection to Charlot through Dorothy, and Charlots's connection to Rivera, Sally and Alfred undoubtedly socialized in the Rivera/Kahlo "Bohemian" circle.

At that time (and as now), the cost of living in Mexico, was very low. Sally and Alfred were able to live well on their savings during their five months there. An artist friend from the Savilla [sic] Moving Picture Studio, Miguel Alonso Machado, showed them the sights. In addition, Alfred was able to study music theory with the Mexican composer and conductor Julian Carillo (1875-1965). Carillo was famous for his promotion of "the thirteenth sound." The octave is traditionally divided into 12 pitches. Carillo, while working with his violin, found that it can be arranged into different intervals enabling musicians to go beyond the twelve notes. He was nominated for the Noble prize in Physics in 1950 for his theory of microtonal music.

Sally became pregnant almost as soon as they arrived in Mexico. Of course, she immediately told her mother. Edithe responded with an invitation for the two of them to come and live near her in Hawaii, along with a job offer for Alfred to manage one of Edithe's three photographic stores. They decided to take her up on the offer and booked passage on a Matson Company ocean liner, which was to leave from San Francisco on December 9, 1941. Alfred's memoirs continue:

> **Mr. Savilla drove us to San Francisco. We had tickets for Honolulu, Hawaii on December 9th. [On] December 7th, Pearl Harbor was bombed, so we moved to Des Moines, Iowa for the duration of the war.**

SALLY AND ALFRED MOVE TO IOWA

Iowa made sense as their next move, especially to Sally. There was a war going on in Europe and another in the Pacific. The United States mainland now had the possibility of being invaded on both coasts, and Iowa, Alfred's home, was in the remote center of the American continent. Being fearful about the future progress of the war, they got on the next train for Iowa, choosing Des Moines, the capital of the state, as their home base.

When they arrived in Des Moines, Sally was three months pregnant. Sally took it easy throughout her pregnancy. Interestingly, when she was introduced around to the nearby Harned family relatives, a number of them remarked at how much she resembled Alfred's mother, Anna Harned.

Alfred was now 38 years old and too old for the draft. As was typical of most non-combatant males during World War II, he did war work. He found employment at the Des Moines Ordnance Plant making tracer bullets and worked there for the duration of the war.

It was a good move for Alfred. He was also able to continue some of his music activities. According to his memoirs:

> **I became the music arranger for the [Des Moines] Palace Vaudeville Theatre. This was because Norman Swartswald in Chicago had issued an order that all vaudeville acts must have more modern orchestrations for State and Lake Theatres, using trumpets, trombones and saxophones instead of strings and woodwinds, or their acts would be cancelled. So, I was kept busy, arranging the music for the Orpheum theatre, which had also modernized.**

Sally, however, was in completely unfamiliar territory. Iowa, in the 1940s, was culturally very different from the exciting international life she had led. Having moved recently from New York to an exotic extended honeymoon in Mexico, she was now homebound and pregnant in Iowa in what was essentially farm country. In those days, there was no television and only radio to connect one to the broader world.

SALLY AND ALFRED HAVE CHILDREN – MARYANNA AND ROBERT

Sally's first child, Maryanna Bernice Phipps Harned, was born in Iowa Methodist Hospital on June 26, 1942. The 1943 Des Moines City Directory lists the Harned address as 945 8th Street, Apartment No. 21. Two years later, a son, Robert Alfred Laurence Phipps Harned, was born in the same hospital on May 4, 1944. By then, the Harned family had moved to a house at 2211 High Street.

Sally with baby Robert and Maryanna, Iowa, 1944/1945

SALLY AND ALFRED'S FAMILY MOVES TO HAWAII

When V-E day came on May 8, 1945, ending the war in Europe, it was only a few months before the war with Japan would be over in the Pacific. The Harneds were still eager to go to Hawaii. Edithe's invitation was still open, and the Harneds were at the top of the list of passengers on Matson Company's registry because their previous December 9, 1941 sailing had been cancelled. After the Japanese surrender on August 15, 1945, and the subsequent peace treaty signing on September 2, Alfred and Sally were free to choose a sailing date. They were to leave for Hawaii on the Matson Line's S.S. Monterey from San Francisco on October 31, 1945 and arrive in Honolulu on November 5.

The Harned family packed up, boarded a train from Des Moines, and arrived in San Francisco in time to embark on the ship. When they got on board, they were not surprised to see that it was still outfitted as a troop ship with many of the usual amenities missing. Robert, although only 1½ years old, remembers wandering around the ship with his 3½ year-old sister Maryanna and seeing old tires and hardware lying on some of the hallway floors. However, many years later, when Alfred told his son that Halloween was celebrated on the ship that first night of the voyage and that he had gone trick-or-treating, Robert did not remember doing that.

Edithe's dream was to consolidate her family in Hawaii. Lane, Edithe's son, and Elinor, his wife, already had made their trip to Hawaii in late 1944, even though the war was still raging. They now had two children - Betty, born in 1938, now six years old and Bruce, born in 1940, now four. Lane and Elinor heard that some troop ships were leaving from San Francisco, travelling through enemy waters, and then docking in Honolulu. They decided to make the trip in stages. Lane went first, aboard the S.S. Maunawili. His ship left from San Francisco on October 2, 1944 and arrived safely in Honolulu on October 12. Elinor and the two children went on the S.S. President Tyler, leaving San Francisco on December 20, 1944 and arriving on December 29. But it was not a smooth sailing. Betty and Bruce remember standing on deck one day outside their cabin while enemy Japanese airplanes attacked their ship. They could see the large red balls painted on the sides and wings of the attacking airplanes, the insignia of the famous Japanese "Zeros." Betty vividly remembers seeing one of the attacking planes being shot down and falling into the ocean. Needless to say, the children were terrified. In order to calm them down, Elinor explained away the incident to them as merely a friendly American aerial maneuver and nothing to worry about. Years later, when they were older, Betty and Bruce were told the truth and found it hard to understand why their parents had made the trip at that time, endangering all of their lives.

Edithe was thrilled that Sally and Alfred and their two children would be joining the rest of the family. By late 1945, she would have four grandchildren to make a fuss over, a number that would soon expand to five, since Elinor was again pregnant. Elinor gave birth to her second son, Jack, in Honolulu on June 13, 1946.

Meanwhile, Edithe was busy setting up a home for Alfred and Sally in the Waikiki section of Honolulu, at 221 Kapuni Road (today called Kapuni Street). The house was built in the bungalow style and was only a short walk to Honolulu's popular Kuhio Beach. It had a typical feature of many Waikiki houses close to the beach, an outside entrance giving direct access to the bathroom and a shower, which helped to reduce the amount of sand coming into the house. The house was surrounded by a large garden with many kinds of fruit trees, including mango.

The Harned Waikiki house, Honolulu (Maryanna out front)

Everything seemed to be just right for Sally and Alfred to make a fresh start in a new environment – family close by, a new house, and a new job for Alfred. Edithe had offered Alfred the job of managing her downtown Eastman Kodak photographic store at 129 South Hotel Street, one of her three "Color Art Shop" stores. Since Alfred did not have a car, he would take a short bus ride to work. Sally would stay home with the children.

Advertisement for Edithe's Color Art Shop

Trouble started as soon as they got off the ship. Alfred, years later, related his impression to his son Robert, "We were such a happy family until we arrived in Hawaii." It started with Edithe. She had remembered a svelte Sally with extremely fashionable clothes, befitting a woman who had been someone important in show business. Sally, however, had given birth to two babies within two years, and caring for a 3½-year-old daughter and a toddler boy had left her undoubtedly stressed, overworked, and possibly somewhat depressed. Understandably, she had not been able to give much time or thought to her own personal needs. Furthermore, she was still nursing Robert, who in early November 1945 was only 1½ years old. When the family walked down the gangplank, Alfred leading Maryanna by her hand and Sally carrying baby Robert, Edithe felt embarrassment instead of joy. Edithe later told her grandson Robert how shocked she was when she saw how much weight her daughter had gained, and how frumpy her clothes looked. She made a deal right away with Sally that she would buy her a whole new wardrobe if she would immediately go on a diet. Sally reluctantly agreed. However, this pressure to diet must have brought back unpleasant memories of her Hollywood days at Fox, where weight consciousness was an important part of her employment contract. Overall, Sally began her life with Alfred in Hawaii experiencing disappointment with her reception, feeling overwhelmed by the added stress of dieting, and being faced with the concerns of settling down in a strange place with two young children.

Edithe disliked Alfred immediately. She thought that Alfred did not help Sally enough around the house or with the children. In addition, she did not find him assertive enough as a store manager. The axe fell when Alfred noticed that certain employees at his store were pocketing money from the cash registers. He dutifully reported it to Edithe. Instead of confronting or firing the delinquent employees, Edith fired Alfred. Years later, Alfred told his son Robert that "they were robbing her blind, and she didn't believe it." Fortunately, Alfred was able to find a new job quickly, as a clerk at a competing photographic shop called Wadsworth's Photo Materials, located a few blocks away in the same downtown area.

Alfred and Sally soon found that they disagreed about disciplining the children, now nearly four and two. Sally was quick to spank when the children acted badly, while Alfred tried to "talk" the offending child out of her or his bad behavior. Edithe completely disagreed with Alfred about his methods and sided with Sally on this matter. Sally, home all day with the children, was finding them more and more difficult to handle and was losing patience with their constant demand for attention. One day, Alfred came home from work and heard Robert screaming and crying at a side screen door. Sally was completely ignoring him. When Alfred asked why, Sally said he had been following her around all day, and, tired of his neediness, she hoped he would stay outside, play by himself, and leave her alone. When Alfred checked on Robert, he found that Sally had locked Robert out of the house using the screen door, but accidentally had caught part of his hand in the door. Too young to talk, Robert could only scream and cry to get attention, which Sally had decided to ignore. Needless to say, Alfred was furious with Sally, with what he considered totally neglectful behavior.

Sally became more and more unhappy with living in Honolulu. Hawaii had natural beauty, temperate weather, and resort atmosphere, but Honolulu was not exactly a high cultural center. All the major cultural activities were centered around Hawaiian themes, and these were presented, at that time, mainly for commercial tourist exploitation. Music, song, and dance were particularly emphasized, sometimes in native Hawaiian language and sometimes in English.

Sally found life in Honolulu provincial and limited, and after a while, repetitious and boring. She had known great success in film and on the stage and was also a world traveler. She was increasingly feeling the small-time aspect of Honolulu and was starting to get restless for more stimulation. Also, she did not think that there was a high standard of English speech in the public schools, where her children were soon to enter.

On the other hand, Alfred, a musician, orchestrator, and musical scholar, thoroughly embraced Hawaiian culture, particularly the music, as a brand new territory to explore and be part of. Since he was originally from a small town in Iowa, Alfred found the slow pace of life and gregariousness of the local people in Honolulu quite comforting, especially after his many hectic years in New York. In addition, he envisioned Honolulu as a beautiful place to bring up children.

Then came the disastrous tidal wave of April 1, 1946, less than five months after the Harneds had arrived in Hawaii. Caused by an earthquake in the Aleutian Islands, the tidal wave hit the big island of Hawaii by surprise early in the morning, with waves ranging from 30 to 50 feet high. It left 159 people dead, mostly in the city of Hilo on the Big Island of Hawaii. Honolulu was not badly affected, but it scared Sally out of her wits.

SALLY HAS NERVOUS BREAKDOWN

Soon after, Sally started acting strangely. One often-repeated incident has her getting into a taxicab dressed only in a sheet and then throwing the sheet out of the window. Sally was obviously having a nervous breakdown and needed help. However, mental health care in Hawaii in the 1940s was still in the dark ages. Psychotropic medications did not come into wide use until the 1950s. Before that, fewer than 25% of patients in psychiatric hospitals were admitted voluntarily.

Edithe and Lane pressured Alfred to have Sally committed, which he was reluctant to do. Finally, he gave in. She was committed on April 15, 1946 to the Territorial Hospital in Kaneohe, Oahu. (Hawaii was still a territory. It became a state in 1959.) She stayed there for 7 ½ months. She was discharged as "recovered" on November 29, 1946. Sally's memories of that time were not totally unpleasant. She remembered opportunities to help the staff and to be of some service in certain hospital activities.

Alfred continued work at Wadsworth's but decided to put his children into day care. He was fortunate to find McKinley Day Care Center, a place where he could easily deposit his children in the morning on his way to work and then pick them up after work. The Center was located at the corner of King Street and Victoria Street and was housed in a group of Quonset huts on the campus of McKinley High School. Edithe frequently helped out with the children's care, despite the continuing animosity between Edithe and Alfred. She began to act as surrogate mother, a role she would continue to play for many years, one that Alfred begrudgingly but resignedly allowed. Edithe provided the loving mothering that both Maryanna and two-year-old Robert craved. It would be a long time before Maryanna and Robert would become fully aware of the animosity between her and Alfred.

SALLY MOVES OUT ON HER OWN

When Sally was released from the psychiatric hospital, her attitude toward Alfred and her children had changed. She was no longer willing to live with Alfred. She was particularly concerned about the possibility of having another child, which she knew she did not want. Although she loved her children, she found it difficult to return home even to see them. For a while she stayed with Edithe. Then, she got her own apartment.

Maryanna and Robert remember feeling deep longing to see their mother during this period. If they saw a woman in a photograph or in a film that looked even vaguely like Sally, they would often remark on the resemblance. Robert vividly remembers one incident at a chamber music concert at the Honolulu Academy of Arts. Alfred had just arrived with Maryanna and Robert, and they had taken their seats before the music began. During the program, Robert by chance spotted his mother seated in another section of the audience and started screaming, "There's Mommy," completely interrupting the music performance. Alfred, embarrassed, immediately removed both children and took them home, never once interacting with

Sally. The children cried continuously during their trip home, incredulous as to why they were not able to communicate with their mother.

Meanwhile, Sally, still under Edithe's wing, found employment. Edithe sometimes gave her photographic coloring work. When not doing coloring work, Sally was employed mainly in secretarial positions, first at the KGU and KULA radio stations and then later at B. F. Dillingham Insurance Company. For a while, she worked behind the pastry counter at the fancy, touristic Alexander Young Hotel in downtown Honolulu.

Within a year or two after Sally came out of the hospital, Edithe sold the Kapuni Road house, which she had provided for the Harned family and where Alfred and the children were still living. Edithe's reason was that business was slow, due to the post-war slump, and that she needed the money from the proceeds to continue running her three shops. Needless to say, Alfred was surprised that Edithe would take away her grandchildren's home, but he gave up the house without a fight and rented an apartment. He found a one-bedroom apartment in a recently built apartment building complex on Kalauokalani Way, not far from the intersection of Kalakaua Avenue and Kapiolani Boulevard, within easy access to the bus to work and to the day care center for the children. The apartment building stills stands -- 1697 Kalauokalani Way. During their stay in the apartment, the children slept in separate beds in the one bedroom, while Alfred slept in a large day bed in the living room. During the Harneds' roughly one-year residence there, Robert and Maryanna remember having chicken pox, in particular putting calamine lotion on each other. The Harneds then moved to another one-bedroom apartment at 1034 Apt.A Lunalilo Street, near the corner of Victoria Street in the Lower Punchbowl area, keeping the same sleeping arrangements as they had in their previous apartment.

Three and a half years after the separation, on Christmas Day, December 25, 1949, while they were living on Lunalilo Street, Maryanna and Robert woke up to find Sally and Alfred sleeping together in Alfred's large bed. The children were surprised but supremely happy to see them together. And, in addition, each easy chair in the living room was filled with Christmas presents for each of them. Maryanna was 7½ and in the middle of second grade at the nearby Lincoln Elementary School, and Robert was 5½ and in kindergarten in the same school's annex. But Sally did not intend to move back in, and they did not know it was the last Christmas that all four would celebrate together.

SALLY DECIDES TO LEAVE HAWAII, DESERTING ALFRED AND CHILDREN

Sally was having trouble finding work in Honolulu, and the Korean War had just started in the summer of 1950. Being a fearful person, she did not want to be in Hawaii so close to a war zone. She began to think about going back to the mainland. She and Alfred were still married. She had done nothing about a divorce, and there were still the children. However, she finally made the decision to leave.

She wanted to do something particularly special for the children before she left, because, when summer came and they were on vacation from school, she started to take them to the beach every day. Both she and the children loved the beach.

Every morning she would come by bus to their apartment, pick them up, ride with them by bus to the beach, and then drop them off at home at the end of the day. Her favorite beach was Gray's Beach, in front of the Halekulani Hotel in Waikiki, where they would sit all day, sun tanning, playing in the water, and eating.

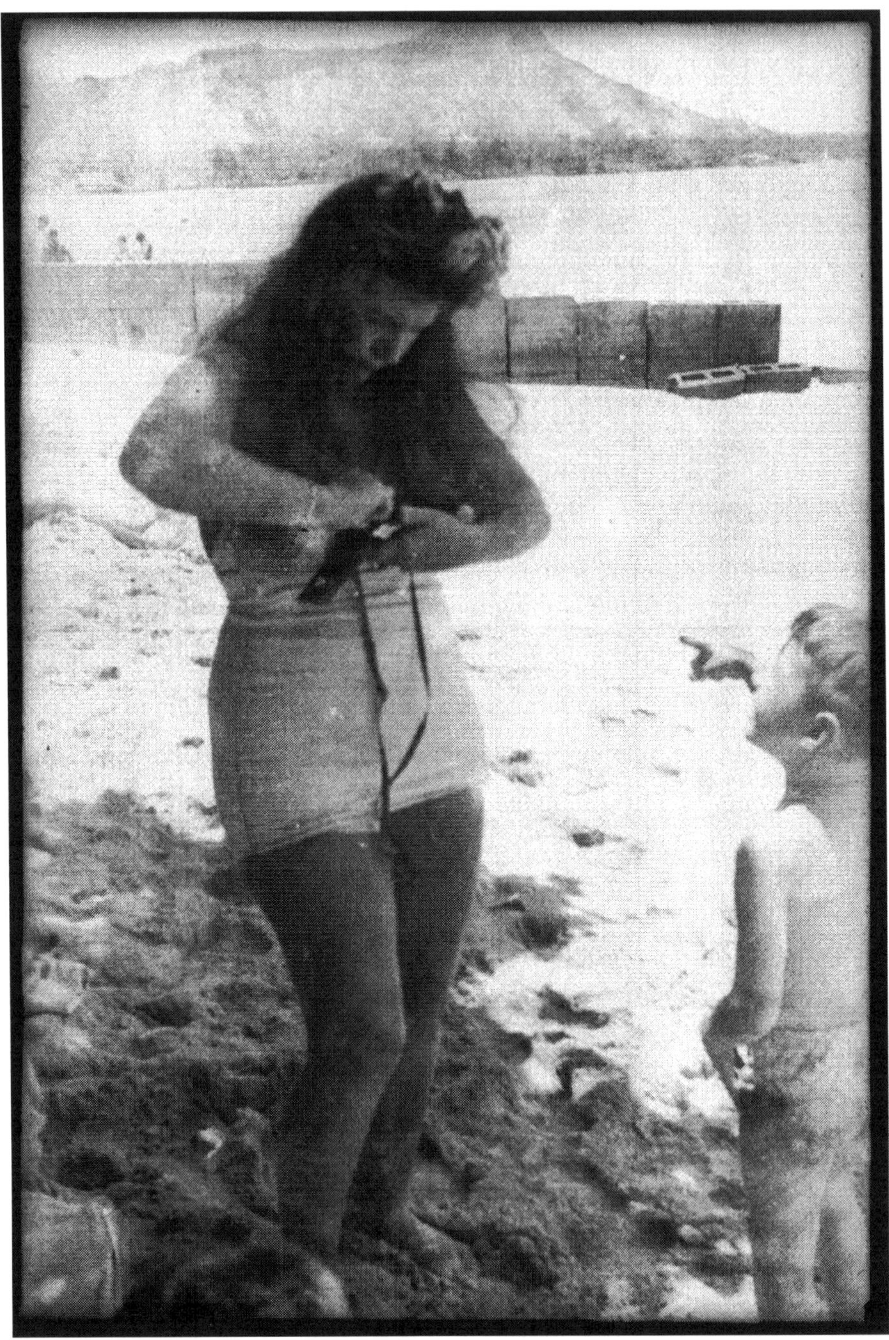

Sally and 6-year-old Robert at Waikiki Beach, 1950

Robert also remembers very well that during these summer visits Sally taught him and his sister The Lord's Prayer. For some reason, she felt it was important that they learn it before she left.

Then suddenly, on the morning of August 18, 1950, her ninth wedding anniversary with Alfred, Sally did not show up. When Alfred called Edithe to find out what she knew, Edithe explained that Sally had flown out that morning for California, with the understanding that she was not going to return. Alfred later told Robert that Sally, unbeknownst to him, had cashed in a number of bonds that they held jointly, leaving Alfred and the children with very little in savings. Sally fled, leaving behind her shocked family.

Chapter 6
Colorado – And On The Road

SALLY MOVES TO DENVER, COLORADO

On August 19, 1950, Sally's plane landed in Los Angeles, where she stayed for a few days visiting friends, although she had already made plans to move to Denver. She was drawn to Denver because her father, Albert Bogdon, had lived there with his second wife, Adele, and their daughter, Violet, from 1920 until his death in June 1927. Living in the city where her father had once lived and where he was buried made her feel closer to him, a closeness she always longed for. There were several parallels in their lives. They both had theatrical careers in their teens, interrupted by a marriage near age 20. Poignantly, they both deserted their respective spouses, leaving behind two children, a girl and boy, who were almost exactly two years apart.

Sally in Denver, early 1950s

When Sally arrived in Denver, she rented an apartment and began looking for work. She found a secretarial position in a company called McQuay-Norris Manufacturing Company at 1085 Galapago Street in downtown Denver. This was the Denver branch of a company that had its head office in Saint Louis, Missouri. The company made automobile parts, such as piston rings, valves, and pumps, among other things. Sally was hired as the secretary to the manager and stayed five years in that position. On one of her employment resumes, she described her work:

> **Became secretary to McQuay-Norris Mfg. Co., largest motor parts company in USA and Canada out of St. Louis. Set up the Denver Branch files, books, and billing for surrounding 16 states. This business entailed distributing auto parts to some 300 customers over the counter, by post and via bus, truck and railroad. Dealt with these customers over long distance phone and acquired a knowledge of all makes of cars and their parts for same. Worked at Denver for the last five years acquiring considerable experience in dealing with business houses in the surrounding region, including Nebraska, Utah, Texas, New Mexico, Wyoming, Arizona, Kansas, Idaho, etc.**

Now that Sally had an apartment and was settled in a new job, she was free to find out more about her father -- his life after he and her mother separated, and after he joined the Navy. Edithe never wanted to tell Sally anything about her father, except the basics – that he remarried, had another daughter, and spent the last seven years of his life in Denver before being killed. Now, she had access to people who knew her father. His second wife and daughter still lived there, and she visited them. She also visited her father's mausoleum in Denver's Crown Hill Cemetery. Furthermore, since Bogdon had become part of Denver history, as one of its state senators, the local libraries and historical societies provided information. Sally was good at research and learned a lot about her father.

ALBERT BOGDON'S LATER LIFE

Bogdon entered military service in the United States Naval Reserve Force on April 4, 1917, just two days before America entered the First World War. He was first assigned to the cruiser U.S.S. St. Louis and shortly afterwards to the battleship U.S.S. Kearsarge. The Kearsarge was originally launched in 1898 and was modernized in 1909. During the war, it was used to train armed guard crews and naval engineers in waters along the American East Coast, from Boston, Massachusetts, to Pensacola, Florida. After a few months, Bogdon earned the rank of Chief Petty Officer and became one of the ship's quartermasters.

Bogdon as a naval officer – ca. 1918

Bogdon on the U.S.S Kearsarge – ca. 1918

Four months after he joined the Navy, the following newspaper article appeared in the Indiana *Valparaiso Porter County Vidette*, August 1, 1917:

WELL KNOWN YOUNG MAN NOW SHIP QUARTERMASTER

Albert E. Bogdon, for years a student in Valparaiso University, and quite well known here from the fact that he was a magician of ability who often gave entertainments locally, is now quartermaster on the U.S.S. St. Louis, according to a letter received by Mark L. Dickover.

Bogdon's rise has been rapid. When leaving Valparaiso, he entered lyceum work, and his friends are surprised to learn that he is in the Navy and in so important a position. While in New York City, Mr. Dickover caught sight of the ship St. Louis lying in the harbor there, and had he known his friend was aboard, he would have visited him.

Bogdon appears to have been fondly remembered in the small academic town of Valparaiso, Indiana. He was a student at the University for a short time and while there, he joined a number of Masonic organizations, where he befriended Mark L. Dickover, a prominent local banker. Bogdon kept up his Masonic relationships with the Valparaiso lodges until he died.

Bogdon's second wife, Adele Evelyn Fowler (1897-1994), was attending nursing school at Mt. Sinai Hospital in New York City when she met him at a dance for servicemen, while he was on leave. His ship had docked in the Brooklyn Navy Yard, and Adele was living near the Navy Yard in the Clinton Hill section of Brooklyn. Bogdon proposed soon after they started dating and wanted to marry immediately. Adele refused, explaining that she had only a few months left before graduation and could get expelled if she were to marry before then. Bogdon, afraid he would lose her to someone else during the uncertain war times, persisted about getting married as soon as possible, through several weeks of correspondence.

Adele finally gave in, and they were secretly married on August 25, 1917 at St. Mary's Episcopal Church, also in the Clinton Hill section of Brooklyn. Bogdon was 26, and Adele was 20. On the marriage certificate, both indicated that it was their first marriage. Obviously Bogdon lied. Ever since he joined the Navy, his child support payments were automatically deducted from his military paycheck each month and sent to Edithe. Since the support payments were automatic, Adele did not know about them, and he did not tell her about them until much later.

Adele Fowler Bogdon

Somehow the nursing school found out about Adele's marriage, and even though Albert was back at sea, she got expelled. However, she was still able to find part-time nursing work despite not having completed her formal training.

Bogdon was eventually promoted to Lieutenant Junior Grade, and, when the war ended in November 1918, he was transferred to Washington, D.C. Going on ahead of Adele, he found a rented apartment for the two of them, as well as a secretarial job for her in the Navy Department. In April 1919, Bogdon, who was already a member of the California Bar, received a highly prestigious appointment in the Navy Department's Office of the Judge Advocate General.

While working in the Judge Advocate General's Office, he attended law school at American University's Washington College of Law. While in law school, he was admitted to the Bar of the Supreme Court of the District of Columbia on May 8, 1919. Because he had already been admitted to the Bar of the Southern District of California in Los Angeles on September 29, 1916 and had maintained a law office there for a short time, his D.C. certificate states that he was of the "California Bar."

Adele became pregnant and left her job with the Navy. Their daughter Violet was born August 9, 1919. Albert chose her name. When his sea duty reenlistment came up, Adele did not want to live alone in Washington with Violet, so Albert decided to resign from the Navy, effective late April 1920. After graduating from Washington College of Law, Class of 1920, with an LL.B degree, he was ready to start a new career as a lawyer.

Bogdon and baby Violet -- 1919

Bogdon, a Washington College of Law graduate -- 1920

Albert and Adele were not sure where they wanted to go. But Adele's father, Burt Fowler, was living in Omaha, Nebraska, and wanted to see them. They decided to visit him and explore law practice possibilities there. They planned to have Adele and Violet stay with Adele's father, while Albert, drawn by his ethnic roots, visited a Lithuanian colony in Sioux City, Iowa, in hopes of finding a new home. By the time Albert came back to Omaha, Fowler's new wife, Maud, decided that she did not want them to stay any longer and asked them to leave. Adele's father then gave them some money to travel further west. They chose Denver, because Albert, who had been there on tour as a magician, said he always liked it. They arrived by train. Albert was 29. Adele was 23. Violet was only nine months old.

Bogdon and Adele visit family in Omaha, Nebraska, 1920

Albert quickly got a job in the legal department of the Denver Tramway Company for $100 a week. Always ready to find employment for his wife, he found a job for Adele selling Fuller Brushes.

Adele wrote in her memoirs:

> **Then I had to find someone to look after Violet while I worked. That hurt more than anything.**

Shortly after they moved to Denver, Albert received a letter from Edithe telling him that the child support payments she had been receiving for Sally and Lane had stopped when he resigned from the Navy. It was then that Adele learned for the first time that Albert had been married previously and had two children. "What a shock!" Adele noted in her memoirs. Albert decided that it would be best if Adele wrote a letter to Edithe, telling her about his new family, and that he would continue the payments. She says in her memoirs that he dictated it and also says, "I don't remember what I said, but we never heard from her [Edithe] again." That would probably be, according to her daughter Violet, because Adele ended up dutifully sending Edithe's support payment checks every month until Bogdon's death in June 1927.

Working in Denver as a lawyer meant he would have to be admitted to the Colorado Bar. Albert concentrated all of his efforts on passing the Colorado Bar exam. He chose the local Westminster Law School as a place to study for it, a school which provided an evening program. On June 10, 1921, he passed the bar exam and was admitted to the Colorado Bar on June 30, 1921.

He continued working at the Denver Tramway Company. Then in early 1924, for a short while, he joined the law firm of John C. Vivian. He was now able to make enough money to buy a house, and Adele could stop working and be with Violet full time. "What a joy," Adele wrote in her memoirs. "She was the only joy that kept me going."

Bogdon, Denver lawyer – ca. 1922

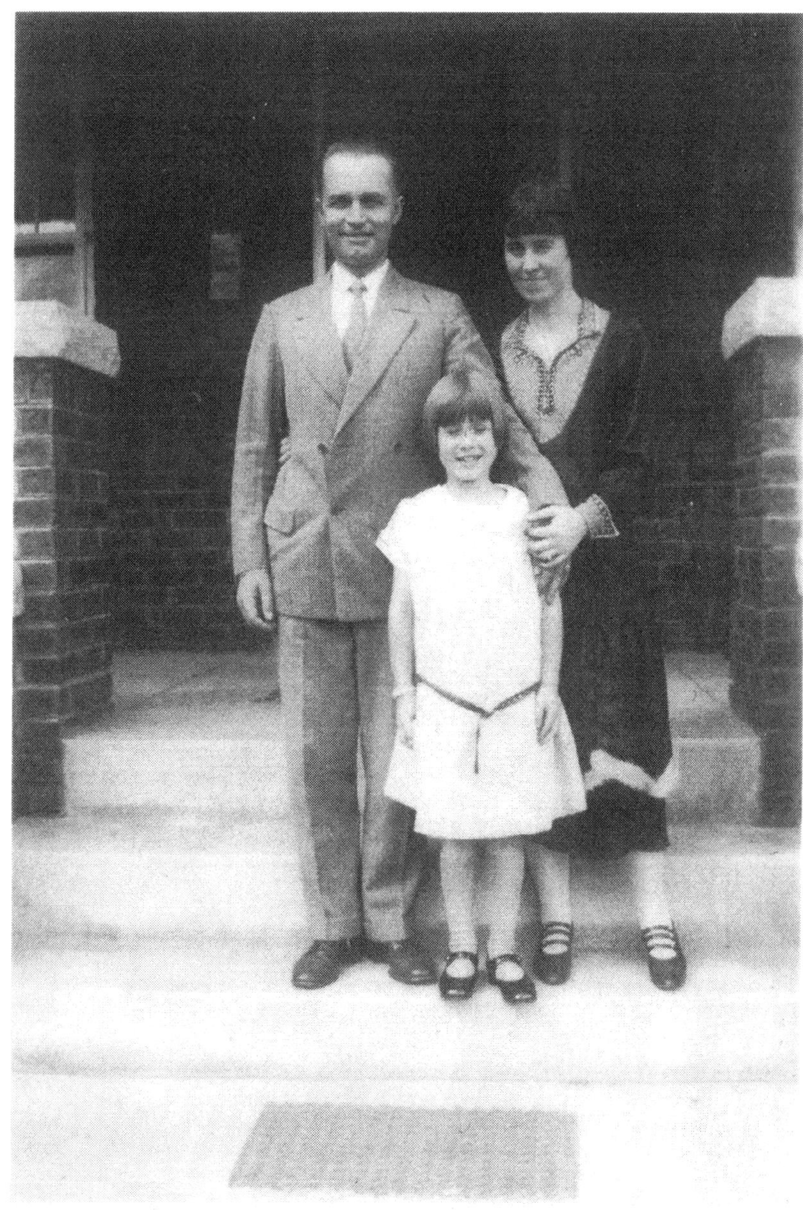

Bogdon, Adele, and Violet -- 1927

Albert's next move, later in 1924, was to join the law firm of Henry E. May. May was a powerful Republican Party attorney, born in Denver, as well as a 32nd degree Mason. He had developed big political ambitions over the years and had also fostered ties with important local politicians. May served as a member of Denver's Civil Service Commission between 1919 and 1924, and, beginning December 1, 1924, served as City Attorney of the City and County of Denver, in addition to maintaining his own law office.

Henry E. May, Bogdon's employer

Joining the May firm in 1924 was a turning point in Bogdon's life. He now, by association, had become a significant public figure in Denver and Colorado politics. Within a short time, Bogdon decided to run for State Senator for the Denver area in the upcoming November 1924 election. However, in order to get elected to any important position in this area in the early 1920s, one had to become a member of the Ku Klux Klan. He dutifully joined. (Bogdon is listed as No. 565 in the Denver Ku Klux Klan Member List, currently housed in the Denver Historical Society.)

Albert rose rapidly in his career, mainly due to Klan backing. He won the 1924 election for State Senator. In 1925 he became head of the Civil Service commission. There was even talk of a path to a judgeship or the governor's office. It is entirely possible, however, that the Klan membership also caused his murder.

Bogdon – official photo as state senator, 1925

Because his work kept him busy during the day, both as State Senator and as head of the Civil Service Commission, Albert usually made his private law practice appointments in the evening, which Adele was used to having him do. On the night of Thursday, June 9, 1927, he had scheduled an appointment at the apartment of Helena Minter, a client he was representing in her divorce from her husband Joseph. The Minters had been separated for several months. Joseph Minter, unhappy with their separation and distrustful of his wife, had been regularly lurking outside her apartment building to spy on her, believing his wife was entertaining other men. When he saw Bogdon entering the apartment, he suspected a romantic tryst and, in a jealous rage, broke down the door and shot Bogdon three times, killing him.

After the shooting, Bogdon's body was found partially clothed, and the press and the court assumed a romantic tryst. Adele believed adamantly that Bogdon's murder was set up by his political enemies to look like a romantic assignation and that the perpetrators undressed Bogdon quickly after the shooting. When she spoke publicly about this, she received threatening phone calls.

Another possible theory is that, after the shooting, Minter, realizing Bogdon's innocence, may have undressed Bogdon himself in order to make it look like a romantic tryst. Minter certainly expected that there would be a jury trial because of the shooting, and he trusted in the power of the "unwritten law" to win the sympathy of judge, jury, and the Denver public to award him a light sentence. The "unwritten law" is the belief that if a husband finds his wife in the arms of another man and he kills the other man on the spot he cannot be convicted of murder.

After the trial, Minter was convicted only of involuntary manslaughter and sentenced to a mere one day to one year in jail. "The unwritten law" was cited continually during the trial, in spite of the fact that the Minters had been separated for months and a divorce was in process. Adele continued to believe completely in her husband's innocence, as she declared in the *Denver Post*, October 17, 1927, a day before the trial began:

> **He was the victim of a cruel plot perpetrated by his political enemies. Minter was but a pawn. Of these things, I am certain and time will prove them.**

She may well have been right. At the time of the shooting, the tide was turning against the Klan. Even though a large majority of the Denver populace was originally enthusiastic over the Klan control of local politics, Denver was slowly waking up to the Klan's dangerous excesses, and there was still an abundance of animosity directed at Bogdon, not only from anti-Klan people but also from certain high-level Klan members.

Of course, the scandal created a feeding frenzy for the newspapers. They were filled with sensational reports of the shooting. These were the same Denver newspapers that Edithe showed to Sally when she was on location in Los Angeles, back in June 1927 filming *Gentlemen Prefer Scotch.*

First in the Morning Field—in Circulation, Advertising and Reader Buying Power

UNITED PRESS
Serves the Rocky Mountain News. It is the world's biggest telegraph news agency.

THE ROCKY MOUNTAIN NEWS
Colorado's First Newspaper

CITY EDITION

VOL. LXVIII: NO. 161 — DENVER, COLO., FRIDAY, JUNE 10, 1927—24 PAGES — PRICE 2 CENTS

STATE SENATOR BOGDON IS SLAIN

Prominent Colorado Solon Shot to Death in Room With Woman

HUSBAND OF MATRON RUSHES INTO APARTMENT, KILLS VICTIM, NOTIFIES POLICE AND FLEES

Joseph Minter Fires Bullet Thru Lawyer's Chest Near Heart; Body, Partly Clad, Is Found on Floor; Assailant Was Seen Lurking at Door of Death House

BY HARVEY T. SETHMAN

STATE SENATOR ALBERT E. BOGDON was shot to death at 9:45 p. m. Thursday in the apartment of Mrs. Helen Minter in the Airose apartments, 1951 Lincoln st.

Police are searching for Joseph Minter, who fled from the apartment immediately after the shooting. The slayer himself called the police before disappearing.

When police arrived Bogdon was dead, lying on the kitchen floor of the little apartment, only partially clad. Mrs. Minter, who had been living at the apartment under the name of Brandenburg, was in hysterics.

The Minters had been separated for some time, according to police.

Ed Kirkham, proprietor of the Astor hotel, 1960 Broadway, abutting the Airose hotel, told police that a man answering Minter's description rented a room late Wednesday morning under the name of R. V. Mandell.

The room was so situated that actions of occupants in the Minter apartment could be plainly observed. The shade [illegible] police entered the room. They are working on the theory that Minter took the room, and watched Bogdon enter his wife's apartment. Up to 11:15 p. m. Thursday, the occupant of the room had not returned.

Minter Seen Listening at Apartment Door

Frank L. Riley, of the Airose, a Littleton druggist, arrived at his apartment at 9:15 p. m., and after the shooting told police he saw the slayer listening at the Minter apartment door.

"There's a man in there with my wife," Riley quoted the man as saying.

Riley, thinking it a joke, entered his own apartment.

A moment later, he and other residents heard a crash.

That was the slayer breaking down the locked apartment door.

Then three shots—and a man's voice called:

"Help! Call a doctor, call the police, call the coroner."

Riley rushed into the hall. He saw the slayer standing in front of the Minter apartment, and the slayer called to him:

"Come. Hurry. I have just shot that man. I think I killed him."

Riley followed the slayer into the apartment, and saw Bogdon lying on the kitchen floor. Mrs. Minter was weeping.

"Oh, God, can't you do something for him," was all she said.

"I looked at the body, and turned it over to see where the bullet had entered," Riley told police. "I saw in a moment that it was all over, and I told the man so.

"He went out into the hall right away and used the public phone. He called police, asking for a surgeon, and also for the coroner. Before I left the apartment, he had disappeared."

Bullet Pierced Bogdon's Body Below Heart

Police Chief Reed was with the first officers at the scene.

There were two bullet holes in the wall of the bedroom. One of these passed clear thru the wall into an adjoining apartment, that of Mrs. Irene Vickery, and crashed into a Victrola. The other bullet imbedded itself in the outer wall of the bedroom halted by the bricks.

There were no signs of a struggle.

As police re-created the crime, the shots are believed to have been fired from the small entry hallway of the apartment, into the bedroom. Bogdon is believed to have been standing facing the door, as the only wound found by Deputy Coroner George Bostwick was in Bogdon's chest, just below the heart.

Two shots evidently passed very close to Bogdon, but missed him, causing the holes found in the walls.

After being shot, Bogdon is believed to have staggered into the kitchen, a few feet away, and to have fallen there in the position Riley found him.

Crowd Flocks to Scene of Shooting

A few minutes after the shooting, the Airose was a scene of the wildest chaos. Almost every resident of the apartment house was at home, and most of them were out in the hall before the police arrived. Police said they were greatly hampered by the crowds, not only of apartment residents, but crowds who thronged in from the street.

Detective M. D. Corney was in charge of the preliminary investigation. He at once called Coroner Bostwick, and officers of the identification bureau, who photographed the scene from every angle.

Bogdon was lying in a pool of his own blood, and police at first believed he had been shot several times. Blood covered

(Continued on Page 2, Column 1.)

PRINCIPAL IN TRIANGLE SLAYING AND HIS WIDOW

ALBERT E. BOGDON, Denver attorney and state senator, who was killed Thursday night, and his widow, Mrs. Adele Bogdon. Mrs. Bogdon also is a practicing attorney. Bogdon was shot to death in the apartment of Mrs. Joseph Minter, 1951 Lincoln st. Police are searching for Mrs. Minter's [illegible]

MRS. BOGDON'S LOVE TRIUMPHS OVER DEATH AND INFIDELITY

Widow of Slain Senator Visits Scene of Shooting, Then Collapses

BY MARY COYLE

LOVE triumphed Thursday night—over death and infidelity.

A few moments after a clanging ambulance had rolled away from an apartment house at 1951 Lincoln st., bearing the body of State Senator Albert E. Bogdon, a small brown-eyed woman crept noiselessly in.

She walked into apartment No. 7 and stood for a moment gazing quietly at the blood-covered floors—Albert Bogdon's death chamber.

"I am Albert Bogdon's wife," she told Officer Madigan. "What have they done with him?"

"He's gone to the hospital, madam," said Officer Madigan kindly.

"No," she repeated, "I feel sure that he is dead."

"Don't hesitate to tell me. I have known all about this affair all along. Please tell me everything. I love him in spite of it and wish to go to his side."

Tribute to Wife

Silence reigned in the tiny apartment, crowded to overflowing with policemen, detectives and spectators aroused by the shooting. A silence that was full of awe and wonder—mute tribute to the courage and fineness of a slim, brown eyed little woman who is facing the greatest tragedy of her life.

The officers, fearing she would collapse, placated her with the news that her husband had been wounded not killed.

She walked from the room, thru the corridor and out into the street.

The cries of the newsboys yelling "State Senator Albert E. Bogdon murdered" were filling the air.

She gave a startled cry, of "Oh, Albert," and fell into a limp heap on the pavement.

Adele Bogdon is a strange contrast to the plump little Helen Brandenburg.

Woman of Strength

Adele Bogdon is a woman of strength and integrity—the kind who rates constancy above pleasure and love above all else.

She is a slight, almost girlish figure, dressed modishly, but conservatively—her brown hair curling slightly and her mouth a small faint line of warm rose.

At the Bogdon family home, 3103 W. 38th ave., a curly-haired baby girl, Violet Bogdon, 7, slept soundly in her nursery, a rosy-cheeked doll flung at the foot of her little white bed. She had gone to bed at 9 o'clock, one-half hour before her father's death.

Mrs. Bogdon was notified over the telephone by police that her husband had been injured. The call came a few moments after the shooting. She called to a neighbor to care for her little girl, jumped into a car and rushed to the Lincoln apartment.

Mrs. Bogdon One Of Few Women Lawyers in City

Matron Passed Colorado Bar Examination With High Honors in Aug., 1925

Mrs. Adele E. Bogdon, widow of Senator Albert E. Bogdon, is one of Denver's few practicing women attorneys.

Passing the Colorado state bar examination with an average of 80 on her first attempt, Aug. 28, 1925, Mrs. Bogdon was given her oath and was formally admitted to the bar by the Colorado supreme court Sept. 14 of the same year.

Mrs. Bogdon ranked 12th in the class of 83 applicants for admission to the bar, being only seven points behind first place in the examination.

A romance of the Washington College of Law in Washington, D. C. culminated in the marriage of Mr. and Mrs. Bogdon in Washington in 1917. Mrs. Bogdon, then Miss Adele E. Fowler, studied for two years in the Washington college of law.

She completed her study under her husband and Henry E. May, now city attorney.

She has been associated with her husband, carrying on the active practice of her profession in addition to her duties as mother of a 7-year-old daughter.

Will Rogers Wires—

BEVERLY HILLS, Calif., June 9.—There are two types of men in the world that I feel sincerely sorry for. One is the fellow that thinks he "knows women," and the other is the one that is always saying, "I know the Mississippi river."

The bolsheviks used to sponsor bomb throwing.

That's when they were doing the throwing. Now that they are on the receiving end, it's inhumane. Yours,

The Mayor on the job, WILL.

P. S.—Will Hays is here supervising production and divorces.

HELEN MINTER PACES JAIL CELL

Blond Woman in Bogdon Slaying Hides Face From Visitors

BY HELEN BLACK

Fear and shame clutch so tightly the heart of Mrs. Helen Minter, that the sight of a human being is unbearable.

The type that gentlemen prefer—round, soft and of the cuddly build, Mrs. Minter is being held at the city jail for investigation in connection with the murder of State Senator Albert E. Bogdon, Thursday night.

Frantically she paces up and down the matron's quarters or falls in a strained position for a moment on the bed. With frenzied effort she tries to bury her head in her chest or covers it completely with a white rag provided by the matron.

Sobs Hysterically

Only incoherent words escaped her lips and the hysterical sobbing seemed never to cease save to be replaced by a wailing, "Oh, Oh," as she crumbled in a heap or jumped suddenly up to begin again the pacing.

"What do they want me for?" was her piteous inquiry as the detectives lead her from the matrons quarters to the little room leading to that of the captain of detectives.

When told that she would merely be asked a few questions when the witnesses had been examined she exclaimed, "There were no witnesses!" and fell back into the crying.

"Not All Night!"

She seems unable to comprehend what is going on about her. The only thing that matters is that her face must never be shown. Nothing would induce her to remove her hat and she seemed not to realize that she would remain in the jail all night.

When assured that she would have a rest and be away from the confusion when under the matrons' care she screamed, "Not all night, Oh my, not all night."

Woman Plans to Fly From New York to Rome

United Press.

NEW YORK, June 9.—Miss Nuba Phillips, a New York woman flier, arose before the meeting of American aces at the Hotel Astor Thursday night and announced her intention of flying from New York to Rome and Vienna in the near future. She is a protege of Maj. Gen. William Haskell, whom she first met in Russia during his relief work in that country.

BOGDON'S WAS VARIED CAREER

Commenced Livelihood as a Magician, Served in Navy and in State Senate

Senator Albert E. Bogdon, magician, attorney and politician, had been a resident of Denver for more than seven years.

Born in Mahanoy City, Pa., Feb. 18, 1891, Bogdon spent many of the early years of his life on the stage. The stage had had a natural attraction for many members of the Bogdon family, and young Albert early became successful in the profession.

He spent several years traveling on the Keith vaudeville circuit as a magician and filled many engagements abroad during his early life.

He was graduated from the Washington College of Law, Washington, D. C., with an LL. B. degree.

Following his graduation, Bogdon served in the office of the judge advocate general of the navy. During the World war, he was an ensign in the navy.

Represented Tramway

At the close of hostilities he went to Los Angeles, where his mother, his step-father and a sister are living.

Bogdon was an assistant attorney for the Denver Tramway Co., and was associated in 1924 with Attorney John C. Vivian. He was at the time of his death, a law partner of Henry E. May, city attorney.

Bogdon was elected state senator on the Republican ticket in 1924, as a Ku Klux Klan candidate, at the time Dr. John Galen Locke and the klan swept Governor Morley and virtually an entire klan ticket into office.

Was Active in Klan

Bogdon served in the 25th and 26th general assemblies. His term would have expired with the fall election of 1928.

He had for years been prominent in the klan, and at the time of the internal rift in the organization, became one of the national attorneys for the organization. He held that post until recently. He was one of the klan officials who stayed with the klan, while those of Dr. Locke's faction seceded and formed the Minute Men of America.

In the 26th general assembly, Bogdon served as chairman of the committees on the City and County of Denver, corporations and enrollment. He was a member of committees on insurance, judiciary, military affairs and reapportionment.

The district judges, sitting en banc, appointed Bogdon a member of the city civil service commission on Jan. 17, 1925, to succeed Henry May, who had been named city attorney by Mayor Stapleton.

CAPITAL READY TO OVERWHELM COL. LINDBERGH

Social Crowd That Snubs President's Reception Scrambles For Tickets to Flier's Event

BY RAYMOND CLAPPER
United Press Staff Correspondent

WASHINGTON, June 9.—This cold, hard-boiled city, which snickers at the little faults of the president and looks with fishy eye on all heroes, is prepared to break all precedent and take Colonel Lindbergh to its heart at 100 per cent face value. If the Memphis keeps up her speed, Lindbergh should come down the gangplank at Washington navy yard about 11 a. m. Saturday, the center of the most genuine outpouring of honor and affection that has been visited upon a returning hero within memory.

It will be a tribute not only from the half million or so persons who will see him in the flesh but also of the millions of Americans in every corner of the land who will be listening in on the greatest radio hookup ever arranged.

Capital All Set

All the superlatives of a circus press agent are feeble to describe the welcome that is waiting. There are outward evidences everywhere in Washington, the flags which line the streets, the stands being erected on the tremendous green around the Washington, the pictures of Lindbergh that crowd merchandise out of show windows, the arrangements for the huge reception to be given by the National Press club whose 8,000 tickets are far inadequate to meet the demand, the gathering of celebrities from all corners of the country and the arrangement of a program of the most simplicity and dignity possible.

But there is something more to the Lindbergh reception than these theatrics. You get hints of it in snatches of conversation on the sidewalks and in street cars, in the thousands of letters and telegrams coming in. His letters will have been hauled by the truckload.

Tell Real Tribute

Telegraph wires are crowded to capacity with telegrams. This, rather than the erection of grandstands, tell something of the real tribute that America is about to pay to the boy aboard the Memphis.

It is not the regular hubbub that every four years ushers in a presidential inauguration and those other formalities which Washington considers as part of its routine incidental to being the nation's capital. Aristocrats who scoff at White House receptions because they are so common and turn their invitations over to their servants are begging for tickets to the few receptions for Lindbergh. This welcome for Lindbergh is a labor of admiration.

For Washington, and probably for the nation, this young colonel who three weeks ago was just a foolhardy kid defying death alone, is now the spirit of America—the clean, sensible, modest youth, daring but also equipped with skill and knowledge and who knows how to stand success—he is what all would like to be and thru him the nation honors its own ideal. He is for us what the Prince of Wales is to England, and something more.

Well, he is in for it whether he wants it or not. Just one moment [illegible]

(Continued on Page [illegible], Column 8)

San Luis Fighters Face Most Serious Blaze of Years

20 Men From Saguache Spend Night on Firing Line

Special.

SAGUACHE, Colo., June 9.—Men from Salida and Saguache faced the task Thursday night of fighting one of the most serious forest fires in the history of the San Luis valley.

The fire started Thursday afternoon near the old Biedell mining camp and in an hour several hundred acres of forest were being swept by flames.

Twenty men from Saguache, led by Nick Fuson, went to the scene after the first call for help, and expected to remain on the fire front thruout the night.

It was believed here late Thursday night that sufficient men were on hand to control the flames.

The fire is 15 miles south of here, on the Line creek.

THE WEATHER

FRIDAY, JUNE 10, 1927.

(6 P. M. Forecasts.)

Denver and Vicinity—Friday unsettled and cooler, probably local thunder showers; Saturday probably fair.

Colorado—Friday fair west, unsettled and cooler, with local thunder showers east portion; Saturday probably fair.

Wyoming—Friday fair west, unsettled east, probably thunder showers southeast portion; Saturday probably fair, little change in temperature.

New Mexico—Friday and Saturday generally fair, [illegible]

Nebraska—[illegible]

Kansas—Friday mostly fair, cooler; Saturday partly cloudy to cloudy, unsettled in west portion.

Temperatures at Denver (Last 24 Hours)—Highest, [illegible] degrees; lowest, 58 degrees; mean, 68 degrees.

Sun rises 4:[illegible] a. m.; sun sets 7:28 p. m. Moon rises [illegible] p. m.; moon sets 2:[illegible] a. m.

(Complete Weather Report on Page 23.)

ROCKY MT. NEWS BAROMETER — RAIN · UNSETTLED · CLOUDY · FAIR · STORMY

THE NEWS IN SUMMARY

Local

State Senator Albert E. Bogdon slain while visiting woman; slayer, believed to be woman's husband, evades police.

Suit to oust Barry F. Chrysler from city council seat is filed.

Waldman apartments sold for $600,000.

Two automobile accident victims die at General hospital.

Three injured in bus crash near Brighton.

State

Prowler mutilated in Walsenburg miner's "dynamite trap" may die.

State highway bridge at State Bridge, Colo., falls, killing one.

Telegraph

Chamberlin and Levine to fly from Berlin to Vienna at head of triumphal procession Sunday.

Hard-boiled Washington and New York prepare to extend regal welcome to Colonel Lindbergh.

Wisconsin youth kills father and minister.

Slashing by 'gorilla man' on coast may be hoax by actress, police say.

Financial

Hogs make sharp upturn, killing cattle higher, lambs weak, on Denver livestock market.

Selling pressure ends rise in wheat. Denver stock list gains on nervous market.

Sports

[illegible] pitches Bears to [illegible] victory over Des Moines in debut with Denver.

Yankees trounce White Sox third time, 8 to 3.

Nungesser Search Plane Takes Off on Grim Task

HALIFAX, N. S., June 9.—The Jeanne d' Arc, airplane of the Cotton Expedition which is beginning a search for Captains Nungesser and Coli, lost French transatlantic fliers, took off at Quidi Vidi lake, Newfoundland at 5 p.m. Newfoundland time (3:35 p.m. Eastern Daylight saving time.) A search of two weeks for the lost French airmen will be made.

'Shipwreck' Kelly Is Still Up in Air on Flag Pole

United Press.

NEWARK, N. J., June 9. Alvin "Shipwreck" Kelly was still flying at the top of a 30-foot flagpole over an eight-story hotel Thursday. He went up Monday and plans to stay for eight days. His wife was still sitting on the hotel roof looking up at him. Arguments were rife in the streets below about which helpmate was undergoing the greater endurance test.

Front page story of Bogdon's murder – June 10, 1927

After Bogdon's death, Adele had a long and full life. She died in 1994 at the age of 97. She married twice more, outliving both husbands. When she died, she requested to be buried with her first husband, Albert Bogdon, in the same marble-faced mausoleum compartment in Crown Hill Cemetery in Denver. The marble slab over their compartment reads:

ALBERT E. BOGDON

ADELE E. KYER

1897--1994

1891 -- 1927

Bogdon and Adele's mausoleum plaque

INTERNATIONAL CULTURAL CENTER

Just like her father, Sally had grand dreams for her future. One of them was to build an international cultural center, similar to the ashram mountain retreats she had seen while she was staying in India, but one with more of a commercial twist. Living in Denver gave her the opportunity to scout for a location. Close to the end of 1952, she found a perfect location in a rural area outside of Golden, Colorado, not far from Denver. The plot, 7.1 acres, was situated on a gentle slope slowly rising up from the main highway. On the deed, the plot was described as in Jefferson County in Section 8, Township 2, South Range, 71 West. Sally was able to purchase it for only $1,800, with $200 down and with $25 monthly payments at 6 percent.

As she was planning her cultural center, she wrote up a description:

OUTLINE FOR DEVELOPMENT OF MOUNTAIN PROPERTY IN GOLDEN, COLORADO

The nine thousand feet altitude acreage to be developed as a self-paying business venture to include manifold cultural possibilities. To be developed as a center where scholars from every corner of the earth may come, visit for a while and gaze at the sky through the huge observatory to be erected at the peak of the estate. (A telescope has already been donated.) A Library and Study Halls are linked with the Observatory through passages. All facilities are available for astronomers, scientists through the adjoining Lodge with its open air a amphitheater, available for square dancing and entertainment by singing cowboys and cowgirls who also will accompany the guests on the trails.

The Tourist Lodge may be as sumptuous as desired, with the huge outdoor bonfires and the huge fireplace within, surrounded by familiar western mountain decorations for the entertainment of the guests at dinner and drinks. Spacious accommodations may be included here. For those who wish their own homes, a number of smaller guest houses may be erected with large walls of glass looking over the mountains. There would, of course, be a vast stable, where the horses to transport the tourists would be kept.

As for the business interests, these would mainly be carried on along Highway 72, where a lake could be dredged, and a swimming pool for a popular outdoor garden dining place with an attendant Souvenir and Curio Shop, which caters to the tourist, could be placed. Since this road is used to reach Central City (15 miles), and, during the summer, travelers come from everywhere up to this famous resort, the possibilities for making money should not be overlooked. Colored pictures of the surrounding scenery, with art objects made of the native drift wood, acorns, pine cones, holly, etc. as well as minerals, could profitably be sold to the tourists if interestingly developed. A public relations officer would be placed in charge of this as soon as the place was established.

It is a natural spot for a sanitarium also, as there are three natural springs (also a means of revenue, selling the spring water) and could be used for those persons who wanted to recuperate in the mountain air in the summer.

The possibilities are so vast and limitless for developing this property, but somehow, I feel, even though it is generally known, that oil has been found very close there, and probably also, is present on the acreage; we know that gold lies on the surface of the ground and uranium abounds – (I brought samples here in my car and a great mineralogist has taped each sample as a valuable mineral) but even so, I prefer to let those things lie temporarily.

As the years passed, Sally continued working at McQuay-Norris and determinedly paid the $25 monthly mortgage payments on her mountain property. In addition, she found time to moonlight as a baby sitter and do other part-time jobs as they came available. Needless to say, she did not accumulate enough money to build her cultural center.

However, the cultural center plans continued to occupy her thoughts. In the spring of 1955, she was able to interest an engineer friend of hers from India to visit Denver and give her an evaluation of her unimproved property. This was T. S. Chathunny, who at that time was the Superintending Engineer of Irrigation Projects of all of Trichur, India. Trichur today is called Thrissur, an important city in Kerala State, in southwest India. Mr. Chathunny visited in late June or early July of 1955, while Sally was living in an apartment in the Baker Hotel in downtown Denver. He may have stayed in the same hotel where Sally had an apartment. Long after his trip to Denver, he wrote a letter to Sally, in April 1956, to ask how she was doing in general. In one part of the letter, he fondly recalls the trip to the property site:

> **How about your Rocky Mountain Estate. Have you started building your Ashram there? How I wish to see that beautiful and romantic place again.**

Sally was well-prepared for his visit. She had gotten her driver's license, and she even purchased a car to make the short trips with Mr. Chathunny to the property. This visit and her association with Mr. Chathunny may have been the reason she was fired by McQuay-Norris. Sally, in her naivité, completely forgot that she was living in extremely conservative and racist Denver. Her distinguished visitor from Southern India, Mr. Chathunny, had dark skin, and, as far as the Denverites were concerned, he was just another Negro man. Sally, who was a world traveler and who had actually lived in India for a short while, was truly "color-blind," and she only saw Mr. Chathunny as a dear friend. She probably hugged him publicly to greet him and may even have innocently kissed him on the cheek at times, which was, in Denver, a true social transgression. Sally felt that the "word" must have gotten around that she was "dating" a black man.

Very soon after Mr. Chathunny's visit, she got a termination notice at work. The "excuse" was that the company was replacing her position with a man. Sally was fired, but with a velvet glove, from a company in which she had been happily employed for five years. This all happened in mid-July, but she was able to stay on in her job until the end of July. Before she left, she asked for a letter of recommendation. It is dated July 19, 1955 and is from her immediate boss, Mr. A. B. Ball, the Factory Branch Manager, who wrote:

> **To Whom It May Concern:**
>
> **Due to a change in business conditions, the Company feels that it is to their advantage to replace Sallie Phipps Harned in the Denver Branch.**
>
> **Miss Harned's ability as a secretary has been entirely satisfactory during the five year period she had been with the Company.**

In addition to this letter, she asked for other letters of recommendation from the part-time employers where she had recently worked, who also gave her positive comments. J. Wasser of the Approved Baby Sitters Service, 3335 Olive Street, wrote on August 1, 1955:

> **Sallie Harned has worked through our Service since December, 1954. All reports from our clients regarding Miss Harned have been excellent. She has been very trustworthy and reliable in our own contact with her, is very conscientious, and handles situations intelligently.**
>
> **We recommend Miss Harned most highly in any work which she might undertake.**

The Baker Hotel, where she was living at the time, was also a part-time employer. R. I. Sheldon, the manager of the hotel, wrote the following on August 2, 1955:

> **Sally Harned has been both a guest and employee at the Baker Hotel for several months, and we have found her to be not only a pleasant guest but also an efficient employee.**
>
> **We would highly recommend her for any position for which she may apply.**

SALLY DECIDES TO LEAVE DENVER FOR NEW YORK

Having suddenly lost her job, Sally knew she had to make a quick decision about her immediate future. Should she stay in racist Denver or move to another city? She knew the answer: There could be no place for her to feel truly comfortable other than New York City.

She still had her small piece of land in Golden where she was planning to build an international cultural center. However, rather than sell, she continued her small monthly payments and kept the land as an investment property. Years later, she was able to sell it for well over $12,000, making a considerable profit.

Now, of course, she needed a new job, and again she immediately found one, this time as the fund-raising director of small-town amateur talent shows. Redpath-Horner Company recruited talent show directors in ads placed in *Billboard* magazine, such as the one published on November 27, 1954:

> **DIRECTOR, OLD REDPATH-HORNER Chautauqua organization. Openings for women, 23-50; direct pre-arranged local talent benefit shows, small towns. Free to travel. Hotel, meals, transportation paid plus $200-$400 monthly. Write Etta Wilson, 3419 Broadway, Kansas City 11, Mo.**

The following magazine article, *VFW Magazine* (the magazine for the Veterans of Foreign Wars), published in July 1955, was found in Sally's personal archives and describes in detail her new work:

> **There's Fun In This – Fund Raising Stunt**
>
> **With An Audience Of Friends And Relatives – Your Home Talent Show Is A Sure-Fire Box Office Hit**

By Bryan R. Horner, as told to Henry C. Sivewright

> Bryan R. Horner is the president of Redpath-Horner, 3419 Broadway, Kansas City, Mo., a company that has been producing and managing both amateur and professional talent for nearly 50 years. The business was founded by Mr. Horner's father, Charles F. Horner, who was one of the foremost operators of the old Chautauqua show circuits that flourished throughout rural America in the early years of the century. Featuring varied programs of music, comedy, drama, education and politics, the Chautauqua reigned for many years as one of the most popular forms of entertainment for millions of people. It was one of the great influences in the development of our American culture.—The Editor.

"On stage," the director shouts. "House lights off! Stage lights on!" The hubbub out front and back stage subsides into hushed silence. Chorus girls, making last minute adjustments in costumes and make-up, stand ready to enter on cue. Actors take a final quick look at the script. The curtain rolls back, and the show begins!

No, this isn't Broadway or a scene from a big Hollywood musical. The locale is Hometown, U.S.A. For this is a typical hometown amateur variety show, a local production featuring just about all the home-grown talent available. It happens every week in small cities and towns all over the country.

The production of an amateur show affords one of the most satisfactory methods there is of combining fun with a profit making activity. For this reason, it is an ideal project for V.F.W. Posts, Auxiliaries and other organizations seeking means of raising funds for various worthwhile civic programs.

Too many fund raising plans fall short of expectations; principally because the financial risk is too great and the guarantee of success too slim. That an amateur show can produce a fair reward for the time and effort required has been proven through the years in hundreds of communities. Of course, as in any other endeavor, the profits vary, but in show business, perhaps more than in any other, the old adage that "you get out if it what you put in" fits pretty well.

Organizing a local talent show, complete with singers, dancers, specialty acts, "meller-dramer" and what have you, is a refreshing and stimulating experience. People tend to get a little tired of spectator sports and the ready-made entertainment on television screens and in the movie houses. The chance to take part in a real-live stage show offers an exciting means of self-expression, an opportunity found all too infrequently in modern life.

The producers of an amateur variety show may be surprised to find plenty of eager young would-be actors and entertainers right in their own back yards, but they certainly won't be sorry. There's a good deal of

theatrical "ham" in all of us, and while many citizens may take part in a show because of a sense of civic duty, the majority simply want to have fun. Most of them soon get "grease paint" in their blood and thoroughly enjoy every minute before the footlights. No one knows how many stars of the entertainment world have appeared in home talent shows, but it is quite likely that most of them faced their first audience in an amateur production.

Although it is entirely possible to produce an amateur show with no outside help, it is not often practical. The many details involved – procuring scripts, direction, casting, costumes, make-up, etc. – usually necessitate the services of experienced people who are familiar with every phase of the business. Fortunately, because of the demand, such professional service does exist. It is offered on a "wholesale basis" and is made available at nominal cost through large volume operation.

Several organizations now offer management services in the amateur theatrical field. Their usual methods of making contacts is through booking representatives who travel from town to town making the arrangements for shows to be staged. Information on these professional companies can probably be obtained from the following sources in the community: the public library; English teachers or dramatic coaches in schools; the Chamber of Commerce. Those interested may also write to *Billboard* Magazine, Cincinnati, Ohio, for further details.

The most important factor in the success of an amateur theatrical production is the trained director. This is usually a woman who combines all the qualifications of a business woman, a diplomat, and a dramatic coach. She is thoroughly experienced in the procedures which make for success. The director stays in the community about two weeks, arriving 10 or 12 days before the start of the show, which is held on two successive nights.

People who have seen one of these capable directors in action often wonder how she can accomplish so much in so short a time. It is simply because she knows her job and is working with a positive system, one that has been successfully formulated through the production of thousands of amateur shows.

It is amazing how the end results in amateur theatricals almost invariably give the impression of much longer preparation. This is due to know-how and effective planning on the part of the director. With only two weeks to rehearse, she places the emphasis on simplicity and coordination. To ease her task, somewhat, the shows selected are virtually "actor-proof"; that is, the assigned roles require a minimum of memorization and intricate maneuvers on stage.

Not only does the director conduct rehearsals of the cast, but she also plans and carries out all publicity and promotional activities, attends to all business matters, and organizes the advance ticket campaign.

"The success of our show was due to the very fine director, Miss Mollie Kinsey," wrote Commander E. R. Reasoner, Post 4244, Belmond, Iowa, in a letter to Redpath-Horner recently. "You can be proud of the work she has

done in Belmond. She started working on our show the minute she came to town, and there was no limit to the hours she worked each day."

The prospect of seeing friends and neighbors, and often dignified civic leaders in incongruous roles, on a stage is irresistible. It always assures a capacity audience. In one town, recently, the newspaper editor and a prominent business leader, who had been "friendly enemies" for years, took part in a wedding skit, one as the bride and the other as the broom. It brought down the house. In another community, the Methodist minister played "Toby," a red-headed, slow-witted clown, who is not as dumb as he looks.

One of the attractive features about producing a home talent show, professionally directed, is that there need be no financial risk or guarantee on the part of the local organization. Hundreds of V.F.W. Posts and Auxiliaries have found amateur theatricals to be the answer to their fund-raising problems. One of the attractive features about producing a home talent show, professionally directed, is that there need be no financial risk or guarantee on the part of the local organization. Hundreds of V.F.W. Posts and Auxiliaries have found amateur theatricals to be the answer to their fund-raising problems. Furthermore, they are a definite contribution to the social and cultural life of the community. The sponsoring organization gains not only in prestige and good will, but also stimulates the interest of its own members.

The recent experience of Post 8317, Benton, Pa., in producing a home talent show is typical. With the aid of a professional director, the Post presented "Funnybone Follies," an effort that had the audience rolling in the aisles from start to finish. Children had a big part in the production. A pantomime of "Raggedy Ann's" birthday party featured dozens of talented youngsters. Boy and Girl Scouts of the community appeared in another bit. A number in which Hollywood and TV personalities were mimicked by local wags was the hit of the evening, however. As its share of the proceeds, Post 8317 received $1,013.00, quite a substantial sum for four hours of fun and frolic.

Talent shows do well even in the smallest communities. The Auxiliary to Post 4633 in Hampden, Maine, a village of only 300 persons, realized a profit of nearly $900.00 from a show sponsored several months ago. In Manchester, Vermont, Post 6471 made $781.00 with its amateur talent production. Reports from all sections of the country indicate that such successes are the rule rather than the exception.

Yes, there's a lot of fun in producing an amateur talent show, and a lot of satisfaction. It's a type of activity that develops community spirit; bringing together people with different ideas and different interests for the betterment of the community as a whole. And, since most projects, when utilizing the services of professional helpers, are smoothly geared to the financial needs of the sponsoring organization, the process of fund-raising is made practically painless.

There's Fun in This -- Fund Raising Stunt

BY BRYAN R. HORNER
As Told to Henry C. Sivewright

WITH AN AUDIENCE OF FRIENDS AND RELATIVES—YOUR HOME TALENT SHOW IS A SURE-FIRE BOX OFFICE HIT

Bryan R. Horner

• Bryan R. Horner is the president of Redpath-Horner, 3419 Broadway, Kansas City, Mo., a company that has been producing and managing both amateur and professional talent for nearly 50 years. The business was founded by Mr. Horner's father, Charles F. Horner, who was one of the foremost operators of the old Chautauqua show circuits that flourished throughout rural America in the early years of the century. Featuring varied programs of music, comedy, drama, education and politics, the Chautauqua reigned for many years as one of the most popular forms of entertainment for millions of people. It was one of the great influences in the development of our American culture.—The Editor

"ON STAGE," the director shouts. "House lights off! Stage lights on!"

The hubbub out front and back stage subsides into hushed silence. Chorus girls, making last minute adjustments in costumes and make-up, stand ready to enter on cue. Actors take a final quick look at the script. The curtain rolls back and the show begins!

No, this isn't Broadway or a scene from a big Hollywood musical. The locale is Hometown, U.S.A. For this is a typical hometown amateur variety show, a local production featuring just about all the home-grown talent available. It happens every week in small cities and towns all over the country.

The production of an amateur show affords one of the most satisfactory methods there is of combining fun with a profit making activity. For this reason it is an ideal project for V.F.W. Posts, Auxiliaries and other organizations seeking means of raising funds for various worthwhile civic programs.

Too many fund raising plans fall short of expectations; principally because the financial risk is too great and the guarantee of success too slim. That an amateur show can produce a fair reward for the time and effort required has been proven through the years in hundreds of communities. Of course, as in any other endeavor, the profits vary, but in show business, perhaps more than in any other, the old adage that "you get out of it what you put in" fits pretty well.

Organizing a local talent show, complete with singers, dancers, specialty acts, "meller-dramer" and what have you, is a refreshing and stimulating experience. People tend to get a little tired of spectator sports and the ready-made entertainment on television screens and in the movie houses. The chance to take part in a real-live stage show offers an exciting means of self-expression, an opportunity found all too infrequently in modern life.

The producers of an amateur variety show may be surprised to find plenty of eager young would-be actors and entertainers right in their own back yards but they certainly won't be sorry. There's a good deal of theatrical "ham" in all of us, and while many citizens may take part in a show because of a sense of civic duty, the majority simply want to have fun. Most of them soon get "grease paint" in their blood and thoroughly enjoy every minute before the footlights. No one knows how many stars of the entertainment world have appeared in home talent shows, but it is quite likely that most of them faced their first audience in an amateur production.

Although it is entirely possible to produce an amateur show with no outside help, it is not often practical. The many details involved — procuring scripts, direction, casting, costumes, make-up, etc.—usually necessitate the services of experienced people who are familiar with every phase of the business. Fortunately, because of the demand, such a professional service does exist. It is offered on a "wholesale basis," and is made available at nominal cost through large volume operation.

(Continued on page 41)

It's hard to tell who has the most fun at a home talent show —the audience or the performers. And the biggest laughs aren't always in the script. These are scenes at a typical show produced with the aid of a professional director. Funny costumes and weird make-up guarantee an hilarious evening.

***VFW Magazine* article -- 1955**

SALLY EMPLOYED BY REDPATH-HORNER WITH "FUNNYBONE FOLLIES"

Sally's new job required her to go to Kansas City, Missouri, for training at the head office of the Redpath-Horner Company, at 3419 Broadway. This was where all the talent show directors, like Sally, were trained and were later sent out on directorial assignments to towns far afield from Kansas City.

The company was run by Bryan R. Horner (1914-1986), the then 40-year-old son of the founder, Charles F. Horner (1878-1967). His business associate was Barbara Lee Brooks. Together, Horner and Brooks wrote a script, called "Funnybone Follies," for the directors to use wherever they were sent. They copyrighted the script in August 1954, and it served as the guide for all the directors to follow in casting, directing, and producing. "Funnybone Follies" was a combination of musical revue, variety show, and local talent show, and, depending on the talent assembled, the running time of the "Follies" was usually about two hours. Directors were sent out to small towns all over the United States and into Canada. The heyday of "Funnybone Follies" was late 1954 to late 1956.

All the directors needed to have a car (Sally had already purchased one in Denver) and had to be able to drive long distances to the towns to which they were assigned. Sally usually arrived in the town two weeks before the performances, which were generally scheduled for two successive nights. During those two weeks, she had to arrange for the rehearsal and performance spaces, cast and rehearse the shows with available amateur local talent, and carry out all publicity and ticket sale campaigns. It was a grueling schedule, requiring much organizational ability, and, as the previous article says, requiring the director to be a combination of "business woman, diplomat, and dramatic coach." After the final performance, she then had to move on to her next two-week assignment, sometimes a long drive to the next town, and the routine would start all over again.

After Sally's training in Kansas City throughout August 1955, she was sent out in early September on her first assignment to Sigourney, Iowa, about 250 miles away, about a 4½ hour drive by car from the head office. During the next three months, she did five two-week assignments in a row, ending in Hermitage, Arkansas, on November 23. During this three-month period, Sally chose not to use her real name. Instead of Sallie Phipps Harned, she called herself Sallie Nonah Enayah, a name she felt had numerological advantages and, at the same time, a name she felt would allow her to keep a low show business profile.

The following summarizes her five small-town directorial assignments:

September 13-14 -- Sigourney, Iowa -- V.F.W. Post 2308 & Ladies Auxiliary -- Memorial Hall

September 27-28 -- Harlan, Iowa -- Harlan Kiwanis Club -- Harlan High School Auditorium

October 18-19 -- Petersburg, Illinois -- V.F.W. Post 6871 & Auxiliary for the benefit of the P.T.A. Milk Fund -- Petersburg Harris High School Gymnasium

November 4-5 -- Elkins, Arkansas -- Elkins School -- Elkins School Gymnasium

November 21, 23 -- Hermitage, Arkansas -- P.T.A. -- Hermitage School Cafetorium

Today, "Funnybone Follies" is considerably dated. The script incorporated impersonations of then-familiar film and television personalities of the mid-1950s, such as Dean Martin and Jerry Lewis, Doris Day, Roy Rogers and Dale Evans, Ma and Pa Kettle, Grace Kelly, and George Gobel. The script included a brief old-fashioned melodrama where everyone gets a chance to hiss the villain. There was an all-male wedding, drag always being popular with audiences. And, there was ample opportunity for patriotic and specialty acts. The following is an article that appeared in the *Harlan Tribune*, September 30, 1955, which gives a summary of the Harlan, Iowa, September 27-28 shows, examples of a typical "Funnybone Follies":

Small Crowd Liked Funnybone Follies
Skits, Specialties, Drama, Burlesque By Local Talent
by Elsie Graves

"Funnybone Follies," a review of specialty acts, skits, drama, and burlesque, played to a sparse but appreciative audience Tuesday and Wednesday nights to the high school auditorium. The cast of approximately 100 persons includes local talent selected by members of the Harlan Kiwanis club, which sponsored the show.

The 2½ hour show was a "take-off" on a combination of several TV shows, with the call letters, F.U.N. It features such TV performers as George Gobel (Monty Pitner), Grace Kelly (Jane Graves), Dean Martin (George Schack), Jerry Lewis (Forrest Petersen), Roy Rogers (Wayne Bauerle), Dale Evans (Prudence Fredericksen), and Doris Day (Patty Jo Jacobsen). Also Ma and Pa Kettle (Carolyn Larsen and Joe Moran).

The opening feature had a toyland setting with third grade pupils dressed as dolls. Mrs. Elmer Norgaard was the "Magic Lady" who narrated the story of "Raggedy Ann's Birthday Party." Suzanne Pundmann played the part of Raggedy Ann and Richard Lorenzen of Raggedy Andy. Entertainers were baton twirlers, song and tap dancers and the "No Time Four" barbershop quartet.

Striking a serious note with a patriotic theme, the second part of the show was a tribute to the "Stars and Stripes," led by the Rev. Clifford Atkinson. Girl scouts and boy scouts took part in the ceremonial with audience participation, in patriotic songs. Closing this portion of the show was an excellent tap dance number by talented Bernice Appel.

Monty Pitner, dramatic instructor at the high school, pepped up the show with his surprise performance of acrobatic dancing opening the third portion, "Stars on Parade." His splendid act, and impersonation of George Gobel in a quiz program, gave it a professional touch. Jane Graves as Grace Kelly was his able assistant on the Gobel show.

Don Haley, with his "Commercial," delighted the audience. He was teamed with Mrs. Milford Rold in this comedy skit.

Also in the "Stars on Parade" were the Ma and Pa Kettle skit and the Martin and Lewis act that had the audience roaring with laughter. The top performance in this portion of the show was the old fashioned "meller

drammer," a take-off of the "Snicker Flicker" silent movies with Monty Pitner providing the patter.

"Round-Up Time," the fourth portion of the show, featured Roy Rogers and Dale Evans (Wayne Bauerle and Mrs. Fredericksen) in western costume, singing pantomime songs and directing the show. The highlight of their show was the novelty dance by talented Barbara Paulsen.

The fifth portion of the show was "Here Comes The Bride," a comedy skit with an all-male cast. The wind-up after the woman-less wedding, was a burlesque show staged by Mr. Pitner. The "Dimpled Darlings of "Broadway" were Charles Summers, Fred Nelson, Robert Rasmussen, Robert Miller, Doug Larsen, John Miller and Darryl Van Duyn. Their performance had the audience almost rolling in the aisles.

"Funnybone Follies" was produced by the Redpath-Horner theatrical company of Kansas City. It was directed by Sallie Nonah Enayah, a representative of the company. Music was furnished by the Harlan high school band directed by W. W. Pundman. Pianist was Jim Polozis.

Vocalists were Patty Jo Jacobsen and Janie Campbell. Tap dancers Bernice Appel, Leah Hervey, Pattie Blum, Lois Blum, Kaleen Petsche, Mary Ellis Petsche.

The chorus girls were Linda Hammes, Mary Lou Knapp, Donna Larson and Karen Haskell.

The barber shop quartet was composed of Leo Koestler, John Smith, Dr. Joseph Spearing and George Schack.

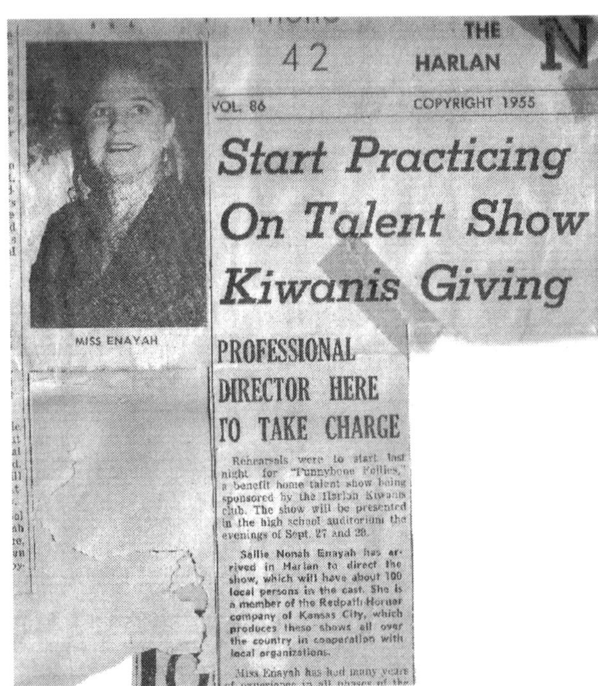

THE HARLAN N

42

VOL. 86 COPYRIGHT 1955

MISS ENAYAH

Start Practicing On Talent Show Kiwanis Giving

PROFESSIONAL DIRECTOR HERE TO TAKE CHARGE

Rehearsals were to start last night for "Funnybone Follies," a benefit home talent show being sponsored by the Harlan Kiwanis club. The show will be presented in the high school auditorium the evenings of Sept. 27 and 28.

Sallie Nonah Enayah has arrived in Harlan to direct the show, which will have about 100 local persons in the cast. She is a member of the Redpath-Horner company of Kansas City, which produces these shows all over the country in cooperation with local organizations.

Miss Enayah has had many years

Sally in the 1955 *Harlan, Iowa News* about her "Funnybone Follies"

"FUNNY BONE FOLLIES" TUES. - SEPT. - 27 & 28

MUSICAL DIRECTOR MR. E.W. PUNDMANN

****

Pianist Jim Polozis

Overture - Harlan High School Band

Cast in the order of their appearance

AMERICAN BEAUTY CHORUS - Linda Hammes, Mary Lou Knapp, Lila Parker, Donna Larson, Karen Haskell

DORIS DAY------------------------------ Patty Jo Jacobsen
MAGIC LADY------------------------------ Darlene Norgaard
RAGGEDY ANN------------------------------ Suzanne Pundmann
RAGGEDY ANDY------------------------------ Richard Lorenzen
TOYS------------------------------ 3rd Grade Elementary Students
TRIBUTE TO FLAG------------------------------ Rev. Cliff Atkinson
TRUE AMERICANS------------------------------Boy Scouts & Girl Scouts
GEORGE GOBEL------------------------------ Monty Pitner
GRACE KELLY------------------------------ Jane Graves
COMMERCIALS------------------------------ Don Haley
MA KETTLE------------------------------ Carolyn Larsen
PA KETTLE------------------------------ Joe Moran
DEAN MARTIN------------------------------ George Schack
JERRY LEWIS------------------------------ Forest Petersen
ROY ROGERS------------------------------ Wayne Bauerle
DALE EVANS------------------------------ Prudence Fredericksen
NELLIE------------------------------ Mrs Rold

SPECIAL ACTS

Leo Kester
Dr. Spearing
Baton Twirlers
Pattie Blum
Lois Blum
Kaleen Petsche
Barber Shop Quartette
Jane Campbell
Barbara Paulsen
Bernice Apple
Charlotte Reise
Twyla Savereide
John Smith

"HERE COMES THE BRIDE"

MRS. FANNIE GOOGLEHEIMER - Aunt of the Bride -- Charles Summers
MR. WILL B. TREMBLIN ----- Groom ------------- Ron Jensen
MR. HEP M. OUT ----------- The Best Man-------- Roger Huffman
MISS WANDA MANN ---------- Jilted Sweetheart -- Fred Nelson
FLOWER GIRL ------------------------------ Bob Rasmussen
BRIDESMAIDS --------------------- Bob Miller & Doug. Larsen
MAID OF HONOR ------------------------------ Bob Hurley
JUSTICE TYE-D-KNOTT ------------------------------ John Miller
MISS DAINTY ANN GRUESOME ------------------------ Darryl Van Duyn

THE DIMPLED DARLINGS OF BROADWAY - Staged by Monty Pitner

The Kiwanis Benefits wish to thank all those who have contributed toward making this show a success.

director - SALLIE NONAH ENAYAH

"Funnybone Follies" program -- 1955

After her last performance of "Funnybone Follies" in Hermitge, Arkansas, on November 23, Sally decided she had had enough of "trouping" for the Redpath-Horner theatrical company. Even though the company paid well, and she was really good at her job, she did not see herself continuing in this grueling work. Fortunately, because of the approaching cold weather, she had a short seasonal break to think about her future. She decided to stick to her original plan and head for New York City to see if she could again make a go of it there. She held off resigning from Redpath-Horner Company just in case New York City did not work out well.

Chapter 7
New York

SALLY RETURNS TO NEW YORK

Sally drove directly from Arkansas to New York City, about 1,300 miles. She arrived in early December and got herself an apartment at 124 East 72nd Street. She quickly sold the car, gaining much-needed funds for living expenses.

Soon after, Sally received two memos from Redpath-Horner describing upcoming plans and the future of the company. It is obvious from the memos that the executives were happy with Sally's work and wanted her and even expected her to continue her directorial work with them:

> **We are working on schedules and are going to send assignments out early, so you will have plenty of time to get ready to start trouping again. We are counting on you, and I know there will be wonderful shows ahead for you in 1956.**

Sally decided she did not want to continue with Redpath-Horner and, instead, stayed in New York. Until the end of her life in early 1978, she never again lived anywhere but in her beloved New York City.

SECRETARIAL WORK IN NEW YORK

According to Sally's memoirs, she attempted to return to show business in New York, but, impatient as always, she gave up when nothing turned up immediately. Although she still had her looks, she was now 44 and no longer right for the ingenue roles that had made her famous.

She returned to secretarial work to make ends meet, the kind of work that was always readily available in New York City. She began her employment by using temporary agencies, and, if the hiring company liked her, she could be kept on longer. An examination of her resumes reveals a varied list of employers: Brown Temporary Agency, British And Irish Railways, Inc., Camp Fire Girls, Inc., Hypo Surgical Supply Corp., Postage Stamp Machine Company, State Insurance Fund, Transportation Vehicles, Inc.

In 1963, after an almost 10-year period of short-term secretarial gigs, Sally found a permanent position at Emerson Television and Radio Company. Her office was located at 14th and Coles Streets in Jersey City, New Jersey. She became the private secretary to Jerome Roth, the company's National Service Manager. Since the late 1950s, she had been living in a residence hotel called the St. George Hotel in Brooklyn Heights, immediately across the East River from Wall Street. Unfortunately, getting to her new job involved a two-fare commute, first by subway from Brooklyn to Manhattan and then by bus from the Port Authority Bus Terminal to Jersey City. She stayed with Emerson until she resigned on June 1, 1973, after having decided to take an early retirement at age 62.

Sally, head shot by Kesslere again, 1956

While she was at Emerson, the company's in-house publication did a feature story on Sally:

> **Sally Phipps-Harned of the Service Department is more than casually interested in electronics as well as people. A film actress from the early age of four, she became curious about the mechanics of radio, motion pictures, and TV. Light particularly interested her and has brought her right into the technological field of electronics.**
>
> **Like us in childhood, she cannot recall much of her playing as a baby star in westerns... What she does remember vividly is lights flashing in her eyes constantly -- huge sun-arc lamps, used today in Hollywood premieres, and, in the daytime outdoors on location, silver papered reflectors.**

Hundreds of technical people were required to film a simple scene which added to her bewilderment as a child. Numerous carpenters, grips, electricians, directors and assistant directors, property men, technical advisors, producers, script girls, cutters, business managers, wardrobe mistresses and designers, makeup artists, hairdressers, as well as the camera men, all of whose attention was directed at the artist while portraying the scene. Before the cameras started rolling, everything was dark on the set. But once production began, so many lights were required that many directors and artists could not stand the glare of the prolonged exposure and had to leave the film industry.

Lighting became even more important as Miss Phipps-Harned graduated to color films. While playing in "None but the Brave" on the Fox lot and appearing as Miss United States in an international beauty pageant, she found that a brilliant blaze of light was required to accentuate the colors of the flags of the various countries and their costumed models in the color segment of the film. Each vehicle required a different lighting pattern of the different black and white productions in which she appeared, her most famous were in the "The High School Hero" and "Why Sailors Go Wrong."

Leaving Hollywood and coming to Broadway, she found an altogether different technique applied in the legitimate theatre in the uproarious Moss Hart/George Kaufman satire on Hollywood (particularly aimed at the talking films) "Once In A Lifetime," in which she appeared as the original ingénue.

Once here in the East, she enrolled at Columbia University and later the University of Pennsylvania. Great strides were being made in electronics both here and abroad. She went to Europe for further studies and acquired secretarial skills at the Gregg Business School. With these skills, she was enabled to travel all around the world and attend universities in the Far East.

Today Miss Phipps-Harned has achieved fulfillment in her studies and has applied them to her work at Emerson. She knows the entertainment world. Now that radio and TV are found in every home, the early films are available to all, as well as any conceivable type of entertainment, educational feature, or cataclysmic world event through Telstar via satellite. She is a real Emerson fan.

SALLY'S FRIENDS

Over the years, Sally made many friends whom she cultivated in person or through correspondence. Those who lived outside New York City frequently came to visit her.

One of them was her best friend since high school, Dorothy Day, who married Jean Charlot in 1939, and by 1946 had four children -- Ann Marie (1940), John (1941), Martin (1944), and Peter (1946). The Charlot family lived in many different places, because Jean became a popular art lecturer and visited many universities. In 1949, a year before Sally left Hawaii, the Charlot family moved to Honolulu after Jean was offered a permanent professorship at the University of Hawaii. Sally, still in Hawaii, found it a great comfort to have her best friend living in the same city.

Dorothy now preferred to call herself "Zohmah," a name given to her by an astrologer, or some mystic, during a visit she and Sally made together in the late 1920s. She never liked the name Dorothy. Zohmah sounded so exotic.

Throughout Sally's early life and before Zohmah married, she and Zohmah often roomed together. Zohmah was with Sally in New York during most of the run of "Once In A Lifetime." For a time, the two of them shared an apartment while Sally lived in London. And Zohmah came to visit Sally during her summer stay with Edithe in Hawaii in 1936. Whenever living apart, Zohmah and Sally were devoted correspondents. Over the years, Zohmah made a number of trips from Honolulu to New York City to visit Sally, and they always relished their visits with each other.

Another close friend who lived out of town and visited Sally in New York City was her former supervisor at the Federal Theatre Project, Harriet B. Meyer. After the closing of the Project, Harriet worked at a number of federal government jobs, which eventually required a move from New York City to Washington, D.C. While there, she developed an interest in Far Eastern art, in particular Chinese, and became quite an expert and collector. Harriet admired Sally very much, particularly Sally's devotion to the study of Sanskrit, Eastern religion, and astrology. Harriet also gave Sally much useful advice about personal finance and about being a woman working in the business world, all of which Sally found extremely helpful.

After Sally left New York City in 1941, she also kept in touch with another former employer, George Maillard Kesslere, the famous New York City portrait photographer of the entertainment world. When she arrived back in New York City in December 1955, he offered to do a series of headshots for Sally, for what turned out to be her short-term attempt to return to show business. Kesslere remained one of Sally's closest friends for many years and, up until she passed away, she often visited him or attended parties at his magnificent townhouse at 131 East 62nd Street.

Another friend was Gustav Davidson (1894-1971) and his wife Mollie, who also lived in Manhattan, at 200 East 36th Street. Davidson, a Polish Jew, came to America as a child. Educated at Columbia University, he became a renowned poet, writer, and publisher. Sally met him in the late 1930s while he was associated with the Federal Writers Project and she was with the Federal Theatre Project. Although his poetry was widely published, his most famous work is *The Dictionary Of Angels*, which came out in 1967. Sally and Davidson remained good friends until his death in 1971.

Sally met another Manhattan friend through her associations with the occult world. This was Rolla Nordic (1898-1995), the professional name of a woman born in Cardiff, Wales. Widowed early in her life, after a marriage to a Norwegian named Berulfsen, Rolla changed her name from Murielle and became a professional reader of Tarot cards and the runic stones. She also became knowledgeable about witchcraft. Furthermore, she published in these areas. *The Tarot Shows The Path*, which came out in 1960, and *Let's Talk About The Tarot*, which came out in 1992, are her most famous publications. She resided at 121 West 72nd Street and lived to the age of 96. Sally's son Robert paid a visit to her only four months before she passed away in 1995, and, at the time, she was in excellent mental and physical health.

SALLY'S FAMILY BACK IN HAWAII

Alfred Harned, Sally's husband, remained bewildered for many months by Sally's desertion. She had suddenly left in August 1950. He tried to track her down from Honolulu, but she remained elusive. After a few years, he gave up and started dating. He soon met a woman he liked and entertained the idea of marrying again. However, he needed first to initiate divorce proceedings against Sally, which he did in 1956, on the grounds of desertion. The divorce became final on August 2, 1956. In the end, he and his girlfriend never got married, but they continued to date for many years. Neither Alfred nor Sally ever remarried.

Alfred Harned, newspaper photo, early 1950s

Edithe, on advice from her son Lane, sold all her Color Art Shops and her house in Waikiki by 1952. Lane failed to foresee and understand the boom in tourism and land prices in Honolulu that were then beginning and continuing to build as Hawaiian statehood approached and was eventually attained in 1959. Lane and his family had already given up on Hawaii by 1949 and had moved back to Los Angeles. After the sale of her house, Edithe went on a travelling spending spree that lasted almost three years, not returning permanently to Hawaii until 1955. Her travels included a European tour, with luxury ocean voyages both to and from, and an American cross-country road trip from Florida to California, on which she picked up a brand new Cadillac Coupe DeVille in Detroit.

Alfred and Sally's children continued their schooling during these years. They both attended Lincoln Elementary School, although two years apart. Maryanna spent her junior high school years at Robert Louis Stevenson Intermediate School and graduated from Theodore Roosevelt High School in 1960. Robert attended Washington Intermediate School and then, for his high school years, he went to Punahou School, a private school, graduating in 1962.

Maryanna, age 16 (1958)

Robert, age 22 (1967)

Both Maryanna and Robert grew up interested in the theater. They also were avid movie fans, especially for musicals. In school activities, they were constantly active in theatricals. Maryanna was particularly talented in performing serious dramatic roles, while Robert excelled in dancing and the lighter comedic roles.

Maryanna also excelled in athletics, especially swimming, diving, and running. She was fearless and had great physical endurance. Anecdotally, when Robert was in the third grade and was sitting in his classroom, he once remembers observing his sister in the school playground hanging upside down on the Jungle Gym and revolving several times and his thinking, "Wow, how courageous! I could never do that! I don't have the nerve."

Maryanna eventually gave up theatrics to become a champion track runner. Her running speed was quickly noted by her high school physical education teacher, who suggested she join one of the women's track and field clubs. Maryanna joined the York XDR Club in 1958, organized by a physician, Dr. Richard You, and a university coach, Moses Ome. Together they sought to revive women's track and field competition in Hawaii, which had been inactive since 1929. Furthermore, the goal for their girls was national success at the upcoming Amateur Athletic Union (AAU) competition in 1959 and international success at the upcoming Olympics in 1960. The Amateur Athletic Union is an organization that works closely with the Olympic movement to prepare athletes for the Olympic Games. The York XDR Club organizers trained the girls on their team very well, and there were several who were selected to compete at the AAU women's track competition to be held in Cleveland, Ohio, on June 27 and 28, 1959. Maryanna was at the top of the list. Although only 16, she already held the women's amateur record time in Hawaii for the 800 meter run at 2:39.1 minutes and the 880 yard run at 2:35.2 minutes.

Honolulu female track team, 1959 (Maryanna, 2nd row, 2nd from left)

SALLY HAS REUNION WITH DAUGHTER

Maryanna's athletic success made possible a reunion with her mother, whom she had not seen in nine years. The reunion was an event that both Maryanna and Sally eagerly anticipated. Ever since Maryanna was eight years old, they had only corresponded by mail and had not even talked with each other on the telephone. Because Cleveland was so close to New York City, it was relatively easy for Sally to get to the competitions and also to celebrate her daughter's 17th birthday, which would fall on June 26, the day before the competitions began.

Unfortunately, the reunion turned out to be both a psychological and physical disaster for Maryanna. Maryanna's life had been conservative, and although she had been interested in the theater, she had no experience with Hollywood and New York glamour and glitz. She was embarrassed by Sally's flamboyant clothes, dramatic make up, and her theatrical affectation of wearing dark glasses all the time. It was a further embarrassment when the other girls on her team started to make fun of Sally.

Then, Sally, accustomed to the clever and novel, arranged a birthday party for Maryanna and her teammates, choosing a watermelon with candles as a birthday cake instead of a normal cake. Typical of teenagers, Maryanna and her teammates found it totally stupid rather than funny and clever, resulting in another embarrassment for Maryanna.

The biggest disappointment of all, however, was the fact that Maryanna got all the way to Cleveland to compete, only to end up not being able to. While in training one day before the track competition, Maryanna pulled a calf muscle and was in agony, not only physically but also emotionally, for the whole competition weekend. When Maryanna said goodbye to Sally after the competition and the visit was over, she went home feeling defeated and disheartened over how she felt about her mother. Maryanna and Sally never saw each other again, but continued a cordial correspondence until the end of Sally's life in early 1978.

Maryanna returned to Hawaii, finished her senior year of high school, and entered the University of Hawaii. She then met her future husband, Bob Funes, and married him in Honolulu in November 1962.

Funes worked for the U.S. Army as a civilian employee and, as a result, he was sent with his family to many different locations, including Okinawa, Japan, and Heidelberg, Germany. Bob and Maryanna, soon after their marriage and influenced by close friends, became converts to Mormonism. Over the next 15 years, they had seven children together: Laura (1963), Jon (1966), Bobette (1968), Lee (1970), Angela (1973), Joylyn (1975), and Bob, Jr. (1977).

Maryanna Harned Sets Track Mark

Maryanna Harned of the York XDR Club returned to competition yesterday and smashed the 800-meter run record as the first phase of the Hawaiian State women's track and field championships got under way at University of Hawaii's Cooke Field.

Miss Harned, who was sidelined the past two months with a leg injury, won the 800-meter open in 2:30.1 to break by nearly six seconds the mark held by Isabelle Gonzalez.

Muriel Strauss of York XDR and Annette Bayne of Kailua also bettered records yesterday.

* * *

MISS BAYNE was a triple winner, capturing the discus, broad jump and shot put in the girls' 14 to 17 years group. She won the shot put with a toss of 35 ft. 11¾ in., topping the old record by 3 ft. 2¼ in.

In the broad jump she leaped 15 ft. 7½ in. to clip the old mark by a half inch.

Miss Strauss won the open broad jump with a leap of 16 ft. 8 in. to take a half inch off the old record.

Puanani McKee of York turned in the fastest time of 8.1s in winning the 60-meter open while Isabelle Gonzalez, also of York, won the 200-meter open in 28.3s.

Results:

[illegible]

Robert Young

MARYANNA HARNED

Maryanna, track champion, in the newspaper -- 1959

Bob Funes and Maryanna on wedding day – 1962

SALLY HAS REUNION WITH SON

While Maryanna was pursuing her athletic activities, Robert was spending his free time performing in school theatricals and in the local Honolulu Community Theatre. During one summer musical production in 1960, when he was 16, Robert met a fellow male dancer who was 11 years older, and they developed a romantic relationship. The relationship continued while Robert attended high school, the University of Hawaii, and during his course work for his master's degree in library science, which he received during the summer of 1967. They left Hawaii together and moved to Washington, D.C., after Robert got his first job as a cataloging librarian at the Library of Congress. When they first arrived, Robert called Sally and heard her voice for the first time in 17 years. Robert arranged a get-together for the three of them in New York City on September 2 at the St. George Hotel.

From this first meeting, Robert and Sally's relationship was completely opposite from hers with Maryanna. They were soul mates from the minute they met. He had an intense interest in film and Broadway history and saw Sally as entertainment history personified. They met frequently, Robert often going up to New York alone. He spent many delightful hours listening to stories about her past experiences, and they particularly enjoyed attending the theater together. He had spent many years in theatrical pursuits, in his case as an actor, singer, and dancer, and saw Sally's eccentricity as positive. Sally, in turn, was totally unfazed by Robert's homosexuality. She had many close gay friends in her life, both past and present. As a result, he visited with her as often as he could, sometimes in New York City and sometimes in Washington, D.C. In mid-August 1968, Robert obtained a position in the University of Pennsylvania Library. When Robert moved to Philadelphia, his partner also came, but with the commute to New York much shorter, and the visits with Sally increasing, their interests diverged and their ten-year relationship deteriorated and soon ended.

Sally, May 1968

SALLY IN A FILM CLIP ON THE *JUDY GARLAND SHOW*

In early 1964, Sally Phipps' recognizability as a celebrity had fallen so low that when a ten-second film clip of her appeared on *The Judy Garland Show* (1963-1964 season), no one on the show knew who she was. According to Coyne Steven Sanders, in his book *Rainbow's End: The Judy Garland Show* (1990), Ken Murray, an actor and filmmaker, was invited on her show four times in January and February 1964 as a guest star. For each episode, he showed different clips of his home movies of Hollywood celebrities taken during the late 1920s through the early 1960s. As the footage was screened on the show, Judy would make her own delightful comments about the stars, most of whom she knew personally. The following is the verbatim commentary between Garland and Murray as they watched the clip in which Sally appeared:

K: Now, I took one of those [tour] buses when I first came out [to Hollywood] and went through the Universal Studio [i.e. Fox Studio]. The minute I got off the bus, I took this picture. I don't know who it was. It looked like a movie star. Who is that?

[At this point, we see Sally in a close up, wearing a shoulder length reddish-blonde wig, with a flaring, tiara-like white cloth headdress. She is smiling, waving hello, and blowing kisses.]

Sally in Ken Murray Hollywood documentary screen shot -- 1927

J: It looks like a movie star.

K: Look at the fellow with her.

[At this point a tall dark-haired actor in ancient Roman costume walks up to Sally and stands next to her, holding her hand. We now see Sally in a full length, billowy, long-sleeved, white dress, with a veil attached to her tiara, and with a lengthy string of pearls around her neck, dressed very much like an ancient Roman patrician woman. With her other hand, Sally continues to blow kisses.]

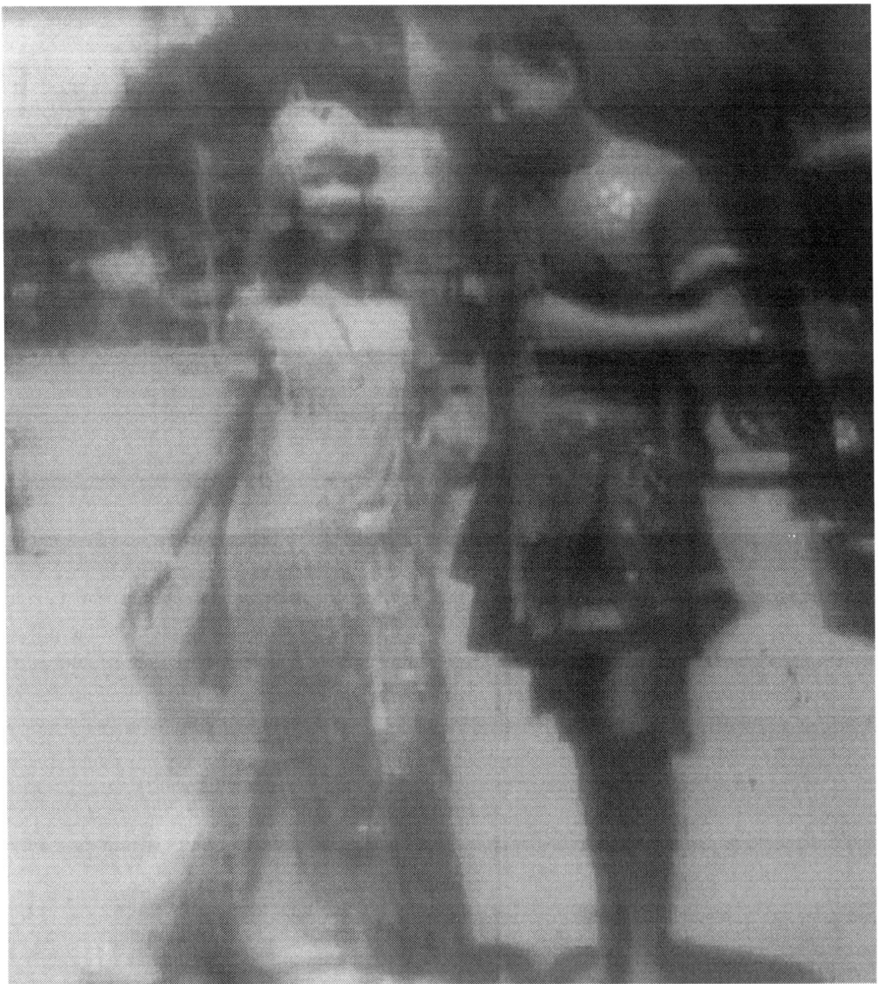

Sally with unknown actor in Ken Murray Hollywood documentary screen shot - 1927

J: It couldn't be Mary Pickford?

K: I don't know who they were. I just took the...

J: It must have been somebody, with that fantastic ... (At this point, the film abruptly cuts to another scene)

This Ken Murray clip, his fourth appearance on *The Judy Garland Show*, is in Episode 22, taped on January 31, 1964 and aired on February 23. In that episode, in addition to Ken Murray, the singer Jack Jones was a special guest.

In 2002, Ken Murray's *Hollywood Home Movies* (with the same clip of Sally) was included as a "Special Bonus Feature!" in the DVD version of the 1963 *Judy Garland, Robert Goulet & Phil Silvers Special.* One day, while watching the DVD, Sally's son Robert recognized the mystery star as Sally. In addition, he noticed that she was wearing a costume from a scene from her 1927 feature film *High School Hero.* According to the scenario of this now-lost film, at one point in the story, the high school Latin class puts on a Roman tragedy. The Roman costumes seen in the Ken Murray clip must have been worn during the Roman tragedy scene, and, on the day that Ken Murray arrived at the Fox studio, Sally and the other Roman-costumed actor were likely serving as greeters for the tour buses.

This clip can also be viewed in Episode 22 (Disc 1) of a 2009 DVD set of 14 complete episodes, entitled *The Judy Garland Show Collection.*

SALLY IS REDISCOVERED

In the 1960s, America began rediscovering silent film in all its aspects – its stars, directors, music -- due to a number of excellent television documentaries and reruns of old films. Film historians tried to contact surviving silent film performers, including Sally, but she was not aware of it, for, by the late 1960s, she was sure that she was forgotten. But she was not.

Robert, who had been living on the East Coast since 1967, grew up quite well-aware of his mother's connection with entertainment history, in film, theater, and radio. While still in Hawaii, Robert found Sally referenced in a couple of major works on silent film. Daniel Blum, in his *A Pictorial History Of The Silent Screen* (New York: G. P. Putnam, 1953), features Sally in a scene still from *High School Hero*, surrounded by her co-stars Nick Stuart, David Rollins, John Darrow, and Charles Paddock. An Italian film encyclopedia, *Filmlexicon degli autori e delle opere* (Roma: Edizioni di Bianco e Nero, 1962), gives her the following entry:

> **PHIPPS, Sally – Attrice del cinema statiunitense. Nata a San Francisco (California) il 24 maggio 1909, figlia di un senatore. Frequentati gli studi a Salt Lake City, nel 1924 si trasferì con la famiglia a Los Angeles. Già nel 1915 conobbe le fatiche del cinema interpretando un ruolo di bambina in un film avventuroso con Broncho Bill [sic]. Nel 1927 fu selezionata dalla "Western Association of Motion Pictures Advertisers of America" e venne scritturata dalla "Fox" che le fece interpretare alcuni film, particolarmente ambientati nella rivista. La P. fu una delle trenta [sic] "Wampus Baby Stars," che ottennero successo come ballerine in molti teatri degli Stati Uniti. Con l'avvento del sonoro, la P. cessò ogni attività artistica.**

FILM – 1927: *The High School Hero* di David Butler, con Charles Paddock, Nick Stuart e John Darrow; *Love Makes 'Em Wild* di Albert Ray. – 1928: *Why Sailors Go Wrong* (Marinai senza bussola) di Henry Lehrman, con Sammy Cohen e Ted McNamara; *News Parade* di David Butler; *None But the Brave* di Albert Ray. – 1929: *Joy Street* di Raymond Cannon, con Lois Moran e Nick Stuart; *One Woman Idea* (Il velo dell'Islam) di Berthold Viertel, con Rod La Rocque e Marceline Day.

Needless to say, Robert was thrilled with the renewed interest in silent film history, which would certainly include his mother.

While Robert was in his teens, his grandmother gave him her personal collection of around 250 scene stills from Sally's movies, all purchased in the late 1920s at the Fox studio store. These scene stills became the nucleus of what Robert would later call the "Sally Phipps Archive." With Robert's devoted care, this archive would eventually grow to include all things related to the career and life of Sally Phipps – books, magazines, newspaper articles, publicity photos, personal photographs, correspondence, postcards, posters, lobby cards, theater programs, movie house fliers, glass slides, and even a little ticket from a weight machine with her picture on the back. Robert encouraged Sally to start thinking about writing her memoirs in a more systematic way, noting important events in her life for each year. Robert was certain that attention from film historians was not far off.

The first attempt to contact Sally was made by Roi A. Uselton (1916-2007), a Hollywood historian from the Atlanta area. He wrote an article about the Wampas Baby Stars and, in addition, made it his mission to track down all the surviving members of that group. The Wampas awards were bestowed between 1922 and 1934, and 140 actresses received the awards. Uselton began his search for the surviving members in the late 1960s. In his search, he also sought group photographs of the members for each year. His article, "The Wampas Baby Stars: Only A Few Grew To The First Magnitude," which appeared in *Films In Review*, February 1970, gives a brief blurb about each member. An asterisk is placed before the names of the 15 he was not able to contact, including Sally. Not yet having found Sally, he wrote the following blurb for her as one of the Baby Stars of 1927.

***SALLY PHIPPS had a few leads at Fox but soon left Hollywood for Broadway. In 1931, she married into the Gimbel (department-store) family. When that ended in divorce, she did not return to films.**

Uselton, who wanted to place updates of his article in subsequent issues of *Films In Review*, continued his search for surviving Wampas members. He finally found Sally in early 1971, through a rather circuitous route. Knowing that one of Sally's former surnames was Beutler, he discovered a Gertrude Beutler in San Francisco. Gertrude Beutler, a relative of Edithe's second husband, Albert S. Beutler, directed her to Edithe in Hawaii. Uselton then wrote to Edithe, who in turn forwarded Uselton's letter to Sally. The following is Uselton's letter:

Roi A. Uselton
746 N. Highland Avenue N.E.
Apt. 6
Atlanta, Georgia 30306

26 February 1971

Dear Mrs. Beutler:

I am a motion picture historian and have recently published an article pertaining to the Wampas Baby Stars, a film historical subject.

One of these former actresses I regret not having been able to locate and contact was Sally Phipps (Byrnece Beutler).

I have been referred to you for possible help. It would make me very, very happy if you were able to tell me the present name and whereabouts of Sally Phipps or to put me in touch with her in some way.

I, of course, want to please her by letting her know she is well remembered and to tell her of my article about that charming subject: the Wampas.

Enclosed is a self-addressed envelope for your convenience in replying for which I would be most grateful.

Sincerely,
Roi Uselton

Sally answered his letter in early April. This initiated a pleasant mutual correspondence that lasted for about five years. During that period, Uselton made two updates to his article in *Films in Review*. In the August-September 1971 issue, in the "Erudition Wanted & Supplied" column, he provided the following new information, "Sally Phipps ('27) resides in NYC." In the February 1973 issue, he published a major addendum to his "Wampas Baby Stars" article:

> **Sally Phipps ('27) sent me a photo of 7 of her group greeting Babe Ruth on his arrival in L.A. to make films, however, the picture of the complete group printed with this letter is from Sally Rand ('27).**

Uselton finally got his group picture of all 13 of the 1927 members, including Sally, from Sally Rand, who became the famous fan dancer. Another 1927 group picture has since surfaced on eBay, and it is now in Sally's son Robert's Sally Phipps Archive (Picture in Chapter 2).

SALLY PHIPPS ARCHIVE

After Roi A. Uselton "rediscovered" Sally, she was immediately bombarded with requests for signed photographs from fans, writers, and cinema nostalgia organizations. The University of Wyoming Library asked her to donate her personal archive to their Division of Rare Books and Special Collections, today part of the University's American Heritage Center. When Sally turned to her son Robert for advice, Robert knew that the archive was not yet ready for donation. A donation, although a good idea, would have to wait for a later time, and maybe even a different library. He could easily handle the requests for photographs, since he was in possession of almost the entire collection. He had already named the collection the "Sally Phipps Archive," and used that name on flyers and correspondence. He made copies of the choicest of Sally's portrait shots and a few of her scene stills. He charged a modest fee per print, had Sally sign the photos, and then had her send the photos out to the fans or to the organizations requesting them.

Some of Sally's fans made contributions to the Archive by sending her gifts of some of their own Sally Phipps memorabilia. These included portrait photos, picture postcards, movie house flyers, and newspaper and magazine articles. Some items were completely new, but some turned out to be duplicates. All were graciously accepted, and Sally wrote everyone a personalized thank-you note.

Today, the photographic material has been put into large, easy-to-use, loose-leaf binders. Robert has digitally scanned all the visual material, which can now be easily emailed, transferred to disc or flash-drive, or printed out as needed.

MORE CONTACTS

By the mid-1970s, word had gotten out to film buffs that Sally Phipps was alive and well and living in New York City. Film buffs published her current full name, Sallie Phipps Harned, and her Brooklyn Heights address at the St. George Hotel (51 Clark Street, Brooklyn, New York). Sally had retired from Emerson in 1973, and she was now enjoying adult education classes, which were conveniently offered every day at her hotel.

In addition to receiving requests for photographs from fans, she was also contacted by writers who were doing "whatever became of" types of publications and stories. There were two writers in particular who stand out, David Ragan and Jess L. Hoaglin.

David Ragan (1925-), the editorial director of a number of entertainment magazines, contacted Sally in the early 1970s when he was writing his latest publication, *Who's Who In Hollywood, 1900-1976* (New Rochelle, NY: Arlington House, c1976). This one-volume reference book (864 pages) gives brief biographical sketches of 20,000 actors and actresses who are credited with American film appearances. The book is divided into two major parts, those alive in 1974 and those who died before that year. He wrote the following profile of Sally in the "Living Players" section:

> **PHIPPS, SALLY (N.Y.) Married to and divorced from an heir of the Gimbel's fortune, this leading lady of the late '20s is now in her 60s and has long been retired from acting. On-screen from 1927. IN: *Bertha, The Sewing Machine Girl; High School Hero; Why Sailors Go Wrong; The News Parade; The One Woman Idea,* more.**

The "(N.Y.)" after her name indicates that Ragan knew that she was then living in New York City. Fourteen years later, Ragan published a second edition of this work in two volumes (1883 pages): *Who's Who In Hollywood: The Largest Cast Of International Film Personalities Ever Assembled* (New York: Facts On file, 1992). Sally's entry is found in volume 2:

> **PHIPPS, SALLY (d. 1978, AGE 67) Saucy, brunette Wampas Baby Star of 1927, who had leads in perhaps ten youth features at Fox between 1927 and 1929; was in *Bertha, the Sewing Machine Girl* (with Madge Bellamy), *High School Hero* (with Nick Stuart, *Detectives Wanted*, *The News Parade* (again with Stuart), *Why Sailors Go Wrong*, *None But the Brave*, *The One Woman Idea* (with Rod La Rocque), *Joy Street* (once more with Stuart), etc; left Hollywood in 1930 for Broadway, to play the ingénue in the Hart-Kaufman comedy hit *Once in a Lifetime*; is said to have later played bits in "many" talkies; had begun her movie career at 3½, playing the Baby in *Broncho Billy and the Baby*, with "Broncho Billy" Anderson; first of her two husbands, from 1931 until they divorced in 1935, was department-store heir Benedict Gimbel Jr.; was later married to N.Y. musician Alfred M. Harned, by whom she has a son, Robert, a librarian at the University of Pennsylvania at Philadelphia.**

Jess L. Hoaglin (1912-1999) was another Hollywood historian who contacted Sally. He also had his own large collection of film memorabilia. In the late 1940s, he published a fan magazine called *The Supporting Cast*, which was comprised of articles about the usually underappreciated character actors of the stage, screen, and radio. The magazine was issued only between early 1948 and late 1950 and then ceased publication. When Hoaglin contacted Sally in the 1970s, he since 1968 had been writing a regular column for *The Hollywood Reporter*: "Where Are They Today?" Later, in the early 1980s, he finished a three-volume set of publications called *Wherever Is . . .?: The Stars Of Yesteryear* (Newell, Iowa: Bireline Publishing Co., 1983). These volumes are filled with mostly half-page articles about former film stars, some well-known and some not. The articles summarize their careers and include information about their current lives. In his frequent correspondence with Sally, he proposed the idea of writing a feature article about her, but unfortunately, he never followed through.

SALLY RECEIVES A ROSEMARY AWARD

In April 1976, less than two years before she passed away, Sally received the following delightful letter:

Tom Fulbright's Rosemary Award Association
A Society of Remembrance to Present Belated Awards to our Beloved Silent Stars

1211 Rally Avenue
Greater Capitol Heights
Maryland 20207
(301) 735-9453

April 7, 1976

Dear Sally Phipps;

My dear young lady – you have been a hard one to find – but we old 'fans' are very much like Uncle Tom's Bloodhounds – we never give up. I am very glad to find you live in a spot very dear to me. I have a great fondness for Brooklyn Heights – lived there for quite a while years ago at the Hotel Margaret – not far from the St. George.

My association has had your name before us for two years now. We are slowly getting around to giving our lovely Rosemary Awards (Rosemary is for remembrance) to all the Wampas Baby Stars. Now, I am so very glad to let you know that come October 5 of this year, we will be honoring you with this remembrance of your Hollywood days. Another great thing is that it will take place right there in the Heights at the Vintage Film Club. As of now, I am sending the list of a few of your films around to see if we can locate one to run at that time. If you have any idea where one can be located, well, it would help? I do think the Canadian Film Institute may be of help. The affair will be informal, and the location will be posted out by the Vintage Film Club's President, Dick Griffo, who also lives in the Heights. Maybe he can call you?

Another former star will be receiving the Rosemary that same night. While he is not a silent star, we give a few to those we feel should have gotten some kind of 'Oscar' – Erik Rhodes. Constance Binney will be helping me and also Butterfly McQueen – both Rosemary people.

I am searching for a good glossy of you for the publicity we hope to get – may have to call on you – but in the meantime, I hope this brings you as much happiness as it brings 'us old buffs' – with such wonderful memories of those Golden Days.

On behalf of the entire association, accept our love and all good wishes,

Tom Fulbright

Sally, of course, was very pleased to hear that she was going to receive the Rosemary Award. Tom Fulbright (1907-1988) corresponded frequently with Sally over the next few months and even wrote to her son Robert when he found out that he was the curator of the Sally Phipps Archive. Sally and Robert learned a number of things about Fulbright. He lived in the Washington, D.C. area and was a film historian and writer for several film buff magazines, such as *Classic Film Collector*,

Hollywood Studio Magazine, and *The World Of Yesterday*. In 1970, he founded the Rosemary Award Association, and by 1976 he had given out a number of these awards to such former silent stars as Lillian Gish, Leatrice Joy, Dorothy Mackaill, Constance Binney, and Betty Compson, and to other movie actresses such as Mae West and Butterfly McQueen, just to name a few. Originally from Ashville, North Carolina, Fulbright spent a few years on Broadway as a dancing chorus boy. He had fond memories of seeing Sally on the screen when he was a young man, and he was now thrilled to find her alive and well and living in Brooklyn. He even felt a bit fatherly toward her and did what he could to give her as much publicity as possible. In fact, the advance planning and preparation for the award ceremony that was to be held in October did much to further Sally's "rediscovery" in the United States and worldwide.

As Fulbright said in his letter to Sally, Erik Rhodes (1906-1990) would also receive the Rosemary Award on the same day. Rhodes was certainly more famous and accomplished professionally than Sally. Born in Oklahoma with the name Ernest Sharpe, he went to New York City with a scholarship to study acting after graduating from the University of Oklahoma. After obtaining parts on Broadway, he adopted his new name. He became an expert mimicker of accents and dialects, and he specialized in playing hyperactive Continental charmers. He is most famous for his appearance in two Fred Astaire/Ginger Rogers films, *The Gay Divorcee* (1934) and *Top Hat* (1935), in which he played this character. These were followed by many more film and Broadway roles. Rhodes, in 1976, at age 70, was still active theatrically. In fact, around the time of the upcoming October Rosemary Award ceremony, Rhodes was rehearsing for a new off-Broadway musical, *Two Of Everything*, with book, lyrics and music by Andrew Rosenthal. The musical was "an Equity approved showcase," which opened at the Marymount Manhattan Theatre, 221 East 71st Street, and ran from October 14 to 24, 1976.

Tom Fulbright had elaborate plans for the Rosemary Award ceremony. The official date was set for Wednesday, October 6. It was to be held in the large reception hall of the First Presbyterian Church, 124 Henry Street, in the Brooklyn Heights section of New York City at 7:30 p.m. This was to be an official function of the Vintage Film Club, a group coordinated by its president, Dick Griffo, a minor film actor who lived in Brooklyn Heights. Clips from each of the award winners' films were to be shown during the event. A number of important people were expected to attend. Besides Tom Fulbright and Dick Griffo, Butterfly McQueen and Constance Binney, actresses who had won Rosemary Awards in 1972 and 1974, respectively, were expected to attend. Fulbright also invited David Ragan, whose new book, *Who's Who In Hollywood, 1900-1976*, had just come out and had included biographies of both Sally and Rhodes. And, of course, Sally's son Robert was invited as a special guest.

To add a little sparkle to the occasion, Fulbright contacted one of Sally's co-stars from her 1927 feature film, *High School Hero*, David Rollins (1907-1997), to write her a surprise congratulatory letter. Rollins wrote the letter and then sent it to Fulbright. Fulbright wrote Sally's son Robert about his plan to mail Robert the letter in advance of the event and then have Robert read the letter to Sally during the ceremony.

High School Hero **scene still (1927) of Sally and David Rollins studying together**

Fulbright, in the course of the planning, also found out that an artist friend of his, Bob Harman (1929-2009), was drawing a 16 by 20 inch portrait of Sally specifically for the occasion. For 13 years, Harman taught art at Concord Academy, a preparatory school in Massachusetts. For five years, Harman also wrote a column called "Movie Memories," which ran in several newspapers. Harman specialized in large-sized pencil portraits, and as a former actor, he began his art career drawing caricatures of his fellow performers. His love of movies prompted him to begin making portraits of film stars. He produced two books of them. The first, *Bob Harman's Hollywood Panorama* (New York: E.P. Dutton, c1971), reproduces his 5x9-foot montage of 1001 caricatures of film stars, all set against a background of famous movie sets and Hollywood landmarks. The book has 30 color plates and several biographical indexes. Sally is not included in this book but she is in his next, *Bob Harman's Enchanted Faces* (New York: B. Harman, c1991). This one has 130 full-page pencil drawings of female stars and four montages of 161 tiny drawings of other famous and not-so-famous actresses. Sally is in Montage III, in a drawing taken from one of her head shots. Harman planned to bring his finished portrait of Sally to the event himself or, if he could not make it, to send it to Fulbright in Maryland with enough time for Fulbright to bring it to the event.

Bob Harman drawing of Sally, 1976

From April to October, there was a considerable number of letters and phone calls between Sally, Fulbright, Griffo, and Robert. During this period, Fulbright also gave Sally's name and address to many of his film buff friends, resulting in an increase in the volume of fan mail and requests for photographs for Sally and Robert to handle. Fulbright also encouraged Robert to begin work on a career article about Sally, which he said was sadly lacking in the film history literature. He added that he would be glad to provide any help with the research. Unfortunately, Robert did not begin work on his mother's much-requested career article until he began writing this book. (It was published in the March 2014 issue of *Classic Images.*)

Tom Fulbright and Dick Griffo were able to obtain publicity for the Rosemary event. An article was placed in *Hollywood Studio Magazine*, September 1976, written by Moody Po Cook, entitled "Rosemary Awards for 1976." This article covers the awards that were given to the former silent stars Doris Kenyon and May Allison earlier that year. It also announces the future event for Sally and Erik Rhodes and includes a lovely full-faced portrait photograph of Sally, among several other photographs of the year's recipients. Tom Fulbright himself wrote an article for *The World Of Yesterday*, October 1976, entitled "Rosemary Awards Selects Four Stars For 1976." The coverage is similar to the previous article, with the same portrait photograph of Sally. Dick Griffo was able to get some publicity for the event in a couple of New York City neighborhood weekly newspapers, *The Phoenix* and *The Gay Scene.* Both sources include pictures of Sally and Rhodes, along with the event details.

Everything seemed to be planned perfectly. On the evening of October 6, around 100 fans arrived at the church. They had read the notices about the event and were excited to have the opportunity to meet Sally and Erik Rhodes. But – on that night, there was no Tom Fulbright, no Dick Griffo, no Bob Harman drawing, no David Rollins letter, and no clips from the films. Of course Sally was there, as well as her son Robert, Erik Rhodes and his wife.

Sally posing at Rosemary Award ceremony -- 1976

Robert got explanations for the absences later, but at the event, the awardees felt awfully embarrassed and not a little bit betrayed. However, at least a microphone had been set up for them, and there were refreshments. Fortunately, Fulbright had the foresight to send the two Rosemary Award plaques to Sally's son Robert a week before the event, just in case he was not able to attend at the last minute. So, the award plaques and the awardees were in the same room, and the three of them realized that nothing else was really necessary, except to put on a good awards ceremony show for the invited audience of fans. This was exactly what Sally and Rhodes did -- like two real troupers. With no master of ceremonies in sight, they decided to take over the program, by giving each other the awards themselves.

Sally and Erik Rhodes receiving their awards -- 1976

The following is the text of Sally's Rosemary Award plaque:

ROSEMARY
PAYS TRIBUTE TO
*
MISS SALLY PHIPPS

WHOSE UNIQUE COMBINATION
OF BEAUTY
SPARKLING AUDACITY WITH
A RARE
DRAMATIC ABILITY
WAS ENCHANTING

A SPECIAL MENTION
FOR BEING VOTED
A WAMPAS BABY STAR
OF 1927
*
THE TOM FULBRIGHT
ROSEMARY AWARD
ASSOCIATION
1976

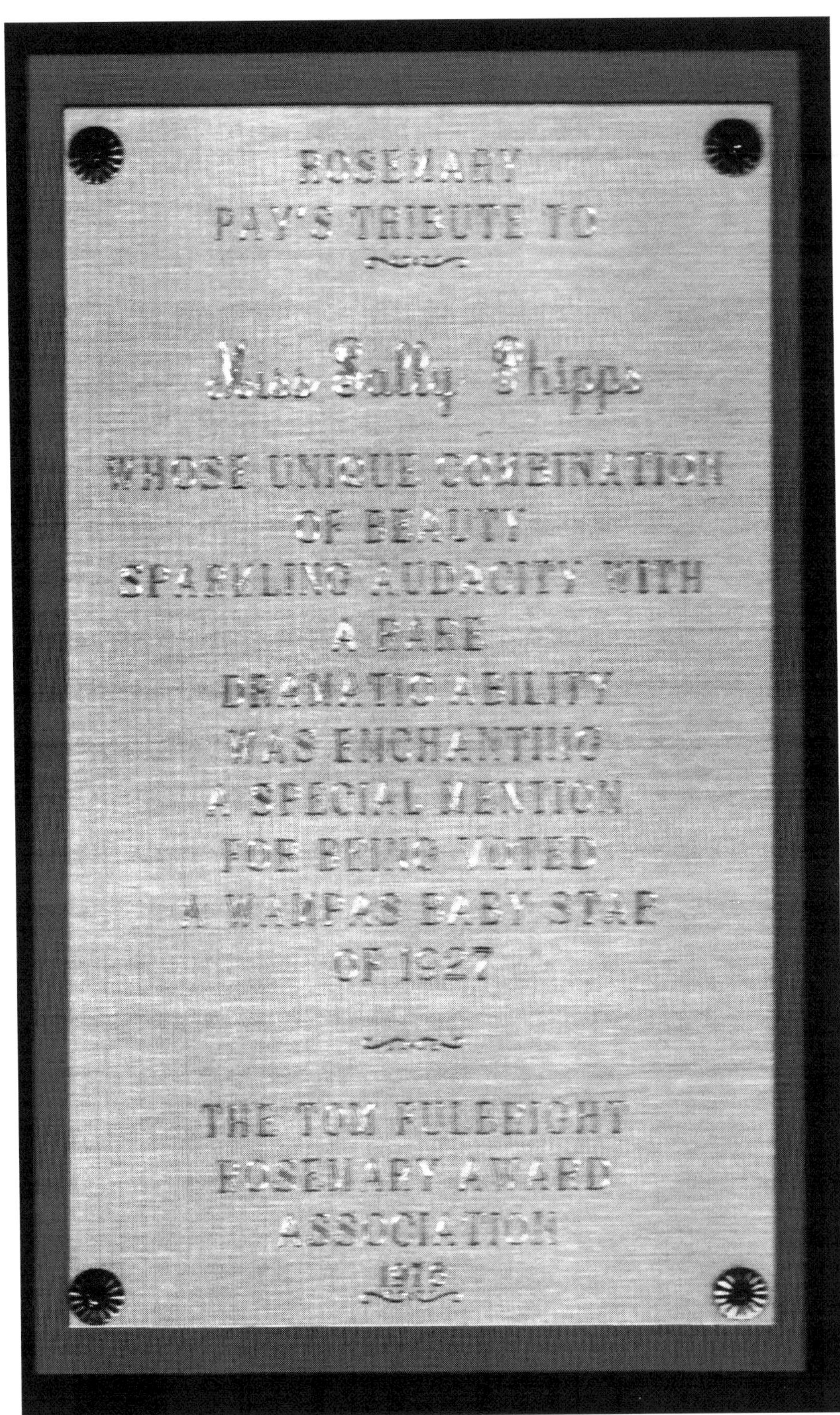

Sally's Rosemary Award – 1976

The handing out of the awards was followed by speeches from each of them, ending with a question and answer period. During the social part of the event, a couple of Sally's fans gave her some vintage four-page Brooklyn movie house flyers, three from the "Park Palace Theatre" at 71-73 Park Avenue and one from the "New Classique" at Marcy Avenue and Fulton Street. Three of these flyers have front-page advertisements for Sally's films, *Love Makes 'Em Wild*, *High School Hero*, and *None but the Brave*, and one has an inside advertisement for *Why Sailors Go Wrong*. Sally was thrilled to see these items still in existence after so many years and accepted them for the Sally Phipps Archive. In the end, the audience found the evening a totally memorable delight. Many photographs taken that night capture the happy mood of the evening. Everyone went home satisfied, but all were still mystified by the "no shows" of Fulbright and Griffo.

Dick Griffo nevertheless later reported on the event in *Classic Film Collector*, Winter 1976, "Erik Rhodes, Sally Phipps Receive Rosemary Awards," under the byline Richard Griffo. The following was obviously supplied by attendees who fed him the details:

> **The Rosemary Award, created by Tom Fulbright, was given to Erik Rhodes and Sally Phipps at a reception held by the Vintage Film Club of the First Presbyterian Church in Brooklyn Heights.**
>
> **On Oct. 6th, this group, coordinated for the past 6 years by myself, Richard D. Griffo, film buff and collector, had previously given the coveted award to Constance Binney (1974) and Butterfly McQueen (1972). This was the first Rosemary given to a male star. Tom Fulbright was unable to come to Brooklyn on account of family problems, and the coordinator fell ill at the last minute. But that marvelous actor, Erik Rhodes, saved the evening and took over the proceedings.**
>
> **The affair was held in a beautiful, historic room of the church, which was replete with memorabilia of Brooklyn from the 1850s to the present and provided a perfect setting for the presentation. In attendance were Mrs. Rhodes, Mr. Robert Harned (Sally's son), Mr. Bruce King of Regiment Publications, there to cover the event for his newspaper, and about 100 people from all parts of the city. The Reverend Sam Taylor (a film buff himself) arranged for a delicious wine punch to be served by one of the most faithful club members, Mrs. Millie Levine.**
>
> **Since much of the proposed 90 minute program had been whittled away by waiting for yours truly to arrive, the actual proceedings only lasted about ½ hour. Corsages were presented to Mrs. Rhodes and Sally Phipps and a boutonniere to Mr. Rhodes. Erik Rhodes gave the Rosemary to Sally, and she, in turn, presented the award to Erik.**
>
> **Sally thanked the many fans who had come out to honor her and introduced her 32 year old son to the crowd. He is especially interested in his mother's career as he is a librarian at the University of Pennsylvania in Philadelphia.**

Unfortunately, I was unable to secure any of her films for the occasion, although we do know that the 1928 production of *Why Sailors Go Wrong* was shown at Bill Everson's film series last Spring held at the New School.

Sally stated that she was especially interested in that film because she had only seen rushes of it, and the leading man had died [comedian, Ted MacNamara (1894-1928)] just after the filming had ended. She was also interested in locating *Broncho Billy And The Baby*, as she was the 3½ year old baby in the film. Also this was one of the early films in which many extras had died in a stagecoach incident while filming was in progress [no one actually died during this incident]. In fact, Sally declared that these set incidents had soured her feeling for the cinema in later years.

Sally was a Wampas Baby Star of 1927. In the early 30s, she married Ben Gimbel of the Department Store chain, and later she married a Mr. [Alfred M.] Harned, whose surname she now holds. Her mother is living in California, and she has a [married] daughter in Heidelberg, Germany.

Sally had bit parts in many talkies and would be interested in hearing from fans who might know of her films. Her address is Mrs. Sally Harned, St. George Hotel, 51 Clark Street, Brooklyn, NY 11201. She would love to hear from those fans who have not forgotten her.

As I am writing this, I have just ordered from Griggs-Moviedrome a print of *Broncho Billy And The Baby* (having just seen it available in that marvelous insert in the latest issue of CFC [Classic Film Collector]) along with a tape from the Essex Film Club. I am planning to have a special Sally Phipps night on Wednesday, February 9, 1977 at 7:30 (tentative night) at which *Broncho Billy And The Baby* will be shown. *Why Sailors Go Wrong* will also be shown, if it can be obtained. For further information, call me at (212) 852-8158 (evenings) or write Dick Griffo, 58 Middagh Street, Brooklyn, NY 11201.

Erik Rhodes declared that he was honored to be the first male to be presented with the award. We had hoped to obtain the AFI [American Film Institute] short, which featured clips from *Gay Divorcee* and *Top Hat* but were not successful. Erik told about a Charlie Chan film which he had made, *Charlie Chan in Paris*, which had recently been found in Czechoslovakia. He then shook hands with everyone in attendance and posed for many pictures graciously. Erik had been a bachelor for 65 years. Five years ago he married a beautiful lady from South Carolina. He then announced that he would appear in an off-off Broadway musical entertainment entitled, *Two Of Everything*, for several weekends in October. Erik told the audience that he was also seen in a segment of *The Adams Chronicles*, the next one to the last.

He has kept quite active in television, commercials and appearances in dinner-theatres. He is still quite friendly with Fred Astaire and Ginger Rogers.

To honor him in a fitting fashion, the Vintage Film Club will present *Top Hat* on Wednesday evening, January 26, 1977 at 7:30 p.m. at which he

will make a personal appearance. For more information, please call or write me at the same address mentioned earlier.

The next Rosemary Award scheduled to be given out next Spring will be to comedy star, Ruth Donnelly.

Why had Tom Fulbright and Dick Griffo not shown up? And what happened to the Bob Harman drawing and the David Rollins letter? In subsequent correspondence from Fulbright and Griffo, Sally and Robert learned that Tom Fulbright had been nursing a sick brother for a number of weeks near his home in Maryland, right outside of Washington, D.C. On the day he was to leave for New York City, his brother had gotten sicker, and he did not feel he could leave him alone. Dick Griffo, in a letter to Sally's son Robert, explained that he "had fallen ill at the last minute due to a nervous condition." As for the Bob Harman drawing that Fulbright still had in his possession, he did not send it to Sally's son Robert until late November. Robert had the drawing framed and gave it to Sally the next month as a Christmas present. Sally later asked Robert to keep it as part of the Sally Phipps Archive. As for the David Rollins letter, Fulbright, who wanted to have Robert read it to Sally as a surprise at the event, had forgotten to mail it to Robert. At the last minute, he mailed it to Sally, hoping it would arrive in time for the event, which it did not. Sally finally got the Rollins letter a few days later, and she kept it as one of her cherished possessions. Following is the letter, sent from 1869 Haymarket Road, Leucadia, California, which Rollins wrote more than four months before the Rosemary Award event:

May 27, 1976

Dear Sally Phipps;

What a surprise, hearing news about you! I guess it has been about 50 years since we starred in "High School Hero." We must be the only two left from that epic. You were such a beautiful redheaded freckle-faced, cute as a button girl. I often wondered whatever happened to you. I guess we both got let out after the 1929 Crash.

Those were the wonderful days of youth, beauty and personality as they billed us, and you were a Wampas Baby Star to boot!!!

I hope and trust this note finds you in good health and happy. Sorry I can't be in New York to see you receive the Rosemary Award. I don't like travelling anymore. New York today is no place to be, tho I'd love to see the Broadway scene again.

With warm affection
Sincerely,

David Rollins

Sally subsequently made a notation on this letter that she answered Rollins on October 23, 1976.

As was mentioned earlier, there were no film clips shown at the October 6 Rosemary Award event, even though they were promised. Nevertheless, during the many months of preparation for the event, the hunt for Sally's films did prove fruitful. Both Tom Fulbright and Dick Griffo headed the search and had their film-buff friends join the cause. They found one company in Nutley, New Jersey, called "Griggs Moviedrome," which was selling a 16mm version of *Broncho Billy And The Baby*. Sally's son Robert and Dick Griffo both purchased copies. As mentioned previously in Dick Griffo's article, one of Sally's 1928 feature films, *Why Sailors Go Wrong*, was traced to William K. Everson, a famous New York City film collector and historian, and University professor. Another of Sally's comedy shorts, the 1927 *Girls*, was tracked down to a listing in the old "Kodascope Library" Catalogue. This *Descriptive Catalogue of Kodascope Library Motion Pictures* describes rental films available in the 1930s through various Eastman Kodak Company's Kodascope Libaries around the country and the world. The catalogue also includes some of Sally's other comedy shorts, *Gentlemen Prefer Scotch*, *Light Wines And Bearded Ladies*, and *A Midsummer Night's Steam*, and one of her features, *Why Sailors Go Wrong*.

VINTAGE FILM CLUB'S "A TRIBUTE TO SALLY PHIPPS"

As mentioned in the previous *Classic Film Collector* article, Dick Griffo made plans to organize a new program devoted totally to Sally Phipps. He wanted it held again by his Vintage Film Club, at the same location, the First Presbyterian Church reception hall, 124 Henry Street, Brooklyn Heights. He would show his recently-purchased *Broncho Billy And The Baby*, then conduct a talk with Sally, and a question and answer session. If *Why Sailors Go Wrong* could be found, he would show it also. After he consulted Sally, who was very excited about the idea, particularly about seeing the films, he set the title and the date: "A Tribute To Sally Phipps," Wednesday, February 9, 1977. He also did what he could to publicize the event, and again he was able to get publicity listings in neighborhood newspapers, such as *The Phoenix*.

The event was held as planned, with Dick Griffo officiating in person. Sally's son Robert, who was in rehearsal for a play in Philadelphia, was not able to attend. Unfortunately, a copy of the film, *Why Sailors Go Wrong*, could not be found for the event. Therefore, only the Broncho Billy film was shown, with Sally following up with a short talk and time for questions. According to Sally, the event was a great success. This was the last event in Sally's honor.

SALLY'S LAST FULL YEAR 1977

Sally did not know, in February 1977, that she had only 13 months to live, although she was certainly aware that she was not in good health. She had gained a lot of weight in her last twenty years and was taking medications for hypertension and diabetes. But she did not expect these to be imminently life threatening. She did complain, however – to herself and in her memoirs – about anemia. According to doctors today, anemia is one of the symptoms of colo-rectal cancer, which led to Sally's death. The cancer was developing rapidly during her last year -- 1977 was decades before routine colonoscopies.

Throughout that year, she continued with her daily life, visiting nearby friends, as well as writing and answering letters from distant friends and relatives. She also answered her fan mail, which had accelerated considerably after she received her Rosemary Award.

Robert worked full time as a reference librarian in Van Pelt Library, the main library of the University of Pennsylvania in West Philadelphia. He lived in Center City Philadelphia at 2029 Walnut Street, close to Rittenhouse Square. His hobby was amateur theatrics, and he performed, in his free time, as a singer, dancer, and actor in several Philadelphia area community theaters: The Gilbert and Sullivan Players at Plays and Players Theatre, Abbey Stage Door, and LaSalle College Music Theatre.

In late 1976, Robert was recruited as a performer by the Playmakers, a community theater connected with St. Giles Church of Upper Darby, a suburb of Philadelphia. He first performed there in a dancing and acting role in their musical production of *Bells Are Ringing* in April and May 1977.

That year, 1977, was the 50th anniversary of the first real "talkie," *The Jazz Singer*, the 1927 Al Jolson film. In April, the Free Library of Philadelphia, celebrating the birth of sound in films, resurrected the 1932 talkie version of *Once In A Lifetime*, starring Jack Oakie and Aline MacMahon. In the film, a starlet named Sydney Fox plays "Susan Walker," the ingénue role originated by Sally on stage. Robert and others from the Playmakers attended the screening and got the idea that it would be a good play for their group. They could even promote it as part of the continuing celebration of the 50th anniversary of sound in films. The Playmakers' administration approved the play, and it was produced in November 1977. Robert played one of the male leads. Unfortunately, Sally was not well enough to come to Philadelphia to see it and bowed out gracefully. Robert, however, although unhappy that his mother could not attend, was immensely pleased to be involved in a play that his mother had appeared in back in 1930-1931.

Sally and Robert usually spent Christmas together, either in New York or in Philadelphia. For the 1975 and 1976 Christmas holidays, they spent several days together in Robert's apartment in Center City Philadelphia. For 1977, however, Robert cancelled their usual Christmas get-together. He was planning on working on another master's degree (Greek and Roman Archaeology) and needed to take the Graduate Record Exam scheduled for early January 1978. He needed to use his Christmas vacation for the necessary intense study time for the exam. Sally, knowing how important this degree was to Robert and to his library career, gave her blessing to the cancellation by saying, "You must not let anything interfere with your getting your master's degree." Throughout late December and January they kept in touch by phone.

SALLY IS HOSPITALIZED WITH CANCER

On February 6, 1978, Robert was notified that his mother was taken by ambulance to the emergency room of Long Island College Hospital, a few blocks from her apartment at the St. George Hotel. According to the hospital report, Sally, two days earlier, while reaching for a light, became dizzy, fell down, and was unable to get up. Although conscious and alert, she felt too weak to move herself. Neighbors who had not seen her for two days finally notified the building's manager, who unlocked her apartment door, found her on the floor, and immediately phoned for an ambulance to take her to the nearby hospital.

After the doctors made a number of tests, she was diagnosed with colon cancer that had spread to her liver. Her health declined rapidly over the next several weeks, while she remained in Long Island College Hospital. She did not want to walk or eat, and she gradually withdrew into sleep.

Robert tried to phone her every day from Philadelphia and took off every Friday from work to come up to New York to visit her in the hospital. She became more and more uncommunicative. Fortunately, early on in his visits, he was able to get power of attorney from her in order to pay her bills and do her banking.

SALLY DIES MARCH 1978 AND IS BURIED IN EVERGREEN CEMETERY

Her last day was Friday, March 17, 1978, Saint Patrick's Day. Robert had just visited her in her room in the hospital and had gone back to Philadelphia by train. He got a phone call about 9 p.m. that Sally had passed away at 8:45 p.m. in her hospital room.

The funeral arrangements were handled by Jere J. Cronin, Inc. of Brooklyn Heights. Sally was interred on Saturday, March 25, at 11:30 a.m. in Evergreen Cemetery, which straddles Brooklyn and Queens, in the cemetery's Mount of Olives section. There was a graveside service, officiated by the Reverend Ronald Myer, Associate Rector of the Diocesan Church of St. Ann and The Holy Trinity, an Episcopal Church in Brooklyn Heights. Robert knew that, although Sally had Eastern religious leanings, she was sympathetic to the Episcopal Church.

In spite of the short notice for the graveside service, Robert's good friend Jack Elias was able to accompany him to the cemetery. They came together on the train from Philadelphia. Sally's loyal 79-year-old long-time friend, Rolla Nordic, came to Brooklyn from her Manhattan apartment. Along with the Reverend Myer, they rode together in a funeral car through the Brooklyn entrance of the cemetery and then crossed the county line into Queens where the Mount of Olives section was located and where the interment was held. After the graveside service, all four rode back to Brooklyn, had lunch together, and then went their separate ways.

Robert and Rolla Nordic at Sally's burial

While he was at the cemetery, Robert ordered Sally's headstone. Should he spell her name "Sally" or "Sallie" Phipps? Then again, she was born Nellie Bernice Bogdon, is credited in some films as Bernice Sawyer, chose Byrnece Beutler in high school, and became Sally Phipps Gimbel after her first marriage. Later in life, she chose Sallie Nona Phipps, became Sallie Phipps Harned when she married again, and even created the name Sallie Nonah Enayah during her Redpath-Horner days.

Robert finally chose "Sallie Phipps Harned." That was the name she used from 1941, when she married his father Alfred Marion Harned, until she died. Her headstone reads:

*

SALLIE PHIPPS
HARNED
1911—1978

*

Sally's headstone in Evergreen Cemetery

OBITUARIES

Obituaries for Sally appeared quickly in the newspapers. The *New York Times* ran one on Tuesday, March 21:

> **SALLY PHIPPS, 67, STAR OF THE SILENT-MOVIE ERA**
>
> **Sally Phipps, who was a star in silent movies of the 1920's, died last Friday at Long Island College Hospital. She was 67 year old and lived at the St. George Hotel in Brooklyn.**
>
> **Miss Phipps made her movie debut as the Baby in the 1915 "Broncho Billy and the Baby," featuring the pioneer western star, G. M. (Broncho Billy) Anderson. She went on to be a principal in such features as "Bertha, the Sewing Machine Girl" (1927), "High School Hero" (1927), "Why Sailors Go Wrong " (1928), "The News Parade " (1928) and "None But the Brave (1928). She also appeared in "Joy Street (1929) and in "The One Woman Idea," the same year.**
>
> **Miss Phipps left Hollywood in 1930 to appear in a featured role as Susan Walker, the ingénue in the original Moss Hart-George Kaufman comedy hit "Once in a Lifetime." She subsequently was seen on Broadway in Allen Rivkin's 1935 Hollywood lampoon, "Knock on Wood."**
>
> **The actress, whose real name was Byrnece Beutler, married Benedict Gimbel Jr., the department-store and radio-station executive, in 1931. They were divorced in 1935. Six years later, Miss Phipps married Alfred M. Harned, a New York musician.**
>
> **She is survived by a son, Robert Harned of Philadelphia, her mother Mrs. Albert Beutler of El Toro, Calif.; a brother and a sister.**

The *New York Post* ran a reduced version of the *New York Times* obituary on the same day. Similar reduced versions appeared on March 22 in both *Variety* and *The Hollywood Reporter.*

***NEW YORK TIMES STYLE MAGAZINE "T"* ARTICLE**

Almost exactly 30 years after Sally died, the *New York Times* honored her with an article in their *New York Times Style Magazine "T"* on February 24, 2008. It was written by fashion writer and novelist Gioia Diliberto and titled "The Flapper Doesn't Change Her Spots." Accompanying the text of the article are six photographs illustrating Sally's professional career from early childhood to Broadway.

ANOTHER *CLASSIC IMAGES* BIOGRAPHY

In March 2014, in the film-buff magazine *Classic Images*, Sally's son Robert wrote an extensive update of the November 1984 Sally Phipps short biography (ca.

575 words), originally written by John Roberts in the same magazine. This time, his article, titled "Sally Phipps, Silent Film Star," was given the magazine's cover display, featuring one of Sally's color lobby cards, and a 3,000-word story extending over 10 pages, with 32 pictures from Sally's career and personal life.

EPILOGUE

Sally Phipps remained strikingly beautiful until the end of her life. In her 60s, even though she was plump, she could still turn men's heads. Robert will never forget one particular day while he was walking with her through the lobby of her St. George Hotel. He overheard a man comment loudly to his friend, "Now that's a beautiful woman!"

FILM, BROADWAY, AND RADIO WORK

FILM

Abbreviations: AFI -- American Film Institute Catalog, 1921-1930; B – Brooklyn Daily Eagle; DK -- David Kiehn, Broncho Billy and the Essanay Film Company, 2003 ; EH – Exhibitors Herald and Moving Picture World, Exhibitors Herald World; F -- Film Daily; MH – Motion Picture Herald; MN -- Motion Picture News; MT – Motography; MW -- Moving Picture World; N -- New York Times; V -- Variety

ESSANAY FILM MANUFACTURING COMPANY – all 1915; all silent; 1 or 2 reels

Broncho Billy And The Baby

Release date: January 23, 1915.
Copyright date: January 8, 1915.
Director: G. M. Anderson.
Cast: G. M. Anderson, Bernice Sawyer [= Sally Phipps], Evelyn Selbie, Lee Willard.

Billy, an outlaw with a reward posted for his capture, rescues a little girl after she falls over a ledge. The grateful mother offers him a room for the night, but her husband recognizes him and wants to turn him in for the reward. His wife holds off her husband at gun point until Billy escapes.--DK.

Reviews:
MT, 1-23-1915:147.
MW, 1-16-1915:411 (story only); 2-6-1915:827-828.

The Western Way

Release date: March 20, 1915.
Copyright date: March 6, 1915.
Director: G. M. Anderson.
Cast: G. M. Anderson, Lee Willard, Hazel Applegate, Bernice Sawyer [= Sally Phipps].

A rancher saves an outlaw from a posse, then discovers he himself may be arrested for a crime committed years ago. The outlaw confesses to the crime to protect the rancher and his family.--DK.

Reviews:
MT, 3-20-1915:463.
MW, 3-13-1915:1644 (story only); 4-3-1915:64.

The Outlaw's Awakening

Release date: March 27, 1915.
Copyright date: March 16, 1915.
Director: G. M. Anderson.
Cast: G. M. Anderson, Neva West, Bernice Sawyer [= Sally Phipps].

An outlaw is about to rob a stagecoach, but when he encounters his wife and young daughter, on their way west to join him, he resolves to end his life of crime.--DK.

Reviews:

MT, 3-27-1915:503.
MW, 3-20-1915:1820 (story only); 4-10-1915:235.

FOX FILM PRODUCTION CORPORATION

Early to Wed (feature)

Release date: April 25, 1926.
Copyright date: April 18, 1926.
Director: Frank Borzage.
Cast: Matt Moore, Kathryn Perry, Albert Gran, Julia Swayne Gordon, Arthur Housman, Rodney Hildebrand, ZaSu Pitts, Belva McKay, Ross McCutcheon, Harry Bailey, [Sally Phipps, uncredited].

Tommy and Daphne Carter, a young married couple, following the advice of a pretentious friend, decide to impress their friends by appearing to be prosperous. Their efforts end in disillusionment when Tommy loses his job, and their furniture is collected for nonpayments. However, by feasting a millionaire with a borrowed dinner and accommodating him for the night in a borrowed bed, they gain his sympathy; and he offers the young husband a substantial position.--AFI.

Reviews:

F, 5-16-26:11.
MN, 5-15-26:2369.
MW, 5-29-26:420.
N, no review found.
V, 6-23-26:18.

The Family Upstairs (feature)

Release date: August 29, 1926.
Copyright date: July 24, 1926.
Director: J. G. Blystone.

Cast: Virginia Valli, Allan Simpson, J. Farrell MacDonald, Lillian Elliott, Edward Piel, Jr., Dot Farley, Cecille Evans, Jacqueline Wells, [Sally Phipps, uncredited].

Louise, a quiet and refined girl, is taunted by her mother, brother, and sister because she has no sweetheart. Finally a bank teller, Charles Grant, falls in love with her and insists upon visiting her family in their apartment. Mrs. Heller drives him away by her talk of the luxury to which her daughter is accustomed, and when he departs Louise accuses her family of spoiling her one chance for romance. Impulsively, she takes a taxi to Coney Island to lose herself in the crowds but is followed by Charles, who has seen through the family's pretense. There she meets two boys who work in her office; and when Charles tries to talk to her, they resent his interference, assuming him to be a masher. Charles is struck down by her companions, but as a result Louise and Charles are happily reconciled.--AFI.

Reviews:

F, no review found.
MN, 7-31-26:414.
MW, 7-31-26:298.
N, no review found.
V, 7-21-26:14.

Light Wines And Bearded Ladies (short)

Release date: November 14, 1926.
Copyright date: October 24, 1926.
Director: Jules White.
Cast: Gene Cameron, Sally Phipps, Harrison Martell, J. Buckley Russell.

Gene graduates from a barber school and gets a job as barber on an aeroplane fitted with a complete shop. He also incurs the enmity of Tony, a tough guy, as both love Sally. Due to mishaps, Gene entirely shaves Tony's head, but sticks hair back on with glue. Tony discovers this and chases him all over the plane until Gene jumps and Tony falls, both landing in a load of hay. (Imperial Comedy).--MW, 11-29-26:288.

Reviews:

F, 11-21-26:18.
MN, 12-4-26:2157.
MW, 11-29-26:288.
N, no review found.
V, no review found.

Bertha, The Sewing Machine Girl (feature)

Release date: December 19, 1926.
Copyright date: December 19, 1926.
Director: Irving Cummings.
Cast: Madge Bellamy, Allan Simpson, Sally Phipps, Paul Nicholson, Anita Garvin, J. Farrell MacDonald, Ethel Wales, Arthur Housman, Harry A. Baily.

Bertha Sloan loses her job as a sewing-machine girl and subsequently is employed as telephone girl with a lingerie manufacturing company. Bertha falls in love with the assistant shipping clerk, Roy Davis, and soon is promoted to chief model for the firm, owing to the patronage of Morton, the wealthy and dastardly manager. Bertha is about to take a position in Paris as designer when Morton lures her to his home. He takes her aboard his yacht, but she is rescued in the nick of time in a thrilling motorboat chase by Roy--who, it develops, is the real owner of the company.--AFI.

Reviews:

F, 1-16-27:7.
MN, 1-7-27:66.
MW, 12-25-26:597.
N, 1-4-27:21.
V, 1-5-27:16.

Big Business (short)

Release date: December 26, 1926.
Copyright date: December 19, 1926
Director: Mark Sandrich.
Cast: Harold Austin, Sally Phipps, Heine Conklin, Grace Goodall, George B. French.

What happened to a live-wire umbrella salesman in a rainless town furnishes the fun... Harold and his dusky valet...are mobbed when they talk rain, placed in a balloon that blows up, and causes the much needed rain, so all ends well, with Harold winning the girl who befriended him. (Imperial Comedy).--MW, 1-22-27:280.

Reviews:

F, no review found.
MN, 1-28-27:318.
MW, 1-22-27:280.
N, no review found.
V, no review found.

Love Makes 'Em Wild (feature)

Release date: March 6, 1927.
Copyright date: March 13, 1927
Director: Albert Ray.
Cast: Johnny Harron, Sally Phipps, Ben Bard, Arthur Housman, J. Farrell MacDonald, Natalie Kingston, Albert Gran, Florence Gilbert, Earl Mohan, Coy Watson, Noah Young, William B. Davidson.

Willie, a spineless office plodder, is told by quack doctors that he will die in six months, so he proceeds to even up scores with those who have bullied him. A real doctor tells him that the only thing the matter with his heart is love, and he proceeds to marry the girl.--MW, 3-19-27:213.

Reviews:

F, 4-3-27:6.
MN, 4-29-27:1585.
MW, 3-19-27:213.
N, no review found.
V, 3-9-27:17.

Girls (short)

Release date: March 27, 1927.
Copyright date: March 27, 1927.
Director: Eugene Forde.
Cast: Richard Walling, Sally Phipps, Ben Hall, George Gray, Nora Cecil.

Tom Drake (Walling) has the unique reputation of being the only kissless senior in a co-ed college, and Louise (Phipps) undertakes to relieve Tom of his kissless halo. Louise plays her cards well, but Tom eludes all of her efforts during a sequence of rapid action scenes, until, after being cornered in the girls' shower, he manages to escape... Louise snares him on the campus, and, after kissing Louise, Tom goes about rampant, kissing all the girls, until Louise captures him again all for herself. (O.Henry Series).--MW, 4-16-27:655.

Reviews:

F, 4-10-27:7.
MN, 4-15-27:1372.
MW, 4-16-27:655.
N, no review found.
V, no review found.

The Kangaroo Detective (short)

Release date: May 15, 1927.
Copyright date: May 8, 1927.

Director: Jules White.
Cast: Gene Cameron, Sally Phipps.

A hotel bellboy keeps a pet kangaroo hidden in the cellar. A mysterious bandit who disguises himself as a mouse terrorizes the place, and, before the final fadeout, the kangaroo escapes and aids in capturing the bandit by knocking him cold with the aid of the bellboy. Add to this a pretty girl, her domineering mother, and a shrimp of a father, and have the girl and boy secretly in love with each other. (Animal Comedy).--MW, 5-21-27:200.

Reviews:

F, 5-15-27:11.
MN, 5-20-27:1964.
MW, 5-21-27:200.
N, no review found.
V, no review found.

The Cradle Snatchers (feature)

Release date: May 28, 1927.
Copyright date: April 24, 1927.
Director: Howard Hawks.
Cast: Louise Fazenda, J. Farrell MacDonald, Ethel Wales, Franklin Pangborn, Dorothy Phillips, William B. Davidson, Joseph Striker, Nick Stuart, Arthur Lake, Diane Ellis, Sammy Cohen, Tyler Brooke, [Sally Phipps, uncredited].

To cure their flirtatious husbands of consorting with flappers, three wives--Susan Martin, Ethel Drake, and Kitty Ladd--arrange with three college boys--Henry Winton, Oscar, and Joe Valley--to flirt with them at a house party. Joe Valley, who poses as a hot-blooded Spaniard, is vamped by Ginsberg in female attire, and Oscar, a bashful Swede, uses caveman methods when aroused. During a rehearsal of the party, the three husbands arrive, followed by their flapper friends, leading to comic complications that are resolved.--AFI.

Reviews:

F, 6-6-27:3.
MN, 6-10-27:2294.
MW, 6-4-27:365.
N, 5-31-27:25.
V, 6-1-27:16.

A Midsummer Night's Steam (short)

Release date: June 5, 1927.
Copyright date: June 5, 1927.

Director: Mark Sandrich.
Cast: Eddie Clayton, Sally Phipps, Fred Spencer, Dorothy Dix, Henry Armetta, W. T. McCulley, Virginia Whiting, Betty Evans, Marcella Arnold, Lucille Miller.

Phipps...appears as one of the six bathing girls who are hired to jazz up a theatre that is about to flop. ...Clayton is the peppy press agent. He starts to the train to meet the girls and his taxi meets with an accident by running into a freshly tarred street. This starts a chase in which a blackhand scare figures, with the chauffeur, a motor copy, and an Italian after him. He dodges into a side show, gets mixed up with the fat woman and a disappearing act. (Imperial Comedy).--MW, 6-11-27:656.

Reviews:

F, no review found.
MN, 6-17-27:2368.
MW, 6-11-27:656.
N, no review found.
V, no review found.

Cupid And The Clock (short)

Release date: June 19, 1927.
Copyright date: June 26, 1927.
Director: Eugene Forde.
Cast: Nick Stuart, Sally Phipps.

Nick is a reporter sent to get a story and picture of Sally, whose legs have been insured for a huge sum. He takes a cameraman along to the seminary where Sally is a student. They chase a fat girl by mistake for Sally, and eventually sneak into the dormitory. (O.Henry Series).--MN, 7-15-27:130.

Reviews:

F, 7-3-27:10.
MN, 7-15-27:130.
MW, 7-23-27:262.
N, no review found.
V, no review found.

Gentlemen Prefer Scotch (short)

Release date: June 26, 1927.
Copyright date: July 10, 1927.
Director: Jules White.
Cast: Nick Stuart, Sally Phipps, George Gray, Tiny Sanford.

The story starts out in modern times but then goes into flashback to Old Scotland, with Sally playing Sally McTavish as a Scottish gal in a blond wig. (Imperial Comedy).

Reviews:

F, no review found.
MN, no review found.
MW, no review found.
N, no review found.
V, no review found.

Mum's the Word (short)

Release date: July 31, 1927.
Copyright date: August 7, 1927.
Director: Eugene Forde.
Cast: Nick Stuart, Sally Phipps, Fred Spencer, Morris Cannon, Harry Dunkinson.

The story is of the very fresh and breezy young masher who tries to "make" the pretty daughter of the stern judge who is opposed to mashing. The youth trails her into a department store and in order to talk to her steps behind the counter and waits upon her. He is apprehended by the store detective and brought before the stern judge, who sentences him to walk the streets placarded as a masher. Later the judge unwittingly enters the wrong apartment and is about to be compromised, when the youth, also involved, conceives a way out for them both, saves a delicate situation, and with an implied threat keeps the stern judge mum as he wins the winning daughter. (Imperial Comedy).--MN, 9-2-27:712.

Reviews:

F, no review found.
MN, 9-2-27:712.
MW, 8-20-27:535.
N, no review found.
V, no review found.

Sunrise--A Song Of Two Humans (feature)

Release date: September 23, 1927.
Copyright date: June 12, 1927.
Director: F. W. Murnau
Cast: George O'Brien, Janet Gaynor, Bodil Rosing, Margaret Livingston, J. Farrell MacDonald, Ralph Sipperly, Jan Winton, Arthur Housman, Eddie Arnold, Sally Eilers, Gino Corrado, Barry Norton, Robert Kortman, [Sally Phipps, uncredited]

At a rural summer retreat, a vacationing lady from the city engages the interest of a young farmer, and soon he is enslaved to her. She persuades him to murder his wife, sell his farm, and join her in the city. He finally makes an attempt to drown his wife but, conscience-stricken, cannot carry it through. The man and his wife ride into the city on a trolley, she in terror, he in contrition; soon love overpowers her fear, and they renew their vows in a church while watching a wedding. They spend a joyous day in an amusement park and that evening return home; a storm overtakes them, and he gives her the rushes that were to provide his own protection while he swims ashore. Later the fishermen search for her during the night and finally give up hope; he searches out the city woman and is about to strangle her when word comes that his wife has been found alive. At her bedside, he watches the sunrise.--AFI.

Reviews:

F, 10-2-27:6.
MN, 10-14-27:1185.
MW, 10-1-27:312.
N, 9-24-27:15.
V, 9-28-27:21.

High School Hero (feature)

Release date: October 16, 1927.
Copyright date: October 10, 1927.
Director: David Butler.
Cast: Nick Stuart, Sally Phipps, William N. Bailey, John Darrow, Wade Boteler, Brandon Hurst, David Rollins, Charles Paddock, Wee Gee, Pal.

Pete Greer and Bill Merrill, rivals since childhood, continue feuding in high school, and their natural friction is intensified by each centering his attention on Eleanor Barrett, a new classmate. Amusing complications involve a sequence in which the high school Latin class, under the egis of Mr. Golden, presents what is intended to be a Roman tragedy but develops as a comic farce. The boys' enmity threatens to disrupt the school basketball team, but loyalty to their school compels them to drop their differences. Eleanor incontinently turns to Allen Drew, a bespectacled, studious type.--AFI.

Reviews:

F, 11-6-27:6.
MN, 11-11-27:1502.
MW, 10-29-27:568.
N, 10-24-27:24.
V, 10-26-27:18.

Hold Your Hat (short)

Release date: January 15, 1928.
Copyright date: January 12, 1928.
Director: Billy West.
Cast: Sally Phipps, Nick Stuart, Thelma Hill, Arthur Housman.

There are all sorts of complications between a married couple of a week's standing and another married couple of somewhat longer standing, and it is all the fault of the dog. Said canine insists upon taking the straw hat of its master and placing it in the room across the hall occupied by the older married couple, the husband of which is a very jealous individual.

The younger married man follows the dog after his hat into the other apartment and is discovered by the jealous husband. When this is repeated two or three times, the husband becomes completely enraged and a lively quarrel ensues. The newlywed decides to get rid of the jinx hat. He wishes it upon the very young son of his employer. The boy, finding it too big for him, pads it with a paper bearing the formula of his dad's latest invention.

Newlywed loses his job and the hat goes with him. The young son later reveals what he has done wth the formula, and the boss and office force start a chase for the hat, whose owner is trying his best to be rid of. The hat invariably returns and is located by the boss, who rewards the newlywed by making him his general manager. (Imperial Comedy).--MN, 3-24-28:965.

Reviews:

EH, no review found.
F, 4-1-28:12.
MN, 3-24-28:965.
N, no review found.
V, no review found.

Why Sailors Go Wrong (feature)

Release date: March 25, 1928.
Copyright date: March 16, 1928.
Director: Henry Lehrman.
Cast: Sammy Cohen, Ted McNamara, Sally Phipps, Carl Miller, Nick Stuart, Jules Cowles, Noble Johnson, E. H. Calvert, Jack Pennick.

In an attempt to win her back, would-be suitor John Hastings invites Doris Martin and her father to take a yacht cruise with him. Her fiancé, James Collier, tries to stowaway and hires two taxicab drivers, Cohen and Mac, to get work on the ship and help him get aboard. When Hastings sees Collier on deck, however, he orders Cohen and Mac to lock him up. Cohen and Mac wake the next morning on the shores of Pago Pago. They wrestle with lions, alligators, and monkeys and are about to be slain by the natives when they are saved by the crew of an American warship.--AFI.

Reviews:

EH, no review found.
F, 4-15-28:4.
MN, 4-14-28: 1213.
N, 4-9-28:18.
V, 4-11-28:13.

The News Parade (feature)

Release date: May 25, 1928.
Copyright date: May 23, 1928.
Director: David Butler.
Cast: Nick Stuart, Sally Phipps, Brandon Hurst, Cyril Ring, Earle Foxe, Franklin Underwood, Truman Talley.

Photographer "Newsreel Nick" pulls an assignment to get some footage of A. K. Wellington, a camera-shy millionaire. Following the man and his daughter to Lake Placid, Palm Beach, and Havana, Nick saves both of them from a kidnaping plot in Havana and gets his footage as well.--AFI.

Reviews:

EH, 5-26-28:125.
F, 6-3-28:9.
MN, 6-16-28:2037.
N, 5-29-28:17.
V, 5-30-28:14.

None But The Brave (feature)

Release date: August 5, 1928.
Copyright date: July 31, 1928.
Director: Albert Ray.
Cast: Charles Morton, Sally Phipps, Sharon Lynn, J. Farrell MacDonald, Tom Kennedy, Billy Butts, Alice Adair, Tyler Brooke, Earle Foxe, Gertrude Short, Dorothy Knapp.

Charles Stanton, a college hero, fails at business. He becomes a lifeguard, falling in love with a concessionaire. When he throws an obstacle race to aid an injured fellow contestant, he is substantially rewarded and wins the girl.--AFI.

Reviews:

EH, 8-18-28:63.
F, 8-5-28:6.
MN, 8-11-28:477.

N, no review found.
V, 9-5-28: 31.

Joy Street (feature)

Release date: May 25, 1929.
Copyright date: May 16, 1929.
Director: Raymond Cannon.
Cast: Lois Moran, Nick Stuart, Rex Bell, José Crespo, Dorothy Ward, Ada Williams, Maria Alba, Sally Phipps, Florence Allen, Mabel Vail, Carol Wines, John Breeden, Marshall Ruth, James Barnes, Allen Dale, Capt Marco Elter, Destournelles De Constant.

Mimi, an unsophisticated American girl attending an exclusive Swiss boarding school, unexpectedly inherits a large fortune, returns to the United States, and quickly begins to live in a wild and reckless manner. Joe, a good-natured, decent fellow, attempts to set her straight, but she keeps right on living riotously. Mimi is involved in a serious accident while joy-riding, however, and comes to her senses. She marries Joe and settles down to a life of domestic tranquility.--AFI.

Reviews:
EH, no review found.
F, 8-4-29:8.
MN, 6-8-29:1967.
N, no review found.
V, no review found.

The One Woman Idea (feature)

Release date: June 2, 1929.
Copyright date: June 6, 1929.
Director: Berthold Viertel.
Cast: Rod La Rocque, Marceline Day, Shirley dorman, Sharon Lynn, Sally Phipps, Ivan Lebedeff, Douglas Gilmore, Gino Corrado, Joseph W. Girard, Arnold Lucy, Frances Rosay, Jamiel Hassen, Tom Tamerez, Coy Watson.

On an ocean liner bound for Persia, Prince Ahmed is attracted to Lady Alicia, the English wife of Lord Douglas, because she wears a ring that is a duplicate of his own, presented to her father by the father of the prince. Returning to his palace, the prince is confronted by Alizar, a dancing girl who is a double for his love, but he is unable to feel a similar affection for her. Meanwhile, Lord Douglas and Lady Alicia visit Persia; his lordship enters the women's quarters of the palace and is discovered struggling with Alizar, but he flees in time to save his life, while the girl kills herself. Lord Douglas is later captured, and while his wife pleads for his life, he is slain by the mother of Alizar.--AFI.

Reviews:

EH, no review found.
F, 6-16-29:8.
MN, 6-15-29:2095.
N, 6-10-29:23.
V, 6-12-29:31.

Detectives Wanted (short – talkie)

Release date: August 1, 1929.
Copyright date: July 5, 1929.
Director: Norman Taurog.
Cast: Bobby Clark, Paul McCullough, Sally Phipps, Alan Lane, Jane Keckley, Jack Duffy, Ernest Shields, Charles Sullivan, Dick Dickinson, Ray Turner.

In this case, they [Clark and McCullough] are dicks who come to clean out a "haunted" house. Trap doors, shrouded figures, secret panels, and all that make up a haunted house are used as Clark and McCullough blunder through. They capture the menaces by letting them fight each other out in a darkened room while [they] stand by and watch.--V, 5-28-30:21.

Reviews:

EH, no review found.
F, no review found.
N, no review found.
V, 5-28-30:21.

WARNER BROTHERS CORPORATION - VITAPHONE

Where Men Are Men (short - talkie)

Release date: April 1931.
Copyright date: ?-?-1931.
Vitaphone Nos. 1207-1208
Director: Alf Goulding.
Cast: Joe Penner, Sally Phipps.

It concerns a clerk who is fired for cutting up in the boss' office and then learns that he has inherited a house in the Wild West. He gets the Carters and Mayfields in separate rooms under his roof without fighting long enough to sell the place for $10,000, then makes a pony-dive for the railroad station. There he learns that the feud was renewed so successfully that all of both families were shot out of existence.--MH, 9-26-31:30.

Reviews:

F, 9-20-31:11.
MH, 9-26-31:30.
N, no review found.
V, 9-15-31:14.

BROADWAY

Once In A Lifetime

Opening date: September 24, 1930 (Music Box Theatre).
Authors: George S. Kaufman and Moss Hart.
Director: George S. Kaufman.
Cast: Hugh O'Connell, Grant Mills, Jean Dixon, Spring Byington, Charles Halton, George S. Kaufman, Sally Phipps.

The action revolves around three members of a failed vaudeville act, who decide to pass themselves off as vocal coaches, during the short period of time in Hollywood when sound films were superseding silent films. Sally plays an attractive though intensely moronic would-be actress, who meets the trio on the train to California and latches on romantically to one of the men in the trio. He is as much of a moron as she is. Amazingly, she and her boyfriend end up becoming the biggest successes in all Hollywood.

Reviews:
B, 9-25-30:25.
N, 9-25-30:22.

Knock On Wood

Opening date: May 28, 1935 (Cort Theatre).
Author: Allen Rivkin.
Director: John Hayden.
Cast: James Rennie, Lee Patrick, Albert Van Dekker, Sallie Phipps, Horace MacMahon.

It is Hollywood satire through the keyhole of the office of a firm of artists' representatives. Schuyler & Hugo are dynamic and extravagant fellows who do business in a boisterous racketeering style and know how to square the opposition by buying off the enemy. It is a giddy play with the routine ribaldries and an occasional gag about buying the talking-picture rights to Beaumont and Fletcher or some such folderol.--N, 5-29-35:16.

Reviews:
N, 5-29-35:16.

RADIO

Jules Verne series of dramatic programs (October 1937 through June 1938)

A Journey To The Center Of The Earth (October 1937 - early February 1938)
Mysterious Island (mid-February - March 1938)
From The Earth To The Moon (April - June 1938)

Men Against Death series (July 1938 through April 1939)

BIBLIOGRAPHY

BOOKS

Barrios, Richard. *A Song in the Dark; the Birth of the Musical Film.* 2nd ed. New York: Oxford University Press, 2010.

Beutler, Edithe and Frank Warren. *Trees and Flowers of the Hawaiian Islands.* Honolulu, T.H.: Outdoor Circle of Hawaii, 1944.

Blum, Daniel. *A Pictorial History of the Silent Screen.* New York: G. P. Putnam, 1953.

Book of Mormon – Doctrines and Covenants.

Bradley, Edwin M. *The First Hollywood Musicals; A Critical Filmography of 171 Features, 1927 through 1932.* Jefferson, NC: McFarland, 1996.

Brunton, Paul. *A Search In Secret India.* New York: E. P. Dutton, 1935.

Davidson, Gustav. *The Dictionary of Angels.* New York: Free Press, 1967.

De Kruif, Paul. *Men Against Death.* New York: Harcourt Brace, 1932.

Descriptive Catalogue of Kodascope Library Motion Pictures. 7th ed. New York: Eastman Kodak Company, Kodascope Libraries Division, 1937.

Directory and Hand-book of the Kingdom of Hawaii. Edited by J. C. Lane. Oakland, Calif.: Pacific Press Pub. Co., 1890.

Dunsany, Lord. *Plays of Gods and Men.* Holicong, PA: Wildside Press, 2002.

Haley, James L. *Wolf; the Lives of Jack London.* New York: Basic Books, 2010.

Harman, Bob. *Bob Harman's Enchanted Faces.* New York: B. Harman, 1991.

Harman, Bob. *Bob Harman's Hollywood Panorama.* New York: E.P. Dutton, 1971. (includes small drawing of Sally)

Hart, Moss. *Act One.* New York: Random House, 1959.

Hawaiian Directory and Hand Book of the Kingdom of Hawaii. Edited by J. C. Lane. San Francisco: McKenney Directory Co., 1888.

Jones, Jack E. *No Rocking Chair Yet.* Meridianville, AL: NightSky Publishing, 2005.

Kiehn, David. *Broncho Billy and the Essanay Film Company.* Berkeley, CA: Farwell Books, 2003. (includes photos of Sally as Bernice Sawyer in scene stills)

Liebman, Roy. *The Wampas Baby Stars; A Biographical Dictionary, 1922-1934.* Jefferson, NC: McFarland, 2000.

Nordic, Rolla. *Let's Talk About The Tarot.* New York: Vantage Press, 1992.

Nordic, Rolla. *The Tarot Shows The Path.* New York: Magical Childe Pub., 1990.

"Phipps, Sally." *Filmlexicon degli autori e delle opere.* Roma: Edizioni di Bianco e Nero, 1962, p. 582.

"Phipps, Sally." Ragan, David. *Who's Who In Hollywood, 1900-1976.* New Rochelle: Arlington House, 1976.

"Phipps, Sally." Ragan, David. *Who's Who In Hollywood; The Largest Cast of International Film Personalities.* New York: Facts On File, 1992, 2v.

Sacramento City and County Directory, 1888-1889.

Sacramento City and County Directory, 1889-1890.

Sacramento City and County Directory, 1891-1892.

Sacred Hymns and Spiritual Songs for the Church of Jesus Christ of Latter-Day Saints. 14th ed. Salt Lake City: Published by George Q. Cannon, 1871.

Sanders, Coyne Steven. *Rainbow's End; The Judy Garland Show.* New York: Morrow, 1990.

Skinner, Frank. *Frank Skinner's New Methods of Orchestra Scoring.* New York: Robbins Music Corporation, 1935.

Solomon, Aubrey. *The Fox Film Corporation, 1915-1935; A History and Filmography.* Jefferson, NC: McFarland, 2011.

*[Stars] *** of the Movies and Featured Players; Two Hundred and Fifty Portraits Alphabetically Arranged.* Hollywood, CA: Hollywood Publicity Company, 1927. (includes photo of Sally)

MAGAZINES AND NEWSPAPERS

APPLETON POST-CRESCENT (WI)
"Comedy Galore In Fox Film At Bijou." May 4, 1927, p. 11.

BILLBOARD
"Director, Old Redpath-Horner Chautauqua Organization [business advertisement]. November 27, 1954, p. 93.

BOSTON POST (MA)
"And After That, What?" June 3, 1928, [page unknown]

BROOKLYN DAILY EAGLE (NY)
Pollock, Arthur. "Once In A Lifetime (review)." September 25, 1930, p. 25.

BUFFALO COURIER-EXPRESS (NY)
Shaffer, George. "What's New In Hollywood." September 13, 1928, p. 3.

BURLINGTON HAWK-EYE (IA)
"Burlington Woman Was Friend of Wounded Soldier." July 23, 1911, p. 14.

CANTON REPERTORY (OH)
"Take Part In 'Jules Verne' Broadcasts." May 4, 1938, p. 10.

CHICAGO DAILY TRIBUNE (IL)
"502 New Cases of Flu Reported in Los Angeles." November 28, 1928, p. 3.

CINE GRÁFICO (Argentina)
January 11, 1928. (cover photo of Sally)

CINE-MUNDIAL (USA)
Guaitsel, Eduardo. "Sally Se Va A La Habana." April 1928, p. 304, 365-366. (story and full-page photo)
"Sally Phipps Con Su Sombrero De Araña..." April 1928, p. 345. (photo of Sally wearing spider hat, p. 345)
March 1929. (cover photo of Sally and Sammy Cohen)

CINEARTE (Brazil)
June 20, 1928, p. 8, 23. (full page photo of Sally and mention in story)
July 4, 1928, p. 12. (half page photo of Sally)

CINELANDIA Y FILMS (USA)
March 1930, p. 20. (full-page photo of Sally)
May 1930, p. 71. (brief career blurb about Sally)

CINEMA ART
"Youth in Fox Pictures." December 1926, p. 3. (photo of Sally)

CLASSIC FILM COLLECTOR
Griffo, Richard. "Erik Rhodes, Sally Phipps Receive Rosemary Awards." Winter 1976, p. x-16.

CLASSIC IMAGES
Roberts, John. "Sally Phipps." November 1984, p. 57, 63.
Harned, Robert L. "Sally Phipps, Silent Film Star." March 2014, p. 6-15, 70. (biography with cover color lobby card and 33 photos of Sally and family)

CLEVELAND PLAIN DEALER (OH)
Kurlander, Regine. "You Can Be Glamorous, Etc." February 21, 1941, p. 14.

CUMBERLAND EVENING TIMES (MD)
Swan, Gilbert. "In New York." November 5, 1930, p. 16.

DAILY ALTA CALIFORNIA (CA)
"The Eastern Shore; News From Berkeley, Alameda, Oakland, and Environs." September 7, 1887, p. 8.

DAILY STAR (Brooklyn, NY)
"Sally Phipps Robbed in Kangaroo Bout." January 14, 1928, p. 6.
W. H. R. "Star Gazing: Mother Aids Sally." March 29, 1928, p. 9.

DENVER POST (CO)
Humphreys, Ray. "Minter Trial to Open Tuesday with Four-Cornered Battle." October 17, 1927, p. 14.

EXHIBITORS DAILY REVIEW
"Newmeyer Gathers Cast." October 15, 1928, p. 3.
Edwards, J. Harrison. "Fox Row Goes Journalistic." November 23, 1928, p. 4.
"Reed Resigns." December 10, 1928, p. 8.

EXHIBITORS HERALD AND MOVING PICTURE WORLD
"Newmeyer's 'Calamity' Superfeature Fox Film." October 6, 1928, p. 44.
"Newmeyer's Fox Film Done." December 15, 1928, p. 42.

FILM DAILY
Blair, Harry N. "Short Shots From New York Studios." October 26, 1930, p. 5.
"Sally Phipps For Short." October 29, 1930, p. 8.
"Sally Phipps, Former Fox Ingénue…" January 11, 1931, p. 5.
"Sally Phipps With Vitaphone." February 8, 1931, p. 5.

"Joe Penner, Vitaphone's Lisping Comedian..." February 22, 1931, p. 5.

FILM FAN
"None But The Brave (review)." March 1, 1929, p. 5. (photo of Sally)

FILM FUN
April 1927, p. 31, 36. (photos of Sally on each page)
Yetsofa, Sonya Ann, as told to Edward Sammis. "You, Too, Can Have a Body Beautiful." May 1932, p. 26-27, 64. (photo of Sally with diaphanous veil)

FILMS IN REVIEW
Uselton, Roi. "The Wampas Baby Stars: Only a Few Grew to the First Magnitude." February 1970, p. 73-97.
Uselton, Roi. "Erudition Wanted And Supplied." August-September 1971, p. 452-454. (mention of Sally on p. 452)
Uselton, Roi. "The Wampas Baby Stars." February 1973, p. 123-124. (photo of Sally with other 12 Wampas Baby Stars of 1927)

GLENN FALLS POST-STAR (NY)
Winchell, Walter. "On Broadway." April 7, 1931, p. 4.

HARLAN TRIBUNE (IA)
Graves, Elsie. "Small Crowd Liked Funnybone Follies." September 30, 1955, p. 1-2.

HEARTS
May 22, 1928. (cover photo of Sally)

HOLLYWOOD STUDIO MAGAZINE
Cook, Mandy Po. "Rosemary Awards for 1976." September 1976, p. 34.

INVICTA-CINE (Portugal)
January 1930, p. [3]. (photo of Sally)

LIBERTY
Smith, Frederick James."Burning Events and Oil Tanks." July 7, 1928, p. 22. (photos of Sally and mentions in story)

LIFE
Hart, Moss. "Famous Playwright's First Awful Flop." August 24, 1959, p. 82-86, 89-90, 92. (photo of Sally in group)

LOS ANGELES TIMES (CA)
"Editors Spend Day In Studios." November 8, 1928, p. A1.
"Hughes Pupil in Talkies." March 17, 1929, p. C32.

"Guardian Named for Actress; Attorney Will Pull Girl Out of Debt; March 29, 1929, p. A5.
"Dancing Contest." June 23, 1929, p. 24.
"Resort and Hotel Notes." September 15, 1929, p. 23.

LYCEUM WORLD

Bogdon, Albert. "Ancient Mediaeval and Modern Magic." Article I, January 1915, p. 644-645; Article II, March 1915, p. 776-777; Article III, May 1915, p. 90-91.

MAGIC CIRCULAR (England)

Bogdon, Albert E. "The Legerdemaniacs." August 1914, p. 209-216.
Bogdon, Albert Edward. ""The Magicians' Creed." October 1914, p. 1.

MODESTO NEWS HERALD (CA)

"Court Asked to Name Guardian for Wampas Star; Sally Phipps Charges Her Stepfather With Cruel Treatment." March 9, 1929, p. 1.

MORNING TELEGRAPH (New York City, NY)

Sullivan, Wallace. "Broadway" [column]. March 2, 1928, p. 3. (photo and mention of Sally); March 3, 1928, p. 3 (mention of Sally); March 4, 1928, p. 9 (mention of Sally); March 7, 1928, [page unknown] (entire column devoted to Sally)
"To Go Ahead." April 24, 1928, p. 3. (photo of Sally)

MOTION PICTURE

April 1927, p. 108. (photo of Sally)
Vreeland, Frank. "A Rush of Red." July 1928, p. 33. (photo of Sally and mentions in story)
Manners, Dorothy. "Join the Movies and See the World; Nick Stuart Did – And Has – And How!" September 1928, p. 50, 116. (mention of Sally in story)
September 1928, p. 88. (photo of Sally with dog)
January 1929, p. 100. (photo of Sally mending tea cloth)
May 1929, p. 102. (photo of Sally roller skating)
Ramsey, Walter. "Does Mother Know Best?" September 1929, p. 55, 122-123. (photo of Sally and mention in story)

MOTION PICTURE CLASSIC

April 1927, p. 60. (photo of Sally)
Manners, Dorothy. "Looking Them Over Out Hollywood Way." July 1928, p. 60-61, 87. (mention of Sally on p. 61 winning a dancing trophy)
"Backbones Of The Industry." August 1928, p. 56-57. (photo of Sally against feather fan)
Manners, Dorothy. "Looking Them Over Out Hollywood Way." August 1928, p. 60-61, 87. (photo of Sally on p. 61 sitting on pedestal holding parasol)

Manners, Dorothy. "Kute, Kool and Kalm; Twenty Years From Now Sally Phipps Might Take Pictures Seriously." October 1928, p. 42, 77. (photos of Sally and story)
November 1928, p. 66. (photo of Sally in Lux soap ad)
"High and Low." May 1929, p. 62. (full page photo of Sally)

MOTION PICTURE NEWS
"Six Fox Shorts For November." October 30, 1926, p. 1679. (mention of Sally with name "Byrnec[e] Beautler")
"Short Feature Players: Handy Biographies for Use of Theatre Managers and Publicity Men in Newspaper Copy and House Programs – Sally Phipps." May 27, 1927, p. 2080. (photo and story about Sally)
"Flynn, Newmeyer, Reed Are Reported Out At Fox." December 8, 1928, p. 1748.
"Fox Execs Shake Dust Off 'Scarehead' For Fixing." February 16, 1929, p. 487.
"Sally Phipps In Short." November 8, 1930, p. 37.

MOTOGRAPHY
"Broncho Billy And the Baby (review)." January 23, 1915, p. 147.
"The Western Way (review)." March 20, 1915, p. 463.
"The Outlaw's Awakening (review)." March 27, 1915, p. 503.

MOVING PICTURE WORLD
"Broncho Billy And the Baby (story only)." January 16, 1915, p. 411.
"Broncho Billy And the Baby (review)." February 6, 1915, p. 827-828.
"The Western Way (story only)." March 13, 1915, p. 1644.
"The Outlaw's Awakening (story only)." March 20, 1915, p. 1820.
"The Western Way (review)." April 3, 1915, p. 64.
"The Outlaw's Awakening (review)." April 10, 1915, p. 233.
"Beauties of the Wampas." January 15, 1927, p. 192. (photo of Sally and mention in story)
"Sally Phipps ..." September 3, 1927, p. 25. (photo of Sally and story)

MUNDO GRÁFICO (Spain)
July 10, 1929, p. [10-11]. (photos of Sally with guitar and in pool)

NEW YORK CLIPPER
"Albert E. Bogdon [business advertisement]." October 14, 1905, p. 878.
"Vaudeville Route List [column]." May 26, 1906, p. 389.
"Out Of Town News [column]." September 6, 1913, p. 5.

NEW YORK DRAMATIC MIRROR
Grau, Robert. "The Passing of the Magician." May 19, 1915, p. 3.
Bogdon, Albert. "The Rise of the Magician." June 16, 1915, p. 3.
Houdini, Harry. "The Magicians In Review." June 16, 1915, p. 3, 6.

NEW YORK JOURNAL AND AMERICAN

Frank, Gerold. "Ex-Film Starlet, Ex-Rich Wife, Happy in $23 Job." June 26, 1938, p. E-3.

NEW YORK POST

Cassidy, George L. "The Reporter At The Play." May 29, 1935, p. 17.

Wilson, Earl. "Wampas Ex-Baby Lives on WPA $23 – And Likes It." June 21, 1938, p. 11.

NEW YORK TIMES

"Film 'Follies'." March 3, 1929, p. 6.

"B. Gimbel Jr. Seeks Divorce." November 23, 1933, p. 18.

"Two Players From 'Knock On Wood'... (photo of James Rennie and Sally)." May 26, 1935, p. X2.

"Gimbel Divorce Granted."June 25, 1935, p. 10.

"Microphone Presents." October 10, 1937, p. 14X.

"Sally Phipps, 67, Star of the Silent Movie Era [obituary]." March 21, 1978, p. 38.

NEW YORK TIMES – MID-WEEK PICTORIAL

April 7, 1928, p. 12. (photo of Sally)

Rawson, Mitchell. "The News Parade is a Comedy Thriller." June 9, 1928. p. 13. (includes photos of Sally and mentions in story)

NEW YORK TIMES -- STYLE MAGAZINE "T"

Diliberto, Gioia. "The Flapper Doesn't Change Her Spots." February 24, 2008, p. 192, 194. (life story of Sally with photos)

NEW YORK WORLD-TELEGRAM

Keller, Allan. "One-Time Cinema Star Returns Here with Secret Tactics of Three Nations." February 18, 1941, p. 3.

OAKLAND TRIBUNE (CA)

"M'Kinley's Message." July 7, 1897, p. 8.

"Benefit For Girl's Home; Program To Be Given At Entertainment To Raise Charity Funds." April 4, 1907, p. 5.

"'Mother Goose' Baby Show To Be Attractive Church Entertainment." April 1, 1913, p. 10. (photo of Sally as Nellie Bogdon)

"Pretty Infant Is Prize-Winner; Baby Show Carnival Feature." August 17, 1913, p. 39. (photo of Sally as Nellie Bogden [sic])

"Oakland Boys And Girls." December 27, 1913, p. 2. (photo of Sally as Nellie Bogdon)

"Oakland Girl Winner Of Exposition Prize." October 3, 1915, p. 20.

"Civic Committees Plan For Big July 4 Celebration; Announce Novel Events For Day Of Patriotism." July 2, 1916, p. 21.

"Garden Benefit Fete Tomorrow." September 24, 1917, p. 1.

"East Oakland Revives Old Spanish Days – Here Is Prize Essay on Early Days in County – Nellie Bogdon, 1749 Twentieth Avenue, Wins Board of Trade Contest." June 14, 1922, p. 18-19.

"Ground Breaking Ceremonies At East Oakland School." November 12, 1922, p. 8A.

Tazelaar, Margaret. "California Girl Enacts Bride Role in Comedy Kidding Screen Colony." December 21, 1930, p. S-9.

PARIS AND HOLLYWOOD SCREEN SECRETS

October 1927, p. 28. (full-page photo of Sally)

PARIS MUSIC-HALL (France)

"Ciné-badinages: l'envers du septième art." April 15, 1928, p. 14. (photos of Sally)

PARIS NIGHTS (USA)

October 1929, p. [13], [15]. (two full-page photos of Sally).

PARIS PLAISIRS (France)

August 1929, p. [158]. (photo of Sally from beauty pageant scene of her film *None But The Brave*).

PHILADELPHIA INQUIRER (PA)

"She Just Couldn't Find Usual Early Bad Luck." September 7, 1930, p. 30.

PHOTOPLAY

"Baby Stars of 1927." March 1927, p. 67, 82. (photo of Sally, has paragraph in story)

York, Cal. "Gossip Of All The Studios." November 1927, p. 42-45, 98, 101-107, 112-115. (paragraph about Sally on p. 114)

"High School Hero (review)." November 1927, p. 54. (includes photo of Sally, Nick Stuart, and Charles Paddock)

"Gentlemen Prefer Scotch (review)." December 1927, p. 147.

"Gentlemen Prefer Scotch (alternate review)." January 1928, p. 10.

"When The Doctors Disagree." January 1928, p. 77. (disputing critics over film *High School Hero*)

"Mum's the Word (review)." January 1928, p. 122.

"A Summary of Sally." April 1928, p. 67. (story and photos of Sally)

"Why Sailors Go Wrong (review)." June 1928, p. 82.

"The News Parade (review)." July 1928, p. 54 (includes photo of Sally and Nick Stuart)

Shirley, Lois. "Handiwork of the Stars." July 1928, p. 68-70, 106. (photo of Sally on p. 68 mending tea cloth and paragraph about her on p. 70)

"Friendly Advice from Carolyn Van Wyck on Girls' Problems." August 1928, p. 18, 137. (uncredited photo of Sally on p. 18 in bathing suit sitting on diving board with dog)

Larkin, Mark. "What Happens To Fan Mail." August 1928, p. 38-40, 130-134. (paragraph about Sally on p. 39-40 and 132)
York, Cal. "Gossip Of All The Studios." August 1928, p. 48-51, 92, 94, 96-97. (paragraph about Sally on p. 94)
"None But The Brave (review)." October 1928, p. 124.
Shirley, Lois. "Making Bedrooms More Attractive." May 1929, p. 66-67, 112. (photo of and paragraph about Sally in her dressing room)

PICTURE PLAY
"Youth in pictures." January 1927, p. 14. (photo of Sally)
"On the Horizon." January 1927, p. 78-79. (photo of Sally on p. 79)
"Those New Wampas Stars." April 1927, p. 64-65. (photo of Sally on p. 64)
"Among Those Present." August 1927, p. 54-57, 100. (photo and mention of Sally on p. 54 under heading "Saved from the Law")
Lusk, Norbert. "The Screen In Review." February 1928, p. 110. (review of "High School Hero")
St. John-Brenon, Aileen. "Manhattan Medley." May 1928, p. 50-52. (photo of Sally on p. 50 and mention in story on p. 52)
"An Infant Paradox." June 1928, p. 23, 114. (two photos and feature story about Sally)
"The Eternal Feminine." August 1928, p. 33. (photo of Sally)
Lusk, Norbert. "The Screen In Review." September 1928, p. 68-71, 94, 96. (photo of Nick Stuart and Sally on p. 70 and review of "The News Parade" on p. 71)
"Music Hath Charms." January 1929, p. 24. (photo of Sally playing mandolin)
"My Gal Sal." August 1929, p. 55. (photo of Sally)
"I Spy." September 1929, p. 27. (photo of Sally with spyglass)
"Childhood's Happy Hour." September 1929, p. 84-85. (photo of Sally dressed as child, sitting in her dressing room on p. 85)
"For No Man's Land." October 1929, p. 62-63. (photo of Sally in silk pajamas on p. 63)
Mook, Samuel Richard. "They Got What They Wanted, But--." December 1929, p. 60-62, 94. (photo of Sally on p. 63 and mention in story on p. 94)
Bystander, The. "Over The Teacups." January 1931, p. 30-33, 111-112. (photo of Sally on p. 31 and mention in story on p. 31-32)

POPULAR FILM (Spain)
"Sally Phipps." March 14, 1929, p. 3-4. (story and photo of Sally and Edithe)
May 2, 1929, p. 5. (full-page photo of Sally dancing)
September 4, 1930, p. 5. (full-page photo of Sally)

ROXY THEATRE WEEKLY REVIEW
Blair, Harry N. "Thou Shalt Not – Divorce! Marry! Fall I Love! Be Bobbed! Grow Obese! Lose Flesh! – Cinema Commandments." Week Beginning March 24, 1928, p. [3-4]. (photo of Sally and mention in story)

SALT LAKE TRIBUNE (UT)
"Dainty Little Sally Phipps, Flapper of Brand New Type, Former Salt Lake City Girl," November 28, 1926, p. 10.
"Three Salt Lake Girls Given High Recognition by 'Movie' Organization." January 16, 1927, p. 8.
Werner, Wade. "Sidelights of the Stage and Screen." October 15, 1927, p. 20.

SAN FRANCISCO CALL (CA)
"May Contest Dr. Lane's Will; Sister Of Late Physician Dissatisfied With Document." February 21, 1903, p. 14.
"Series Of Concerts By Harmonie Club; Initial Musicale To Be Given At Loring Hall." April 3, 1910, p. 29.
"The Sea Wolf." September 12, 1912, p. 9.

SAN FRANCISCO CHRONICLE (CA)
"Oakland School to be Made a Monument to Pioneers – Aged Woman Helps Build Great School – Board of Education Gives Plan of Honor at Ceremonies – Institution to be Memorial for First Settlers on East Bay Shore." November 19, 1922, p. O-4.

SAN FRANCISCO EXAMINER (CA)
"Truck Not Enough To Halt Her Career." June 14, 1938, [page unknown]. (photo of Sally on piano with crutches and with radio script)

SAN JOSE NEWS (CA)
"Cruel Stepfather Is Assailed By Actress." March 11, 1929, [page unkown].

SANS-GÊNE (France)
November 29, 1930 (cover photo of Sally from beauty contest scene in *None But The Brave*)

SCREEN SECRETS
"Peeking in the Keyhole." February 1928, p. 66-68, 99, 106. (photo of Sally)
Tildesley, Ruth M. "Her Companionate Engagement; Sally Phipps Has a New Idea About Love; Will It Become the Rage in Hollywood?" September 1928, p. 73, 88. (story and photos of Sally)
Tildesley, Ruth M. "Society in Cinemaland." July 1929, p. 54-55, 107. (includes photo of Sally in group)

SCREENLAND
May 1928, p. 53. (full page photo of Sally)
De Casseres, Benjamin. "The Stage In Review." January 1931, p. 92-93, 110. (short article on p. 92 about "Once In a Lifetime," including group cast picture featuring Sally)

Reilly, Rosa. "Is The Stage The Port Of Missing Screen Stars." February 1931, p. 28-29, 126-127. (photo, p. 29, of Sally and mention in story, p. 127)

SNAPPY STORIES AND PICTURES
April 5, 1927, p. [4], 36, 45. (photos of Sally)

SPHINX
"Albert E. Bogdon [business advertisement]." July 1905, p. 59.
"Albert E. Bogdon [business advertisement]." August 1905, p. 71.
"Albert E. Bogdon [business advertisement]." September 1905, p. 83.
"Pittsburgh Association Of Magicians, Pittsburgh, PA." August 15, 1914, p. 108.
Wilson, A. M. "[Editorial Column.]" June 15, 1915, p. 70.
Wilson, A. M. "[Editorial Column.]" July 15, 1915, p. 90.
Oursler, Charles Fulton. "Notes From Baltimore, Md." September 15, 1915, p. 124.
Wilson, A. M. "[Editorial Column.]" January 15, 1916, p. 210.

SPRINGFIELD WEEKLY REPUBLICAN (MA)
"Lew Seiler Has Rounded Out His Fourth Week of Camera Work..." February 21, 1929, p. 29.

STANDARD UNION (Brooklyn, NY)
"Sally Phipps Talkie." February 5, 1931, p. 12.

STATEN ISLAND ADVANCE (NY)
"Star Gazing by C.K." March 31, 1928, p. 14.

SYRACUSE HERALD (NY)
"Up And Down the Rialtos." February 3, 1929, p. 3.

TATLER (London, England)
October 23, 1929, p. 189. (photo of Sally and brief mention in blurb)

TECHNICAL WORLD MAGAZINE (USA)
Cary, Harold. "The Bad Man of the Movies." June 1915, p. 480-484. (uncredited photos of Sally, when she appeared in early films as Bernice Sawyer)

THEATRE MAGAZINE
"Youth in Fox Pictures." December 1926, p. 14, 79. (photos of Sally)
"Wampas 'Baby Stars' for the Year 1927." April 1927, p. 39. (photo of Sally)
"This Play's the Thing – Once In A Lifetime [condensation]." December 1930, p. 35-37, 66, 68-69. (photos of Sally and cast members)

TIMES-PICAYUNE (LA)
Tildesley, Alice L. "Youth Losing Out To Experience." April 6, 1930, p. 79.

TORONTO STAR WEEKLY (Canada)
December 24, 1927, Gravure Section, p. 1. (photo of Sally peeking through a Christmas wreath)

VALPARAISO PORTER COUNTY VIDETTE (IN)
"Well-Known Young Man Now Ship Quartermaster." August 1, 1917, p. 4.

VARIETY
"Sally Phipps Engaged to Newspaper Man." March 14, 1928, p. 3.
"Sally Phipps Says Parents Misuse Money; Suing." March 13, 1929, p. 4.
"Sally Phipps Resuming Broadway Career." September 30, 1936, p. 22.

VFW MAGAZINE
Horner, Bryan R., as told to Henry C. Sivewright. "There's Fun in This – Fund Raising Stunt." July 1955, p. 20, 41.

WORLD OF YESTERDAY
Fulbright, Tom. "Rosemary Awards Selects Four Stars for 1976." October 1976, p. 14-16.

ADDRESSES CITED

INDEX

A

B

H

K

L

M

N

R

S

V

W

ABOUT THE AUTHOR

Robert L. Harned was born in Des Moines, Iowa, but grew up in Honolulu, Hawaii. He is a professional research librarian and has worked at the Library of Congress in Washington, DC, the University of Pennsylvania in Philadelphia, and in several universities and law firms in New York City. He now resides in Park Slope, Brooklyn, New York, with his partner, food journalist, cookbook author, and broadcaster Arthur Schwartz. Robert's interests are film history, Greek and Roman archaeology, and singing. He has recorded four CD albums.

Made in the USA
Lexington, KY
19 July 2015